FRAMING SARAH PALIN

Sarah Palin's 2008 vice presidential candidacy garnered tremendous levels of interest, polarizing the American public—both Democrats and Republicans alike. While many have wondered who she "really" is, trying to cut through the persona she projects and the one projected by the media, Beail and Longworth analyze why she touches such a nerve with the American electorate. Why does she ignite such passionate loyalty – and such loathing? How did her candidacy mobilize the electorate and spark debates about partisanship and gender roles?

Using the notion of "framing" as a way of understanding political perception, the authors analyze the narratives told by and about Sarah Palin in the 2008 election – from frontier woman and political outsider to pit bull hockey mom, beauty queen, and post-feminist role model. They discuss where these frames are rooted historically in popular and political culture, why they were selected, and how they resonated with the electorate.

Framing Sarah Palin addresses the question of what the choice and perception of these frames tells us about the state of American politics, and about the status of American women in politics in particular. What do the debates engendered by these images of Palin say about the current roles and power available to women in American society? What are the implications of her experience for future candidates, particularly women candidates, in American politics?

Linda Beail is a Professor of Political Science at Point Loma Nazarene University, where she serves as Director of the Margaret Stevenson Center for Women's Studies.

Rhonda Kinney Longworth is a Professor of Political Science, Associate Provost and Associate Vice President for Academic Programming and Support at Eastern Michigan University.

FRAMING SARAH PALIN

Pit Bulls, Puritans, and Politics

Linda Beail and Rhonda Kinney Longworth

Routledge
Taylor & Francis Group

NEW YORK AND LONDON

First published 2013
by Routledge
711 Third Avenue, New York, NY 10017

Simultaneously published in the UK
by Routledge
2 Park Square, Milton Park, Abingdon, Oxon OX14 4RN

Routledge is an imprint of the Taylor & Francis Group, an informa business

Library of Congress Cataloging-in-Publication Data
  Beail, Linda.
  Framing Sarah Palin : pitbulls, puritans, and politics / Linda Beail and
  Rhonda Kinney Longworth.
      p. cm.
  Includes bibliographical references.
  ISBN 978-0-415-89333-6 (hbk) — ISBN 978-0-415-89336-7 (pbk)
  — ISBN 978-0-203-80679-1 (ebk) 1. Palin, Sarah, 1964—Public
  opinion. 2. Sex role—Political aspects—United States. 3. Political
  culture—United States. 4. Communication in politics—United States.
  5. Women political candidates—United States. 6. Women in popular
  culture—United States. 7. Presidents—United States—Election—
  2008—Public opinion. 8. Public opinion—United States.
  I. Longworth, Rhonda Kinney, 1967- II. Title.
  F910.7.P35B43 2012
  979.8'052092—dc23   2012015196

ISBN: 978-0-415-89333-6 (hbk)
ISBN: 978-0-415-89336-7 (pbk)
ISBN: 978-0-203-80679-1 (ebk)

Typeset in Bembo
by Cenveo Publisher Services

DEDICATION

To our children, Caroline and Joshua Beail, and Colleen and Jack Longworth, who challenge and inspire us every day. Thank you for adding so much love and laughter to our own narratives.

CONTENTS

ACKNOWLEDGMENTS

We are grateful to everyone who has helped us with the research and writing of this book. Thanks to Michael Kerns, our editor at Routledge, for his patience and encouragement; the Wesleyan Center for 21st Century Studies at Point Loma Nazarene University (PLNU) for a summer research grant; the provost's office at PLNU for sabbatical funds; colleagues in the History and Political Science Department and the Women's Studies Program at PLNU for their generosity and support, especially Kelli McCoy for references on Western women's political mobilization, and Rosco Williamson and Lindsey Lupo for their wonderful camaraderie in the trenches of teaching politics. We also want to thank Eastern Michigan University (EMU) for sabbatical leave and research support funds that spurred early work that grew into this project, and the Political Science Department and Women's and Gender Studies Department at EMU for their invitation to present our research as part of their Women's History Month Program in 2011. We are especially grateful to PLNU students in Linda's courses on campaigns and elections, and women and politics, as well as colleagues in the PLNU Social Issues Discussion Group, for reading and discussing early drafts. Enormous thanks to Kelly Kennedy for her invaluable student research assistance and indexing, to Kim Frey for her bibliographic research, and especially to Andrea Nauta for her expert editing efforts and research support.

We owe a special note of thanks to Lilly Goren at Carroll College for putting together the Midwest Political Science Association panel on gender, the presidency, and popular culture for which this work began, and to the Politics, Literature and Film section for hosting us. Thanks, Lilly, for your vision and encouragement to expand the project, and for cheering us on to completion. We'd also like to thank John Nelson at the University of Iowa for encouraging our interest in political communication and popular culture, and for providing generous opportunities to us throughout our careers.

Linda would like to thank:

Rhonda, I'm grateful for the opportunity we've had to work on this project together. Thank you for the many years of friendship, and many hours of thought-provoking and enjoyable conversation about American politics, feminism, and popular culture.

Like all writers, I've discovered what a strong community one needs in order to engage in this solitary task. I am grateful beyond words to the friends who provided support in so many ways: Jennifer Lang, Melissa and Jeff Burt-Gracik, Heather Ross, Catherine Chadwick, and Jo and Bob Birdsell. From listening to my ideas, to letting my kids come and play, to encouraging me to keep going, I couldn't have done this without you. Sylvia Cortez Masyuk, thank you for the many cups of coffee and the one-word email: WRITE!

Most of all, I'm grateful to have the amazing family that I do. My parents, George and Sherill Beail, have always believed in me, and proved it tangibly once again by providing encouragement and countless hours of childcare while I was working on this project. Thankfully, I believe that time was as delightful for them as it was helpful for me. My husband, Eric, held down the fort while keeping my spirits up during the writing of this book. Thank you for being such a generous partner, not just in this endeavor but also in all of our life together. Your love and unwavering support are gifts of incalculable worth, and I hope I return them in kind. My children, Caroline and Joshua, are the lights of my life. Thank you for sharing your mom's time and attention during this project, and for the much-needed distractions of songs, jokes, stories, and hugs. Caroline, your prolific creativity as a budding author yourself was a great example and inspiration for your mom.

Finally, I would be remiss if I did not say a word to honor the memory of two wonderful men. The first is my grandfather, Leland Huggins. His love of talking politics provided my first political narratives, and shaped not only my career but also my life. The other is my father-in-law, Walt Schlumpf, who was one of the earliest and most enthusiastic supporters of this project. I am grateful for his encouragement, and sad beyond measure that he didn't live to see its completion.

Rhonda's acknowledgments:

My professional and personal life would have been far less rewarding if I had not formed a friendship over 20 years ago with Linda Beail. We have been through so many important events together and I have enjoyed the journey so much more as a result of our partnership.

I was raised to believe that family is the core of any well-lived life. My experience has only confirmed the fundamental truth of that belief. My husband, Paul, has supported this project and me every step of the way. I am deeply grateful for such a wonderful teammate. My children, Colleen and Jack, inspired me to "get it done." I am lucky to be your mom. My father, Donald Kinney, taught me that politics matters. He read the newspaper cover to cover every single day of my youth. We almost never share the same viewpoint but I appreciate that he listens and that he cares. My brother, TJ, knows best the balancing act it takes to live this life. My mother, Linda McWilliams, passed away in the months spent writing this book. Her loss served as a constant reminder that we don't have forever to accomplish the goals we set for ourselves and seeing this project through to completion was important as a way to honor my family's support and her memory.

True friendship is a gift. I can honestly say I would never have written a word of this book if it weren't for some very special women. Susan McDonald has been one of the profound gifts in my life. I am grateful to have found my way to you. Linda Kinney entered my life for reasons I quit questioning a long time ago. Teri Green was the friend you wait a lifetime to find, a true soul mate. I miss her passion for life every single day. Another great source of encouragement throughout this project has been Margaret Crouch. I consider it a privilege to share ideas with her on a regular basis. Mary Linblade deserves a special thank you for her willingness to listen and to always tell me the unvarnished truth. And finally, I am grateful to my friend Julie Cook Booten, who reminds me to laugh—life is too serious to be that serious.

Like Linda, the process of writing this book has reminded me of how lucky I am for the community of friends and colleagues who supported this project in ways big and small. Christine Deacons, Chris Foreman, Akosua Dow, and Winifred Martin took on more so I could spend time working on the book. Susan Moeller fought for me when I needed it. I have been fortunate to work for some great folks who encouraged me in a variety of ways: EMU President Susan Martin, Provosts Donald Loppnow and Kim Schatzel, Associate Vice President Bette Warren, and Political Science Department Head Arnie Fleischmann. They each have my gratitude and sincere thanks.

1

INTRODUCTION

Sarah Palin's vice presidential candidacy garnered tremendous levels of interest, polarizing the American public. From the day John McCain chose her as his running mate until now, much of what has been written about Palin has focused on discovering who she "really" is: establishing her credentials and motivations, exploring her issue positions, or predicting her political future. Is she smart enough to govern? Are her policy positions or familial situations hypocritical? Will she run for president?

We are less interested in defining who Sarah Palin is, and more interested in analyzing why she touches such a nerve with the American electorate. Why does she ignite such passionate loyalty—and such loathing? To what degree did her candidacy mobilize new parts of the electorate? Using the notion of "framing" popularized by George Lakoff as a way of understanding political perception, we explain and analyze the narratives told by and about Sarah Palin in the 2008 election—from beauty queen, to outsider-maverick, to pit bull hockey mom. We discuss where those frames are rooted historically in popular and political culture, why they were selected, and the ways in which the frames resonated with the electorate. Generally we seek to answer the question of what the choice and perception of these frames tells us about the state of American politics, and about the status of American women in politics, in particular.

This book centers around the 2008 presidential campaign in which Palin's image was a muddled one to be sure—a web of pictures and perceptions presented by her, her handlers, the McCain and Obama campaigns, political pundits, the news media, entertainers and popular culture communities. These images were made only more complex by the pre-existing views of various audiences both popular and political, and by the lack of firsthand understanding of Palin herself. Over the months of the campaign she was simultaneously understood and debated as a frontier woman, political outsider, hockey mom, beauty queen, and potential postfeminist role model.

Our analysis is situated in the research literature examining the gendered nature of the American electoral context, as well as the double-bind experiences of women candidates for political office. In framing themselves as candidates, women have had to react strategically to this context—to be "tough enough," while still nurturing and feminine. This provides insight into the factors that resonated about each of the Palin frames and the importance of the Palin candidacy. We examine how she was situated among all candidates—male and female, Republican and Democrat—for executive office. We ask what the debates engendered by these images of Palin say about the current roles and power available to women in American society. Finally, we discuss the implications of her experience for future candidates, particularly women candidates, in American politics.

We pay close attention to race, class, and contemporary political geography as they matter greatly in understanding Sarah Palin's candidacy. Her white, rural, and middle-class identity is important to how she is understood and the narratives that voters are likely to situate her within; these qualities also define her in contrast to her opponents. Narrative frames are most often relational and are not often employed or understood in isolation from one another. They intersect with and reinforce each other. Candidates may employ a variety of frames in a single contest, and narratives are chosen with attention to other frames employed in the election. They also reference historically relevant, important, or impactful storylines grounded in partisanship and gender. Sarah Palin's candidacy is best understood not only in reference to Hillary Clinton and John McCain, but also to Joe Biden, Barack Obama, and even Michelle Obama and Tina Fey. Appeals referenced iconic Republican individuals and employed other narratives appropriated from past women candidates for office. The white, rural, working-class appeals of Palin make sense in light of her juxtaposition to Ivy league-educated women and an exoticized black candidate because we know how well they have worked for other Republican presidential aspirants since the 1950s.

Further, frames are not static or easily controlled by those who initiate them. Consumers interpret, respond to, and reimagine them—sometimes in sympathy with the original author and sometimes not. In the 2008 electoral contest, any attempt to comprehend Sarah Palin's framing must include an understanding of Tina Fey's impersonation of her with its resulting reinvention of these narrative frames. Fey's humorous mocking of "mavericky" behavior and beauty pageant activities and mannerisms (e.g., fancy pageant walkin' and talent portions of the competition) defined the Palin frames as much as anything the McCain/Palin campaign did itself.

So along with describing each narrative frame employed in 2008, our analysis explores where those frames are rooted historically in popular and political culture, why they were selected, and how each resonated with the electorate.

Finally, we discuss what the choices and perceptions of these frames tell us about American politics and the status of American women within that arena.

Methodology

The guiding thesis of this book is that narrative frames are important to understanding the experience of women candidates for national political office, and, in particular, the experience of Sarah Palin, beginning with her 2008 Republican nomination for vice president. As noted above, we suggest that frames are selectively employed as mechanisms by which to provide concise cues to consumers of political information in order to assist them in structuring and understanding their observations of candidates and electoral events. As Anderson and Sheeler suggest, these metaphorical narrative constructs serve as both strategic resources and as constraints upon political figures.[1] We analyze Palin's experience as a candidate and political player from this perspective, closely examining those narrative frames employed by and about Ms. Palin.

In order to investigate the thesis, we ground our analysis first in a comprehensive and close reading of news media stories about Sarah Palin. To identify the frames, we reviewed each story published between the date of Ms. Palin's announcement as the vice presidential nominee and the end of the 2008 campaign contained in the *Wall Street Journal*, *New York Times*, *Time*, and *Newsweek*. These sources were supplemented with a broad review of online blogs and discussion boards encompassing those contained on *The Huffington Post*, *cnn.com*, and *Slate. com*, including everything in Slate's *Double X* blog on women's issues. For Chapter 3's discussion of the role of evangelical tropes within the outsider frame, we reviewed the *Christianity Today* website archive on Palin in 2008, in addition to material contained in *Charisma* magazine and the *Concerned Women for America* blog. We also traced the links and threads that arose as the result of reviewing these sources, attempting to follow conversations to their original source—*Saturday Night Live* skits and other television programs, political cartoons, musical lyrics, viral photo-shopped pictures, posts to additional online blogs, articles in *The Weekly Standard*, *Vogue*, *People*, etc. The concluding chapter draws from the same source materials but includes items published since the end of the 2008 campaign.

We then determined the most common narrative frames that emerged within these venues. We paid particular attention to messages and discussions that contributed significantly to Ms. Palin's public perception. Our goal was to not only identify relevant frames (although the group of frames we identify is instructive regarding the forces at work during political campaigns), but to examine the degree to which frames were employed, co-opted and contested in strategic ways. We intend the analysis to provide broader insight into the current and future possibilities for women candidates for executive office.

Our examination of news coverage, online discussions, texts from candidate campaign appearances and other campaign materials revealed a variety of ways in which narrative frames served as strategic tools for Ms. Palin and for others hoping to characterize her in particular ways. Our discussion of longstanding partisan narratives—frontier woman, outsider-maverick, and faithful fundamentalist—suggests that Ms. Palin was placed by herself and others easily within these familiar and time-tested frames with little resistance or objection. On the contrary, gender frames such as average hockey mom, sexy puritan beauty queen, and new style feminist were highly contested and much debated throughout 2008 and in the years since.

Framing and Political Communication

With the rise of the mass media in the twentieth century, citizens, politicians, communication scholars, and political scientists have all wondered (and sometimes worried) about the powerful role the media plays in communicating political information. Is the media biased? In a democratic system where our ideal of governance is "of, by, and for the people," do citizens get the kind of accurate and comprehensive information they need to make wise choices about who should represent them or which policies they support? Numerous studies have shown that the influence of political news coverage on public opinion is a complex process. Most of us are savvy media consumers, not easily convinced to believe everything we read or see on television. Media influence is not nearly as straightforward as presenting slanted information and having viewers uncritically accept those ideas or opinions. Rather than simply telling us "what to think," the media seems to have more influence in suggesting what we think about, what criteria we use to evaluate issues and candidates, and how we structure, organize, and perceive information.

Scholars of political communication call these influences "agenda-setting" and "priming." For example, when the number of stories in the media about crime increases, the percentage of people telling public opinion pollsters that crime is a major problem in America correspondingly goes up. But when the media turns their attention to a new or different issue (healthcare, say, or terrorism), more Americans report being concerned with those issues. By raising our awareness and giving us more information about some issues, the media helps to set the political agenda: it creates an environment where citizens respond by giving those issues greater weight and attention, and perhaps even demanding action or answers from political leaders. "Priming" is a similar process, applied specifically to how we judge political candidates. By reporting on certain characteristics, media reports encourage us to see those qualities as the most important ones to use in evaluating the candidates.[2] If there are many mentions of some candidates being investigated for ethical reasons, it may prompt voters to recall how important honesty and integrity are to them in choosing a leader. But if much of the campaign coverage discusses the candidates' résumés and qualifications, it may elevate experience over honesty as the most important quality voters are looking for.

(Of course, voters desire a combination of many valuable traits in their elected representatives, so this example is oversimplified. But priming does encourage voters to concentrate on certain qualities, while de-emphasizing others.)

In addition to setting the issue agenda, media narratives can also prime how we evaluate political issues. *How* those issues get discussed matters. The words, phrases, and stories associated with an issue can create support or opposition. Scholars and political strategists call this attention to words and narratives in shaping how we present an issue "framing." In the mid-1990s, Republicans in Congress began calling the "estate tax" on large inheritances (affecting 1 to 2 percent of Americans) the "death tax." This simple change in wording, used repeatedly, has a demonstrable effect on citizens' views. Americans overestimate who is subject to the tax, telling researchers they think it applies to nearly half of households (since everyone "dies," while an exclusive few have "estates"), and are thus far more likely to support its repeal.[3] How and what information is presented affects how citizens think about the causes of political problems and, thus, how they should be solved. One experiment found when unemployment is reported on in human interest stories, with the focus on individuals or specific events, the audience is more likely to attribute the cause of poverty to individuals (and thus see little role for communities or government in responding or ending it). However, if unemployment is reported on as a social and political phenomenon, with explanations of its background and long-term implications, audiences were more likely to attribute responsibility to systemic or institutional conditions.[4] Framing of affirmative action policies as redressing past discrimination, or simply providing equal opportunity to all races, engenders fairly widespread support among Americans. Reframing the same issue as giving unfair advantage to some minority groups demonstrates far more opposition.

Media "framing" of issues can affect not just public opinion, but actual policy implementation. Researchers have found that a steep drop in the number of death sentences handed down since the late 1990s can be attributed to several factors—including a real decrease in the number of homicides committed and public opinion less favorable to capital punishment—but that the *most* significant variable was the tone of media coverage, with a steady rise in stories about exonerations of inmates on death row. Media discussions of the death penalty added the "innocence frame," the troubling notion of wrongly convicted persons being executed, to its more traditional frames (debating the morality and/or constitutionality of capital punishment). The rise of the "innocence frame" was about four times more powerful in predicting the decrease in death sentences than the actual number of exonerations.[5] As the authors of that study note, "framing matters."

Frames are the narratives and stories employed in communicating about an issue; they help to structure how we think about that issue by emphasizing some aspects or considerations over others, and by linking details of the issue together in a coherent way.[6] Frames organize the details of an issue. The narrative helps us to make sense of a large, complex problem or issue by turning it into a story we recognize (and know how to evaluate). As scholar and political strategist George Lakoff notes, simple narrative structures, with archetypal characters and events, help us to categorize new information into familiar stories that make sense to us. For example, a "rescue" narrative encourages us to identify a hero who triumphs over some evil misdeed of a villain to save an innocent victim.[7] Framing is a two-sided process, however. The narrative is an external stimulus, evoked or created by the media, a campaign, or political elites. To be influential, the frame works by tapping into a cognitive *schema* already in the viewer's mind. These *schemas* are psychological structures that organize information about social categories and provide a basis for evaluating issues. The *schema*, once tapped, can "fill in the blanks" of missing information, helping us to infer more details about a situation because at least parts of it match the *schema* in our heads, based on our past experiences and knowledge.

Invoking these story frames is less a conscious, deliberate choice than the unconscious work of neural binding in our brains. And these *schemas* are not merely cognitive; they carry emotional content as well.[8] Thus, frames powerfully structure the way in which we react to political events and why they matter to us:

> Politics is very much about cultural narratives. For candidates it is about the stories they have lived and are living, the stories they tell about themselves, the stories the opposition tries to pin on them, and the stories the press tells about them. But in a deeper sense, politics is about the narratives our culture and our circumstances make available to all of us to live ... Cultural narratives define our possibilities, challenges and actual lives.[9]

Psychologist Drew Westen concurs, stressing the importance of these "networks of associations, bundles of thoughts, feelings, images and ideas that have become connected over time."[10] The metaphors and stories that are most influential appeal to our emotional and moral sensibilities. Westen's work urges Democrats, whom he sees as too focused on the rational merits of particular issue positions, to take note of the more savvy ways in which Republicans have couched their proposals in language and stories that connect with voters' hearts and values: "Political persuasion is about networks and narratives."[11] Framing powerfully connects cognitive information and evaluation with affective motivations and responses. From the music and images of biographical films and political advertisements, to the anecdotes told in stump speeches and nonverbal signals such as flag lapel pins, campaigns attempt to frame candidates in ways that will connect emotionally and cognitively with voters' positive *schema*:

> Political campaigns have long used narratives to bind groups, to create personalities, to define events, and to revere history ... Political narratives often tend to revolve around characters who can be judged in terms of the morality of behavior, of who we are and what and how we are (or should

become), of what we value or disdain. Politicians use narratives to enhance techniques of identification and contrast, the use of stereotypes to enhance in-group and out-group distinctions.[12]

These narratives also create the criteria by which citizens judge which political information matters, because "frames influence not only what people think and feel about an issue but what they don't think about."[13] Thus, the frames we employ help us to focus on some factors as extremely important, while discarding other aspects as not relevant.

What makes framing efforts most effective? While many framing experiments have studied citizen response to a single frame, analysis of news coverage of 14 different political issues demonstrated that, on average, 5.09 frames were used in describing the issues.[14] In the real world of politics, a single frame rarely dominates. Rather, different ways of framing an issue compete for influence and effectiveness. When are frames most likely to influence public opinion or policy preferences? In a study of proposals for a state-funded casino, James Druckman found that repetition or frequent use of the frame helps; more importantly, only "strong" frames impact public opinion.[15] Frames gain strength when they are both *available* and *applicable*. Availability refers to how quickly and easily the frame can be connected to the issue. Does this frame access the *schema*? Can it be readily brought to mind? And does it fit the issue at hand?[16] For example, what considerations come to mind when citizens think about an issue? If thinking about whether or not a hate group should be allowed to hold a public rally, does free speech come to mind as one important value or criteria to be considered? If so, "free speech" is an available frame. Then we might ask if "free speech" is the most important consideration, or if others, such as protecting public safety from rioting or incitement to violence, or a rejection of racial prejudice in favor of a commitment to equality of all individuals regardless of group membership, outweigh its importance. This latter question is the applicability issue: which frame, or set of considerations, is the most relevant and best way to assess the issue? If a frame is both available and highly applicable, it is likely to have a strong influence in citizens' political decision-making.[17] Studies suggest that the strongest frames fit with our already existing cognitive biases, highlight specific emotions, contain multiple frequent arguments, and have been used in the past.[18]

Frames may also be most powerful when they are implicit rather than explicitly evoked. When Clarence Thomas characterized his controversial Supreme Court confirmation hearings in 1991 as a "high-tech lynching," he framed the issue racially. Viewers could access what they knew about American history and race relations to evaluate whether or not the hearings had devolved into a racially motivated, unfair attack on an African American man. Was this metaphor applicable and relevant? Was Thomas having a hard time being confirmed because his blackness threatened white power or privilege? The lynching frame competed with a sexual harassment frame that invoked gender, not race, as its most relevant consideration, and many Americans based their support for or opposition to Thomas's nomination on which frame seemed most salient to this particular situation.[19] Yet, Nicholas Winter argues that the framing of other political issues, such as welfare policy, social security policy, and healthcare reform, can implicitly invoke race or gender *schemas*, even if they have nothing overtly to do with race or sex. In the ways that these seemingly non-racial or non-gendered issues evoke ideas about the legitimacy of differences, as well as the power dynamics and emotional relationships between different groups, he demonstrates that the policies are "framed" in ways that tap into deep race or gender *schemas*.[20] The basis for evaluating policy shifts is based on which *schema* is evoked. Yet these shifts based on how an issue is framed are so implicit, so "natural," that interrogating or critiquing the relevance or fairness of the frame becomes almost impossible. The more a frame seems uncontested and normal, the more powerful it can be. As Winters notes: "frames may be more effective when those promoting them do not emphasize the fact that they are engaged in persuasion. Insofar as the speaker conveys the idea that a particular frame is the natural and obvious way to view an issue, the frame will be all the more effective."[21]

Most political scientists have concentrated on the origins of frames (the choices political elites have made in presenting issues to their advantage) or the impact of frames (how they have shaped or changed public opinion or policy-making).[22] Our interest in framing and the candidacy of Sarah Palin is not aimed specifically at either of these concerns. We are not trying to assign credit (or blame) for employing these narrative strategies to either supporters or opponents of the candidate; nor do we examine quantitatively which frames were most effective in moving public opinion regarding Palin. We are applying the notion of framing— usually used to discuss the presentation of political issues—to a candidate. Rather than noticing how frames encourage "pro" or "con" positions on an issue, we want to explore how a variety of narrative frames for this Republican woman vice presidential candidate both shape public response to her and contribute to wider public debates around partisanship, faith, populism, and feminism. The narratives about Palin tap into already existing *schemas*: of self-sufficient, rugged pioneers often referenced by the Republican party, or of the pretty-but-not-too-bright beauty queen in popular culture, or the maverick reformer willing to buck partisan loyalties. Even as Palin's candidacy evoked these *schemas*, the particulars of her narratives and the responses to them by citizens also changed the *schemas* themselves—reshaping them for the future and reinforcing their salience.[23] We are interested in how Palin's candidacy rewrites the familiar narratives, and how they can be used by other Republican and women candidates in the future as a result.

For many American voters, their understanding of who Sarah Palin was as a candidate was inextricably linked to Tina Fey's spot-on impersonations of her on *Saturday Night Live*. As YouTube made watching these skits more accessible, millions of voters found their impressions of what was true or relevant about the Palin candidacy shaped by the quirks and critiques Fey embodied in her performances. While the lines between political campaigning and "infotainment" have become increasingly blurred since Bill Clinton's saxophone-playing stint on *Arsenio Hall*, today's voters have come to rely on media such as *The Daily Show* and *Saturday Night Live* as important sources of political information. Popular culture plays an important role in creating the *schema* that the Palin campaign narratives drew on, and in communicating political information in the twenty-first century. While some wring their hands, worrying about the "dumbing down" of civic discourse or the inferiority of "infotainment" to hard news, political communication scholar Jeffery Jones argues that satirical television cannot only be a source of good political information, but is more effective than traditional media in interrogating and critiquing the powerful.[24] Not only that, but satires such as *The Daily Show*, *The Colbert Report*, and *Real Time with Bill Maher* engage citizens in politics by making them laugh, and allowing them to participate in making meaning of political events in ways that connect to their daily lives. As Liesbet van Zoonen notes: "Politics has to be connected to the everyday culture of its citizens; otherwise it becomes an alien sphere, occupied by strangers no one cares and bothers about."[25] For van Zoonen, citizenship has a lot in common with being a "fan" of some cultural phenomenon: it keeps a person involved in seeking information, talking with other "fans" in order to make sense of what happens or to persuade them of one's own interpretation and preferences, and being emotionally invested in the object, securing continued commitment.[26] There is real value to recognizing that while political issues and ideologies are serious, engaging in politics can be fun. Even when the issues are serious or the stakes of the election are high, there is real pleasure to be gained in talking about politics with others to learn more or have one's own experiences and opinions validated. There is enjoyment and excitement in cheering on one's preferred candidates, or creatively thinking about solutions to political problems, and emotional reward in seeing one's preferred leaders or policies succeed. If politics is not in some ways pleasurable, why would citizens continue to engage in it? The use of popular culture elements, like stories and narrative, are ways in which the media "entertain the citizen; in other words, how they make it pleasurable to engage in politics, and how they maintain the idea that politics is important."[27]

Framing, particularly as it draws on popular narratives that we are all familiar with, provides ways for ordinary citizens to connect with and make sense of political events and personalities using tools from their everyday lives. Jeffrey Jones notes that politics "is increasingly a textual practice," and it is through media and popular culture texts that we access politics:

> They constitute our mental maps of the political and social world outside our direct experience. They provide a reservoir of images and voices, heroes and villains, sayings and slogans, facts and ideas that we draw upon in making sense of politics. They provide the constituent components of the narratives we construct for organizing, interpreting, explaining,

understanding, and adjudicating the realities and illusions we find within the media, but also within our lives. They are ritual encounters with public life that help in our understanding of who and what we are as individuals, a community, a public, and a nation.[28]

Jones is particularly interested in the use citizens make of popular media narratives, arguing that they are the raw material we use to create our own political sense of identity, our "semiotic self-determination:" "The constant and habitual scanning of mediated political culture for persons, issues, values, styles, rhetoric … is the means through which civic identity is increasingly established, constituted, and maintained."[29] Thus, the framing of political issues or candidacies, such as Sarah Palin's, matters not just in helping us to decide how to vote, but in shaping our own citizen identities and values in response to these narratives and frames. In studies of political issues such as abortion and the environment, researchers have found that television narratives become a catalyst for conversation about the issues. People talk about what they have seen with other citizens, and they also use the narratives and situations the television stories provide to respond to the issue—with deeper understanding, agreement, or to articulate back a different point of view.[30] Thus, we have every reason to expect that media and cultural narratives—such as the newspaper and newsmagazine stories about Sarah Palin, blog posts and editorials about her, and *Saturday Night Live* skits and political cartoons caricaturing her—are important resources for viewers and voters. Citizens use the narrative frames they find there to make sense of the 2008 election, to define Republican party values (particularly with relation to populism and faith), to engage debates about gender, parenting, and feminism, and to relate all of these issues to their own lives. We are interested in how Palin is able to draw on these, and how they are tweaked by her differences (particularly gender) from previous Republican candidates for president. Other frames are drawn from popular culture, familiar archetypes of women: the pioneer woman, the supermom, the beauty pageant contestant, and the feminist. These frames occasioned debate over how aptly each of these narratives fit Palin, but also how well they capture modern American women's lives, aspirations, and achievements. Popular culture is, indeed, contested political terrain, "a complex site of citizenship."[31]

In the chapters that follow, we analyze the influence of popular culture, particularly Fey's characterization of Palin, on shaping voters' views of the candidate, and on what we might expect the relationship between entertainment media and political campaigns to look like in the future.

2008 Electoral Contest

Campaigns do not happen in a vacuum, but instead play out within a political environment that can and does influence issue and event selection, candidate strategies, and, ultimately, the outcome of the electoral contest.[32] Political actors and campaign events have the potential to reshape the environment, but most importantly they can leverage certain aspects that favor their own success or diminish the likelihood of success for their opponent. By way of example, campaign organizations possess knowledge about what factors drive voter turnout and behavior. Typically, they shape their messages, strategies, and campaign behavior accordingly by trying to increase the turnout rates of voter groups likely to support their candidate and to decrease the turnout rates of groups likely to support their opponent. Campaign organizations tailor strategy to the environment. Journalists, pundits, and interest groups present or analyze information in attempts to influence the public debate. The framing process we discuss in this book takes place within this interconnected and interactive environment.

As political scientist Stephen Wayne summarizes, voters and other political actors do not approach campaigns with completely open minds; political party identification, in particular, predisposes individual participants:

> [T]heir pre-existing attitudes and accumulated experiences color their perceptions and affect their judgments ... Of the political beliefs people possess, partisanship has the strongest impact on voting. It provides a perspective for evaluating the campaign and for deciding whether and how to vote. It is also a motive for being informed, for getting involved, and for turning out to vote.[33]

Along with partisanship, other relatively stable aspects of the environmental context influence campaigns and elections. These include social group variables such as the racial, gender, age, geographic, religious, and socio-economic composition of the electorate.[34] Certain aspects of the political environment shift more often between one election cycle and the next. Voter attitudes and the degree to which individuals are attentive and motivated around particular issues tend to be more variable and harder to predict in advance. The personal characteristics and stances of the presidential candidates themselves also play roles in the calculus and interact with voters' pre-existing attitudes and convictions.[35] The strategic process of frames being employed, communicated, mediated, received, shared, appropriated, or reinvented all takes place within and in response to this context.

Candidates for national office in 2008 faced an environment absent of an incumbent president or any specific proxy for the current administration in the race. As is typically the case, this resulted in a large slate of candidates competing for party nominations. Many voters were weary after eight years of Republican executive leadership, six years of war in Afghanistan and Iraq with no clear end in sight and Osama Bin Laden still free, a spiraling budget deficit and national debt, and a looming lending crisis that broke open during the fall election campaign. Younger voters continued to grow in importance as World War II era citizens were passing from the scene and Baby Boomers continued to age into their retirement years. Change became the order of the day.[36] Again, the framing process occurred within and in response to the incentives provided by these environmental conditions.

Women Candidates

Women candidates have had to think carefully and strategically about how they frame themselves for the voting public. We know that the public perceives candidates differently according to their sex. Just as party labels serve as cues for voters to assume information about a candidate in the absence of full information, a candidate's gender is used to infer certain personality traits and leadership strengths.[37] Psychological studies show widespread agreement about the division of personality traits ascribed to women and men. A typical woman is seen as warm, sensitive to others, loving, and kind, whereas a typical man is viewed as decisive, self-reliant, willing to take risks, and assertive.[38] Recent studies of gender stereotyping have found that ideals of masculinity have not changed very much over the past 40 years, despite shifting gender roles in the workplace and household since the 1970s. Men then and now are expected to be daring, decisive, strong, self-reliant, authoritative, competitive, and driven.[39] Women are still expected to be "nurturing and nice," exhibiting compassion, warmth, sensitivity, and affection.[40] However, some additional expectations of competency have been added for women: in addition to being emotional and attuned to others, they should also be strong, independent, and enjoy a challenge.[41] As Deborah Prentice and Erica Carranza note regarding similar findings of increased expectations for Princeton undergraduate women:

> As women have moved increasingly into the workplace, they have taken on additional, nontraditional roles. To perform these roles, they need to demonstrate many of the traits that the prescriptive female stereotype deems less important for them than for others—to be highly intelligent, efficient, rational, to have common sense, and so on. However, because they have not entirely given up their feminine roles, they need to demonstrate traditionally feminine characteristics as well.[42]

In their study of mental health counselors-in-training, Susan Seem and M. Diane Clark find that men expect women to be more traditionally feminine than women themselves do, and that the traits deemed appropriate for a "healthy adult" are almost identical to those of a "healthy adult man," but significantly different than what is expected of a healthy adult woman.[43] Women have competing role demands, with the pressure to perform socially expected and rewarded femininity at odds with the pressure to be competent, strong, intelligent, and forceful in the public world of work and politics, while men face no such competing expectations.[44]

Men and women in the political sphere are not immune to such stereotypes. Both survey data and experimental studies of hypothetical candidates demonstrate that female politicians are thought of as more compassionate, caring, honest, empathetic, and accessible than their male counterparts.[45] However, experimental studies show that when asked to assess the qualities of a "good" politician, students ranked tough and aggressive traits as more important than warm and expressive traits.[46] Experimental research regarding women as presidential candidates, in particular, has found that voters prefer masculine leadership characteristics and rate male candidates as more "effective" than similarly qualified women at presidential duties.[47] Thus, women candidates may ultimately be disadvantaged when it comes to gender stereotypes about candidate personality traits. In a historical study of presidential candidates, Erika Falk found that the emotions of women were covered by the media at a much higher rate than men in the same races. Certainly the most-noted aspect of Patricia Schroeder's exploratory bid for the Democratic nomination in 1987 was her tears at the press conference announcing she would not run—reifying the stereotype that women are too emotional. Over 20 years later, tears from another woman presidential candidate also drew huge media attention: when Hillary Clinton's eyes welled up in answering a voter's question in a New Hampshire coffee shop, the press reported on it as if she engaged in a full-blown crying jag. Ironically, this show of emotion did not serve to undermine Clinton's chances in the upcoming New Hampshire primary, but instead was credited with "humanizing" her and giving voters a reason to support her after her defeat by Barack Obama in the Iowa caucuses. Clinton's unexpected victory in New Hampshire kept her in the race and led to a protracted battle for the Democratic nomination. Whether or not Clinton's alleged tears were the reason for her victory, the media framing of her show of feminine emotion (and its sincerity) dominated the political narrative.[48]

While this display of emotion may have benefitted Clinton, rather than hurting her electorally, it is unclear if it was really a sign of progress for female leadership. Clinton's popularity as First Lady reached its zenith in the wake of the Monica Lewinsky scandal, when she was perceived more as the wronged wife bearing her humiliation gracefully, and not as the overzealous architect of the administration's healthcare policy.[49] Similarly, her surge of support in the wake of a bitter loss in Iowa and her exhausted, unguarded moment in New Hampshire—at a time when many in the media were ready to count her out of the race—might seem to indicate that Hillary Clinton was most likeable when weak and vulnerable, not when she appeared strong. As Judith Warner opined for the *New York Times*: "I hate … that [women have] got to see a strong, smart and savvy woman cut down to size before they can embrace her as one of their own."[50] One blogger mocked not only Clinton, but women voters for going "inside the booths and [having] a little cry" while the headline of Maureen Dowd's op-ed column asked: "Can Hillary Cry Her Way Back to the White House?"[51] Fewer commentators raised the possibility that female voters who rallied to Hillary Clinton in New Hampshire might have been reacting in outrage to the sexist coverage of her campaign (and her "crying"), not enacting a weepy solidarity with a beleaguered female.[52] Rather than demonstrating progress toward a political sphere with room for both masculine and feminine styles of leadership, the media debate over Clinton's choking up in New Hampshire was conducted in ways that belittled women voters and reinforced traditional notions of femininity. The press consensus seemed to be that women voters felt sorry for Clinton, as she had turned out to be merely a weepy girl after all—not a legitimate future commander-in-chief. Rather than opening up the gendered stereotypes about power, this incident and its coverage seemed to reinforce the incompatibility of femininity and leadership.

Based on societal beliefs about gender-linked personality traits, women office-holders have been given credit for handling certain political issues significantly better than men.[53] These include issues involving children and family, poverty, health, education, peace, the arts, consumers, the environment, and women's issues. Of course, these beliefs about issue competence may not be based solely and arbitrarily on gender-role stereotypes. Women officeholders can place a high priority on these issues themselves.[54] The electorate certainly could pick up on such agenda priorities. Further, surveys have shown that male politicians benefit from perceptions that they are tougher, know the political system better, and can more ably handle a crisis. These views lead voters to prefer male leadership in dealing with issues of defense, the military, international diplomacy, foreign trade, big business, and crime.[55] Particularly after the September 11, 2001 terrorist attacks, surveys showed a rise in the salience of security issues, a strong preference for male leadership in military crisis, and a drop in willingness to consider a female presidential candidate.[56] Voters in focus groups interviewed by the Barbara Lee Family Foundation in 2002 were likely to trust men gubernatorial candidates more than women with economic issues and budgeting—another foundational issue of presidential campaigns.[57] Kim Fridkin Kahn found that voters applied gendered stereotypes about issues and personality traits to female candidates for the U.S. Senate even more often than they did to male candidates, making these stereotypes especially important in races involving women candidates.[58] Louisiana's 2003 gubernatorial race provided an opportunity to examine how journalists relied on racial and gender stereotypes in their coverage of a non-white man (Bobby Jindal) running against a woman (Kathleen Blanco). While the media decreased their use of race and gender stereotypes, in general, they still associated Blanco more with traditional "women's issues" and Jindal with typically mascu-line issues, despite the fact that these associations did not accurately reflect the candidates' actual previous political experiences or priorities.[59]

More recent research has deepened our understanding of how gender issue stereotypes interact with voter attribution of issue advantage to the Democratic and Republican parties. A large majority of female candidates in the United States are Democrats, and some of the issues associated with women officeholders are also issues associated with the Democratic Party: poverty, health, education, reproductive rights, the environment. Scholars have begun to explore how much of the issue differences are attributable to partisanship and not just gender. Kathleen Dolan's examination of candidate self-presentation on their campaign websites finds few differences between men and women with regard to the issues they prioritize. Congressional candidates of both sexes were very likely to discuss healthcare, taxes, education, and social security in 2000 and 2002. While men were more likely to emphasize defense and women healthcare, those differences turned out to be a result of partisanship and not sex.[60] Dolan concludes, "The similarity of stereotypes about Democrats and women reinforce each other and create the impression, in the difference of means tests, that women behave in a particular way, when in fact it is because many of these women are also Democrats that they behave the way they do."[61] Similarly, Danny Hayes finds no significant sex differences in how voters rate the empathy, compassion, and strong leadership of male and female candidates within the Democratic and Republican parties in the 2006 Senate elections.[62] Democratic men as well as women get higher scores for being caring and compassionate, creating "ownership" of those traits for their party. Republicans, on the other hand, do not get an expected advantage on owning the "leadership" trait, but that may be due to the overall unpopularity of Republican candidates in the 2006 midterms.[63] Women candidates' supposed strengths of empathy and warmth may be a factor of Democratic partisanship, not gender. Republican women candidates were in an especially challenging position: they were seen as less compassionate and weaker leaders than both Republican men and Democratic women.[64]

Other research demonstrates that gender may still have an independent effect.[65] Survey research shows that voters give female candidates of both parties a large advantage in handling education over their male counterparts, while both Republican and Democratic men get more credit than their female partisans for dealing with crime. Women candidates from both parties are also seen as more liberal on abortion, which could put Republican women in a particularly difficult position with their party's pro-life constituents.[66] Indeed, the confluence of gender stereotypes and partisan trait attribution seems to be advantageous to Democratic women candidates, who are given credibility on the issues their rank-and-file voters care about based on their feminine "expressive" traits and their party label, but potentially detrimental to Republican women candidates.[67] Republican women, like Sarah Palin, face conflicting stereotypes about who they are politically based on their party ideology and their gender.

Because voters often characterize leadership, competence, and power as "masculine," women candidates may meet with the most success when they stress those types of traits rather than "feminine" qualities of compassion and honesty more naturally attributed to them.[68] In other words, female candidates have to make strategic decisions in their campaigns: do they play to their stereotypical strengths and build on that support, or do they play against type and emphasize traits and issues voters normally associate with both men and political office-holders? Recent advice to potential women candidates for executive office emphasizes striking just the right balance on that tightrope: successful women must be "effective but appealing," "factual and tough" without being "personal and harsh."[69] In their guidebooks advising female candidates on how to run and win elections, the Barbara Lee Family Foundation bluntly tells them to avoid short hair or a "mannish" appearance.[70] They also warn women about their tone of voice, citing focus group comments: "She was a witch. That was so clear," and "I couldn't stand to listen to her voice … I'd have to move if she were elected."[71] Women candidates are told they need to be strong and assertive, but to avoid seeming aggressive and shrill.

Some research shows that for both men and women, the real advantage comes in playing against party type: the more Democrats are seen as tough and aggressive, the higher they are rated on both strong and caring dimensions. The more Republicans are portrayed as having feminine traits, the higher they score on leadership and compassion.[72] It seems that "voters have strong expectations about the traits that Republicans and Democrats should exhibit, and they reward candidates when they 'overperform,'" overcoming their perceived weaknesses and eroding the advantage of the opposing party.[73] Thus, for Democratic women, like Hillary Clinton in 2008, a reasonable strategy might be to play against the feminine and Democratic stereotypes voters possess, and to pursue an image of assertiveness, strength, and competence. However, the strategy for Republican women candidates seems harder to untangle. Danny Hayes finds that Republican women candidates benefit from *masculine* portrayals in that they are seen as appropriately tough and assertive, traits that voters value in all politicians; but his findings also suggest that Republican women might benefit from *feminine* portrayals that neutralize Democrats' perceived advantage on empathy. How might Republican women negotiate this conundrum?

Of course, women candidates are not completely in control of the messages and images of themselves that voters receive and react to. Frames presented by candidates are not merely accepted at face value. As Kim Fridkin Kahn found, even though women Senate candidates emphasized "masculine" traits 91 percent of the time in their ads, news stories about those female candidates only mentioned those types of traits 41 percent of the time.[74] Those same media reports emphasized masculine traits for male candidates more than the candidates did themselves—reinforcing views perhaps already in voters' minds, but not what candidates were trying to communicate.[75] Historically, women candidates for the White House have received less coverage than similarly qualified men. Men, on average, had twice the number of articles written about them, and those articles were 7 percent longer.[76] Men have also gotten more "issue" coverage, while women candidates are more often described in terms of their physical appearance. Numerous accounts of women's campaigns discuss the "lipstick watch," the attention paid to the candidate's clothing and hairstyles.[77] Media trainer Michael

Sheehan sums up the obstacles in his title for a seminar for potential women officeholders: "Husbands, Hemlines, and Hairdos."[78]

In addition to having their appearance scrutinized, deflecting attention away from political issues and potentially trivializing or objectifying them as women, female candidates are also faced with questions about their personal lives. As Susan Carroll notes:

> Voters are more likely to scrutinize a woman candidate's family situation … When a man runs for office, his family is generally viewed as an important source of emotional and personal support. When a woman runs, her spouse and children are more often perceived as additional responsibilities that the candidate must shoulder.[79]

Women candidates face a double bind with regard to marriage and family. Mary Sue Terry, a single woman running for governor in Virginia in 1993, was lesbian-baited and accused of not being able to understand the issues of ordinary Virginia families, while Jane Swift, former governor of Massachusetts, was criticized relentlessly as too distracted from her job in the statehouse because she had an infant daughter and was pregnant with twins.[80] Media reporting on women running for the presidency highlighted the role of women and their families more often than male candidates.[81] In 1984, Geraldine Ferraro's historic nomination for vice president was eclipsed by unrelenting coverage and questions about her husband's finances, and dogged by concerns about gender roles on the campaign trail. How would she and Walter Mondale interact onstage together—would they hug? What title would they give her husband? In 1999, when Elizabeth Dole sought the Republican presidential nomination, she was criticized for being too ladylike—full of "sugar" and "charm," but too polite, scripted, and a Stepford-like wife to her famous husband, former senator and presidential candidate Bob Dole.[82]

Indeed, early attempts by women to run for the White House fit no workable narrative and were literally unthinkable. In a 1972 editorial entitled "Symbolic Candidacy," the *New York Times* opined: "The presidential candidacy of Representative Shirley Chisholm, the second-term Congresswoman from Brooklyn, is not a venture in practical politics. She candidly recognizes that she is not going to win."[83] In 1937, a Gallup poll revealed that only 33 percent of Americans would be willing to vote for a woman for president of the United States.[84] Enormous changes in social norms, gender roles, and women's professional and political accomplishments accompanied shifts in that attitude, so that by the end of the twentieth century, nearly all Americans—92 percent—expressed willingness to vote for a female presidential candidate.[85] But as the probability of actually having a woman nominee increased in the twenty-first century, with Dole and then Clinton seriously preparing to run, that support seemed to erode a bit. A 2005 Hearst Newspaper/Siena Research Institute poll indicated that only

"81% of Americans would personally vote for a qualified woman candidate from their party," and USA Today reported that same year that "nearly one-third of Americans believe their 'neighbors' are unwilling to vote for a woman."[86]

To lend some external validity and real-world credibility to these attitudinal reports, surveys of Ohio voters in the summer of 2006 pitted plausible female presidential candidates from both parties (Elizabeth Dole and Hillary Clinton) against plausible male candidates from both parties (Rudy Giuliani, John McCain, and John Edwards) in the six different possible general election matchups.[87] In each electoral pairing, the male candidates received a higher percentage of the vote when running against a female opponent than when running against another man. Voters were also more likely to switch their vote from a woman of their own party to a man from the opposing party in mixed-gender match-ups.[88] Respondents rated all three of the men as more qualified than the women, despite relatively similar tenure in the Senate for Dole, Edwards, and Clinton, while Giuliani has never held statewide or national office.[89] These results lend support to the "gender incongruency hypothesis" of executive office: that women are disadvantaged in running for these powerful positions because they have traditionally been male dominated, which has created masculine norms for what a "good" executive looks like.[90]

Indeed, one of the first popular culture endeavors to imagine a female president was the 1964 comedy film Kisses for My President, starring Polly Bergen as the president and Fred MacMurray as her hapless, much-maligned "First Lady." (There is no Palinesque "First Dude" in this depiction. The poster for the theatrical release features MacMurray in a flowered hat and the words "FIRST MALE 'FIRST LADY' TAKES WASHINGTON BY STORM.") The film's focus is not on the challenges or opportunities facing the first woman president, but on the laughs to be had at MacMurray's expense as he is assigned the ultra-frilly "First Lady's Bedroom" and assigned typical First Lady duties, such as planning the menu for a state dinner. Plot complications ensue with the First Family's children running amok and MacMurray's masculinity under threat. The crises are resolved by Bergen's character discovering, to her surprise, that she is pregnant. She immediately and happily resigns the presidency to devote herself full time to her family. The film's message reinforces separate gender roles for men and women, and makes it clear that a male supporting spouse is as ridiculous as a woman president; obviously, women will be happier in their proper domestic sphere as wives and mothers than in the public realm of presidential politics.

Nearly 50 years later, many of the initial analyses of the 2008 presidential primary season focused on this same conventional wisdom regarding the masculinity of the presidency and sexism in the campaign to explain Hillary Clinton's loss to Barack Obama. In June, the Washington Times reported that once Clinton announced her intention to run for president, she was the subject of only 36 stories in major newspapers, while Obama was featured in nearly twice as many (59), a fact that belied a larger pattern of gender bias in the news media and led to Clinton's loss.[91] Michelle Goldberg posited in *The New Republic* that the women's movement was in crisis, with Clinton's failure to win the nomination largely attributed to sexism.[92] Jodi Kantor also reported in the *New York Times* that Hillary Clinton's supporters felt that sexism—both from the media and the Obama campaign—was to blame for her defeat, and mentioned the "classic hurdle" for women politicians of projecting warmth and toughness simultaneously.[93] One campaign strategist concluded that, like female politicians before her, Hillary had seemed uncertain how to reconcile her sex with her political persona: how could she be an authority figure, warrior fighting for ordinary Americans, victim of male domination, and coffee klatsch girlfriend all at once?[94] But what really doomed Senator Clinton, according to this press narrative, was the incompatibility of womanhood and executive power. A winter *New York Times*/CBS News poll had shown that despite her assertiveness, Hillary was still rated lower by Americans than Obama when it came to ability to be commander-in-chief.[95] It is into this gendered context that contemporary women, including Sarah Palin in 2008, situate their candidacies for executive office.

Structure of the Book

The book is organized around two important variables in electoral politics: partisanship and gender. The central Palin frames from campaign 2008 are presented in two groups: frames that have been most often employed by and about Republican candidates for office (Part I), and frames that have been employed by and about women candidates for office (Part II). We utilize this categorization in order to highlight areas of interest, continuity, and difference between Palin and other candidates for higher office. Part I focuses on the ways in which Palin was situated as a Republican candidate for political office. It analyzes the ways in which the narratives that surround her selection and candidacy in 2008 are continuous or discontinuous with those surrounding past aspirants running under this banner. Part II examines the degree to which Palin's framing is like or unlike past women candidates. Does she open new space for women to run, particularly Republican women, who might not have had it available to them in the past?

Part I: Conventional Frames—Republican Narratives

Chapter 2: Frontier Woman

Chapter 2 focuses on the ways in which the 2008 McCain/Palin campaign frequently framed Ms. Palin as a capable and self-sufficient frontier woman. Visually, this frame translated into pictures of Palin hunting, shouldering firearms, sitting on couches with bear skins thrown over the top, or standing by the family seaplane wearing a parka and boots. She was presented at times dressed casually, wearing denim work shirts and jeans. In interviews, Palin revealed her favorite meal was moose stew or moose burgers. The notion of rugged, outdoorsy individualism as an embodiment of the Republican political ideology has been an enduring and successful piece of Republican campaigns for some time. The frame triggers cues employed by Republican candidates in recent presidential elections to appeal to white, rural, often Southern or Western voters. Comparisons can easily be made to pictures of Ronald Reagan on horseback or George W. Bush chopping wood at his Crawford, Texas, ranch. However, Palin and her partisans were not completely in control of how this frame was employed and reproduced over the course of the campaign. While the McCain/Palin campaign tried to present Palin as a guy's girl—sharing masculine hobbies like hunting and not requiring concessions to her femininity (though remaining sexually attractive)—they could not control what others did with these same "frontier woman" cues of firearms and femininity. A much-Googled photo of Palin depicted her clad only in a skimpy red, white, and blue bikini with a rifle draped seductively across her body, raising questions about the limits of this frame for a successful campaign. The chapter also discusses the degree to which opponents can counter the positive impact of particular frames, in this case by focusing on "trigger happy" behaviors that might call into question the fitness of a candidate for service.

Chapter 3: Political Outsider

Chapter 3 analyzes Palin's stance as a normal American who identifies more with the proverbial "average Joe" than with Washington insiders and other elites devoid of practicality and principles. Palin's choice as McCain's running mate itself was unabashedly focused on her status as a political outsider and a game changer. Hailing from Alaska with virtually no national exposure at all, how could it have been seen otherwise? Unlike several of the other frames we discuss, this frame is less visually focused and is, instead, more centered on the rhetoric of Palin's political biography. The implied narrative to this frame is that ordinary American citizens are also political outsiders, and in order to elect someone who truly understands and empathizes with their lives, they need to vote for someone like Palin who has walked in their shoes. Like the average citizen, she was upset with corrupt entrenched politicians, and juggled myriad daily obligations such as driving herself to work and attending her children's sports activities. Throughout the campaign, Palin talked at length of her small-town background and main street values. These were key words and concepts that were clearly meant to convey that she understands and is in touch with ordinary citizens. Her speech was casual and folksy, including an abundance of dropped g's ("our financial system needs some shakin' up and some fixin'"). She's the cool kid making subtle fun of the far less cool intellectual kids in this election contest—no overly cerebral phrasing or carefully detailed answers from her that might intimidate or alienate potential supporters. Sarah Palin aimed her remarks to Joe Six Pack and

Joe the Plumber—average, "real" men. This was even true in her family life. No formal "First Gentleman" title for her husband: he was the "First Dude" of Alaska.

The outsider/ordinary citizen frame is not an unlikely choice for any candidate, especially a woman. This folksy main street appeal has been a mainstay of Republican candidates in recent decades and this chapter provides illustrations of this continuity. Women candidates are almost inevitably viewed as outsiders in the American political process simply as a result of their status as "women." Women candidates have frequently attempted to turn what might be seen as a disadvantaged status into a position of strength. The strategy presents itself easily given the non-traditional paths women often have followed into public office, as well as the issues that drew them into politics initially. The frame also lends itself to discussions of faith as a guiding principle in politics. Palin's stance, much like that of Republicans since Ronald Reagan, was that liberal, intellectual elites, including the mainstream media, had strayed from the core values of the American Founders (individual liberty), Judeo-Christian traditions and values, and patriotic loyalty to the nation.

The McCain campaign viewed Ms. Palin as a kindred spirit to John McCain, particularly in her history of taking heat from fellow Republicans for bucking them on issues and spotlighting their ethical failings. In their view, both candidates were fiercely principled, honest, unafraid warrior-mavericks. The McCain campaign hoped this anti-establishment story and imagery would appeal to 2008 voters who were in a decidedly anti-incumbent, throw-the-rascals-out mood. Of all the frames employed during the campaign, this is perhaps the one that lost the most focus and depth with observers. What it meant to be a "maverick" didn't come through all that clearly as the campaign wore on. This was perhaps best illustrated in the widely viewed, mocking impersonations of Palin by Tina Fey on *Saturday Night Live* (*SNL*). By the end of the campaign, it was unclear to many just what it meant to be a maverick. It had become a concept without impact or solid cultural reference points. The frame became emblematic of a candidacy that many perceived to lack intellectual seriousness or depth.

Part II: Contested Frames—Gender Narratives

Chapter 4: Hockey Mom

Sarah Palin made motherhood a central feature of her potential political appeal. When McCain announced that he had chosen her as his running mate, Palin introduced herself to the crowd (and the nation) as "just your average hockey mom from Alaska." Like many women in politics, she attributed the start of her political career not to deliberate ambition, but to getting involved in the Parent Teacher Association (PTA) at her children's school, which then led to other opportunities. Some voters responded positively to this framing of Palin's maternal qualities and experiences, citing them as a reason to support her. Many found the idea of a working mother so close to the center of power in Washington appealing. Her staunch pro-life position, demonstrated not only in her own decision to give birth to Trig but also in the views she expressed about her 17-year-old daughter's unwed pregnancy, and the large family she juggled along with her high-powered political career, seemed to underscore a commitment to mothering as one of women's primary roles or duties. In fact, one of Palin's initial charms was how effortlessly she seemed to embody not just Everymom, but Supermom. Importantly, Palin described herself as a "hockey mom"—not a soccer mom. Beginning with the 1996 presidential race, the "soccer mom" demographic was identified as an important swing vote in American elections. In 2004, Republican strategists appealed to these white, married, middle-class suburban women's fears about terrorism to turn "soccer moms" into "security moms." But the addition of "hockey moms" to the political lexicon in 2008 lent a slightly different connotation. Hockey moms seem to be more "tough," "competitive," "aggressive," than soccer moms, able to deal with the pre-dawn practices, freezing rinks, and broken teeth that go along with the sport. There is also a class component to the distinction. While hockey is actually a less affordable sport, the image of hockey moms is more working class. Soccer moms might be married to doctors or lawyers and drink wine; hockey moms' husbands were more likely ironworkers or fishermen, and they drink beer. As a self-proclaimed "hockey mom," Palin was making a more blue-collar, anti-elitist, "Joe Six Pack" appeal. The "hockey mom" frame offered voters a narrative in which they could relate to Sarah Palin as an everymom, admire her as a super-mom, applaud her maternal values, or judge her parenting choices, even while reinforcing her conservative, white, working-class appeal.

Chapter 5: Beauty Queen

From the moment she stepped onto the national political stage, Sarah Palin's looks and style have been central focal points in our collective experience of her persona. In past election cycles, this open and direct talk of traditional femininity and attractiveness, sexiness, and wardrobe might have all been viewed as just the type of objectification that women and women candidates for office had experienced in the past. Feminist critics have commented on how these variables have been used to call into question the seriousness, readiness, or qualifications of women candidates and to disadvantage them with voters in some way. Most past women candidates for office in either party paid great attention to appearing strong, prepared, and decisive.

Yet Palin seemed quite comfortable, almost amused, with her beauty queen image—even empowered by it. Her youthful coquettishness set her in direct opposition to Hillary Clinton, who took the more common approach of projecting great strength and demonstrating experience. Rather than confronting and contradicting the stereotypical focus on her appearance, the McCain/Palin camp instead responded by trying to reframe the discussion, turning the focus on femininity to their advantage. Palin herself became a living example that women could be strong without threatening traditional social values and practices, particularly men's traditional sense of masculinity. She presented a narrative potentially appealing to many women in the American electorate who see themselves as capable and equal, but not androgynous. Finally, here was a woman they could relate to in national politics: one who liked cute shoes and enjoyed being a girl, but who was powerful too. Delegates to the Republic National Convention wave buttons proclaiming her the "Hottest VP from the Coolest State," viewing her attractiveness as a political asset rather than a liability. But as this narrative came to dominate perceptions of Palin, it also served to reinforce dismissive and denigrating stereotypes about women and power.[96]

Chapter 6: Post-Feminist Role Model or Victim of Sexism

Sarah Palin did achieve a historic milestone in becoming the first Republican woman to gain the vice presidential nomination of her party. But whether or not this was a victory for gender equality remained a controversial question. Was Palin a feminist role model—younger, with a more expansive and less doctrinaire definition of empowerment—or an anti-feminist throwback? Was she a victim of sexism during the campaign, or a beneficiary of John McCain's chivalrous protection? Framing Palin in terms of feminism involved highly contested narratives throughout the election season.

From the moment she publicly accepted John McCain's invitation to be his running mate, Sarah Palin touted herself as an empowered role model for women. After noting Hillary Clinton's historic achievement in garnering 18 million votes in presidential primaries, Palin deftly cast herself as heir apparent to Clinton's mantle, asserting: "It turns out the women of America aren't finished yet, and we can shatter that glass ceiling once and for all." Other women vehemently disagreed, seeing the Palin pick as cynical tokenism. Palin's supposed feminism was called into question by her absolutist anti-abortion position, her support for abstinence-only sex education, her lack of advocacy for equal pay, flextime, healthcare reform or childcare policies, and opposition to policies that might support women and children. Critics found it hypocritical of her to talk about her daughter's "choice" to have the baby when she would like to outlaw that reproductive choice. Finally, the debate about Sarah Palin as a good feminist example of women's progress quickly turned to charges by the McCain campaign that she was a victim of sexist treatment by the media.

Conclusion

In this chapter we take stock of Sarah Palin's narrative framing of herself since the end of the 2008 campaign, and draw conclusions about what the Sarah Palin phenomenon means for the future of American politics. We are interested in why Palin has touched such a nerve with the American electorate, and how she has embodied so many different narratives that appeal to, or alienate, voters. We analyze what her popularity and candidacy might mean for the future of the Republican Party and for future women candidates. Has she expanded the narratives available to future candidates, allowing a wider range of potential candidates to emerge and to be successful? Has she mobilized a new element in the electorate (the Tea Party?), or is she using familiar tropes that will cement existing party positions and loyalties? We examine the future of Sarah Palin—not only as an individual political persona and candidate, but also what her celebrity and narratives mean for the future of American politics more generally.

PART I

Conventional Frames: Republican Narratives

2

FRONTIER WOMAN

In 2008, the McCain/Palin campaign frequently framed Sarah Palin as a ruggedly capable, outdoor-loving frontier woman. Given her life story and rise to leadership in America's self-proclaimed "Last Frontier" Alaska, it is not surprising that this narrative emerged as an important frame through which the Palin candidacy was presented. Visually the frame translated into photographs and videos of Palin hunting, shouldering firearms, sitting on couches with bear skins thrown over the back, or standing by the family seaplane wearing a parka and boots. Often, Palin dressed casually for these appearances, wearing denim work shirts and jeans. Speeches by and about Palin focused on her geographic roots and her life living in the West, on the frontier, and referenced a lifestyle grounded in these geographic realities. Hardly an article passed without some reference to Palin's home state of Alaska, while Democratic vice presidential nominee Joe Biden's geographical "home" flew relatively low under the radar despite his own attempts to leverage it for political benefit.

Ms. Palin's public appearances highlighted familiar cultural narratives—both historical and currently popular—about folks from the rural frontier. Visual and verbal imagery highlighted the simple, uncomplicated rewards and pleasures of a grounded life lived close to nature. Palin's family and community stories focused on fiercely proud, self-sufficient people taking on and conquering the challenges of their environment—clearing land, harvesting, hunting, or fishing. Stories and anecdotes focused on determination, hard work, faith, and building things that endure and hold lasting meaning. Appeals targeted generations of conservative consciences—seniors first inspired by Barry Goldwater who later comprised the Silent Majority counted on by Nixon, those emboldened by Ronald Reagan, and prodded by the Bush wars on terrorists and liberal social values.

Both traditional journalistic outlets and entertainment sources for news embraced the frontier frame. Coverage grounded in this frame suggested that Palin was no delicate, elite, helpless city girl unable to fend for herself. Instead, she happily embraced the challenges of the wilderness. In interviews, Palin revealed her resourcefulness and implied self-sufficiency, suggesting her favorite foods included results of hunting expeditions—moose stew and moose burgers. Tellingly, the second most viewed article online in the *Wall Street Journal* for the week ending September 5 was about Palin and ran with the title "Midnight Runs and Caribou Dinners."[1] A *Newsweek* columnist opined at the time that "[Palin] has also been drawn as the latest in the proud lineage of frontier women who shouldered physical work alongside men and were renowned for their strength and courage."[2] Taking the storyline one step further, *Washington Post* staff writer Libby Copeland suggested that Palin might even exceed the capabilities of men, comparing her to "pretty prairie wives with rifles who could out-hunt their husbands and still get dinner on the table. (Hot chicks with guns being a beloved American archetype.)"[3]

Indeed, Sarah Palin's political persona was framed in this manner even before her 2008 vice presidential candidacy. A profile written a year prior to her selection as John McCain's running mate introduced Sarah Palin as a rising star in the Republican Party, describing her squarely within this lens:

> "She's as Alaskan as you can get," summarized Dan Fagan, an Anchorage radio talk show host. "[S]he lives on a lake, she ice fishes, she snowmobiles, she hunts, she's an NRA [National Rifle Association] member, she has a float plane, and her husband works for BP on the North Slope."[4]

In the same profile, Palin brought the self-reliance implied by the frontier image to her proposed public agenda: "Alaska needs to be self-sufficient, she says, instead of depending heavily on 'federal dollars' as the state does today."[5] Her embodiment and embrace of what McCain viewed as these shared core values was one of the factors that suggested Palin as a potential running mate to him.

Throughout the fall of 2008, news media outlets followed the campaign's lead, often framing Palin within this perspective. Conservative commentator Kathleen Parker remarked in the *National Review*: "Palin's narrative is fun, inspiring and all-American in that frontier way we all seem to admire."[6] One of the *New York Times*'s first pieces after her selection for the vice presidential slot featured a picture of the governor in her Anchorage office, seated on a couch with a large bearskin draped over the back.[7] In the photo, the bear's head is still attached to the skin—mouth open, as if in mid-roar, with sharp teeth bared—making the bear appear menacingly lifelike as Palin leans back against it. The juxtaposition of a petite, professionally dressed Palin against the enormous, fierce bear served not only to bring a touch of the state's unique, wild beauty into this well-governed space. More importantly, it reinforced how at home Palin felt on this Last Frontier, with a strength and spirit equal to that of the wild creature, possessing a grit and determination that belied her small stature.

These visual and textual messages are underscored by other images of Palin throughout her political career. A photo shoot of political women in *Vogue* magazine depicted her in a down parka and boots, leaning against her family's seaplane, rather than wearing the more predictable power suit and pearls chosen by most women candidates hoping to be taken seriously as competitors. Palin's self-presentation declared her different from the average woman candidate. She appropriated frontier cues traditionally claimed by male candidates, yet she did so in what many might view as perhaps the most quintessential of women's venues—a fashion magazine. Palin's choice to appear and her self-presentation was especially noteworthy in light of Hillary Clinton's controversial decision to cancel her own scheduled *Vogue* appearance that campaign cycle. In early 2008, *Vogue* editor Anna Wintour publically provided that Clinton's refusal that year was made "for fear of appearing too feminine."[8]

As suggested above, the frontier frame was not invoked randomly—the frame provides a mechanism by which authors and audiences, including voters and political and media professionals, parsimoniously present, understand, and converse about candidates. They "rely on this shorthand to quickly comprehend the personality of the candidate."[9] In 2008, the frontier frame worked effectively in that people quickly understood and accepted that Palin lived this lifestyle and possessed these qualities—perhaps because it corresponded well with Sarah Palin's real life story, her long public record of expressing these beliefs and experiences. The descriptive accuracy of the frame remained essentially unquestioned in any meaningful way.

The frontier narrative references an array of characters and storylines—both real and imagined—with which people are familiar. In this narrative, "good guys" wear white hats, uphold law and order, and in the process display quiet power, demonstrate strength of character, and make principled decisions. They discern quickly and ethically when force is required to protect the weak, inno-cent, or dependent. The frontier equalizes individuals. People pitch in and work hard to survive. Early settlers were strong, independent, unyielding pioneers, setting out bravely against the challenges of the uncivilized terrain. Frontiersmen had to be prepared to fight to protect and defend what was theirs from threats presented by weather, animals, thieves, and rustlers. Correspondingly, the modern narrative presents "bad guys" who typically wear black hats. The black hats, while also strong, use their power to take advantage wherever they can, feeding unjustly from the labor and goodness of others. They challenge stability unneces-sarily, shoot indiscriminately, and put others in danger in willy-nilly fashion. The narrative abounds with simple and relatively uncomplicated dichotomies faced by individual actors—good versus evil, right versus wrong, just versus unjust, order versus chaos, self-sufficiency versus taking advantage of others. Governments are distant or non-existent in the story.

The frontier frame presents stark characters in a straightforward manner with sharp distinctions based on which side of the divide you fall on. Consequently, when drawn metaphorically, the frame can dramatize and escalate disagreements. Opponents are depicted as dangerous, menacing, or unethical rather than as people who reach a different conclusion or who hold a different point of view on an issue of interest. Frames, including this one, also motivate voters differentially and affect certain groups to varying degrees. The frontier frame, in particular, has long historical routes as well as a recent and well-documented appeal to a particular political constituency concentrated geographically and culturally.

In addition to discussing how metaphors grounded in this past are applied, this chapter also examines whether or not the frontier frame allows similar benefits to accrue to Palin as it had traditionally to male candidates. In 2008, few questioned whether or not Sarah Palin was a true frontier woman, just as most accepted that Ronald Reagan was a successful frontiersman. But was the result and impact the same for both? Also, Palin declined to abandon traditional notions and accoutrements of femininity and motherhood. As we discuss further in later chapters, Palin embraced her physical attractiveness during the 2008 campaign. Her long hair was well maintained and femininely styled, her nails manicured and pedicured, her heels high and her skirts slim. She eschewed the notion that to be taken seriously, she needed to wear serious hair, clothes, or makeup. Palin wore bright colors, straight fitted skirts, high heels, and open-toed shoes. Marriage and motherhood were also prevalent topics in Palin's speeches, appearances, and in coverage of her candidacy. But we wonder if Palin's experience demonstrates that women can have it all in this regard—can they simultaneously claim strength bred of frontier living in conjunction with sexiness and fertility? By negotiating an image that embraced aspects of masculine strength without rejecting a femininely styled outward appearance, did Palin open more space for herself as a woman candidate in this most public of arenas or compromise her potential effectiveness as McCain's running mate? While not satisfactory to all women candidates, the Palin approach in 2008 does seem to provide a path different from the traditional approach women have been advised to take in recent years. Rather than downplaying her femininity to appear more like men, she embraced it as a contrast and a balance to her relatively aggressive, attacking comments and tone.

We also wonder about how this frame traveled and morphed as time wore on and what any evolution might tell us about American politics, more generally, for women candidates and for electoral politics. At a minimum, we propose that a political geography underlies the use and imposition of this frame and how Sarah Palin experienced it. Choices and behaviors surrounding this frame highlight the deep ideological and partisan cleavages in American political society that are reinforced geographically and demographically: North versus South; East versus West; rural versus urban; liberal versus conservative. By framing Sarah Palin as a frontier woman she becomes more appealing to some constituencies, less appealing to others. Some celebrated her as a result, while others looked down or condescended.

The frame concisely tells a story—one which appeals to some stakeholders while at the same time repelling others in modern politics.

Historical Antecedents

Sarah Palin was certainly not the first candidate for office to adopt or be positioned within the frontier frame. Since the early years of the American republic, presidential aspirants and their biographers have employed narratives and images of the American frontier and the settling pioneers to assert character, competency, and preparation for the office. Politicians as prominent and varied as George Washington, Andrew Jackson, Abraham Lincoln, and John Kennedy all uniquely embraced, employed, or were identified with the values, geography, settlers, and lifestyles of the frontier "West" in constructing their political personae.

Given the centrality of the frontier to American culture, it is not surprising to see the prominence of this frame in American electoral history. In a highly influential essay, historian Frederick Jackson Turner declared the frontier to be a primary determinative force in American development.[10] He compared its influence to that of the Mediterranean Sea on the Greeks, suggesting that the continual pushing back of the frontier line and settlement of these areas formed a unique American nationalism and approach to societal and political institutions. Turner suggested a composite American national identity emerged as European ways grew distant and irrelevant to the challenges of the frontier.

According to Turner, as settlers lived greater and greater distances from coastlines, the country and its residents grew more independent of European traders in port cities.[11] Residents of the port cities turned inward toward the continental interior and increasingly away from Europe as a source of business and influence. The drive of frontier settlers to formally join the United States as settled states in the union pushed the existing conflict over slavery to the forefront of national policy. This and other frontier challenges continually confronted national legislative activity, forcing an "American" approach to emerge that, while it drew from Europe, took on a character uniquely shaped by the expansive and unsettled geography of the United States. Turner noted the importance of religious missionary activities to settling the frontier and finally analyzed the specific traits that in his view came to comprise the American identity as a result of a continual struggle with the frontier:

> coarseness and strength combined with acuteness and inquisitiveness, that practical, inventive turn of mind, quick to find expedients, that masterful grasp of material things, lacking in the artistic but powerful to effect great ends, that restless, nervous energy.[12]

Turner also tells us that the frontier was not about an education focused on theoretical, book-based learning—rather, frontiered living fostered a more practical, applied intelligence, an instinctual and experiential approach and motivation developed in response to real world, practical challenges.[13] Anti-elitist, populist attitudes are an enduring quality of American culture and in American politics. And we see these in the frontier frame applied to Sarah Palin's vice presidential candidacy.

The frontier frame is rooted firmly in the history of the presidency itself, beginning with founding President George Washington. Washington came to prominence as a leader in pre-Revolutionary times in part because of his perceived prowess in the frontier battlefields of the French and Indian War (1754 to 1763). His ability to master and use the frontier to his advantage became integral to his public image regardless of its connection to the full truth of his performance at Fort Necessity. Much like the later stories of Valley Forge, the early biographical portraits of Washington were peppered with tales of his drawing on nature and environmental conditions in the colonial territories to his advantage. His displays of caginess, toughness, adaptability, and fortitude widely circulated before and after the American Revolution. Frontier battlefield stories referenced underlying competencies and values that Washington seemed to convey throughout his military and political career. As a result, they became integral to his public image and central to his claims to leadership.

Andrew Jackson's political biography was also framed in the mythology of the frontier West. He earned his reputation as a vital leader in the largely unsettled areas of Louisiana and in the battle of New Orleans. Like Washington, his military prowess in lands far removed from the original American states provided him a useful reputation in his later run for the presidency. As historian Evan Cornog states: "his story contained a distinctly American tone, with its emphasis on the untutored forces he commanded … and his frontier toughness, memorialized in the nickname 'Old Hickory' bestowed upon him by his troops."[14]

The mythology of Abraham Lincoln's honesty and moral compass originates in a youth spent in a frontier log cabin. Lincoln conveyed stories of wild animals roaming the surrounding Kentucky and Illinois woods where he grew up. Years lived working hard on the prairie, confronting and conquering frontier challenges, led to simple ethical clarity about right and wrong, good and bad behavior. Honest Abe returned money to shop customers when he discovered misbalanced scales and expected the same treatment from customers given more change than they were owed. Americans looked to this man of character in an historical moment of struggle, division, and insecurity about what constituted the right and just path for the nation in part because of their confidence in his understanding of these values and the character of the American nation.

Theodore Roosevelt, while appointed as assistant secretary of the Navy, resigned his post to volunteer for service in the Spanish American War. He led a cavalry unit referred to as the Rough Riders comprised of western cowboys, law men, Native Americans, and elite gentlemen like himself. He returned to the United States (and political office) a war hero after leading the unit on a charge up San Juan Hill. His time as a "Rough Rider" was central to his subsequent claims of competency and effective leadership ability. He honed this identity over the course of his life, embracing leisure activities such as wild game hunts and safaris and by enacting public policies such as the legislation preserving vast lands on the frontier as national parks. His reputation as a frontiersman was routinely reinforced and reproduced by his choices in office.

Commentary during the 2008 campaign included explicit comparisons between Sarah Palin's political brand and Roosevelt's. Communications scholar Karrin Vasby Anderson suggested that:

> Part of Palin's appeal, however, is that she inhabits the Pioneer frame very differently than did her predecessors. Drawing on the frontier myth that has served many male presidential candidates well, Palin presents herself as an independent thinking, rugged Alaskan, and member of the National Rifle Association. In the tradition of Theodore Roosevelt's "strenuous life," Palin is the woman who can raise a large family, reform state government, participate in the PTA, oversee oil exploration, and field dress a moose. This feminine/feminist image retains the novel appeal of the Pioneer while investing it with the more substantive and familiar narrative of classic American exceptionalism.[15]

Blogger Laura Browder, author of *Her Best Shot: Women and Guns in America*, agreed, suggesting that Palin is the logical extension of women from "an earlier time—as one of the pioneer mothers, Wild West shooting stars, or women hunters who were so popular more than a hundred years ago."[16] She went on to make a direct connection to Theodore Roosevelt's adoption of the Western narrative as one of "wildness, freedom and adventure," opining that:

> Palin is in many ways the embodiment of twenty-first century strenuous living: she runs marathons, shoots wolves (albeit from a helicopter), and affects folksy speech patterns, eschewing educated diction whenever possible.[17]

Like Palin, other modern presidential aspirants and candidates have found frontier images enticing as well. Lyndon Johnson regularly sported cowboy hats and boots. Even children of Eastern elites embraced the mythology and allure of the Western frontier. They may have done so more metaphorically than literally, but they attempted to connect themselves to Americans' love of the frontier, nonetheless. Most notably, John F. Kennedy, son of a multimillionaire businessman, applied the metaphor to challenges of the post-World War II world, asking Americans to work together to conquer a "New Frontier" via international outreach, economic development at home and abroad, and scientific and technological development. And in each of his runs for office, George W. Bush, third-generation Yale graduate, whose grandfather was a senator from Connecticut and whose father had served as a congressman, United Nations ambassador, Central Intelligence Agency director, chair of the Republican National Committee, vice president and president of the United States, projected his self-image as a denim-wearing, brush-clearing down-home rancher from west Texas onto his candidacies for executive office. The lure of the frontier frame and concurrent narrative are clearly attractive to political combatants throughout the long history of the country.

The frame's symbolism holds strong allure for many candidates. Stories, lessons, and values drawn from settling the North American frontier are integral to the shared narrative of what it means to be an "American." Americans understand themselves to be a collective nation, defined by a history of delving into the unknown in search of a better life; conquering and taming nature's challenges (rivers, mountains, animals); facing all of these hurdles with optimism, fortitude, tenacity, and hard work. In the American view of the world, the national character shaped the frontier just as the frontier conditioned the American character. Settlers worked harder and longer, displaying grit, ingenuity, and perseverance. Their eventual prosperity derived from hard work, entrepreneurship, adaptability, and confidence in themselves. They did what had to be done. The frontier was wild and Americans conquered it, settled and civilized it. The Western myth frames many of the core values that define American beliefs about the nation itself. Palin and her top-of-the-ticket running mate, John McCain, both tried to fit themselves within this mold.

Republicans Lay Claim to the Frontier

Modern American conservatives, particularly within the Republican Party, have embraced the notion of a rugged, individualistic, freedom-loving frontier cowboy as the embodiment of a particular, more specific, and uniquely *conservative* political ideology. The frontier metaphorically represents a preferred approach to public policy decision-making, one focused on individualism and limited government. Translated into modern terms, this meant reduced tax rates and fewer regulations affecting businesses, smaller devolved government, and a preference for order and continuity in traditional social values over progressive social change.

Frontier imagery and narrative framing has been a noteworthy cornerstone of Republican campaigns for nearly a half century, dating back most clearly to the unsuccessful 1964 presidential campaign of Barry Goldwater. The frame triggers iconic visual images of Ronald Reagan wearing cowboy hats and on horseback in California; George W. Bush clearing brush on his ranch in Crawford, Texas; and Goldwater donning his cowboy garb in Arizona. In the years following the institution of Franklin Roosevelt's New Deal programs, the frame was employed by Republican candidates in presidential elections to emphasize their connections to a conservative movement grounded geographically in former frontier lands.

In this more particular form, the frame has garnered considerable interest from rural and working-class white voters, particularly those centered in southern and mountain west states. Sarah Palin's desire to mobilize support from these voters for the McCain presidential effort led to a similar approach in the 2008 campaign.

Conservatives have also tended to contrast this frame with Democratic counterparts. For example, in 2008 their portrayal of Barack Obama's life story focused on his Ivy League "elite" education, and his years spent in the big city, Chicago, conducting community organizing activities and working his way via the urban Democratic machine on his path to the Senate. One need only recall Sarah Palin's sarcastic tone during her nomination acceptance speech as she contrasted Barack Obama's political undertakings with her own as mayor of Wasilla, Alaska, to get a sense of how different she and her co-partisans wanted these biographies to appear:

> Before I became governor of the great state of Alaska, I was mayor of my hometown. And since our opponents in this presidential election seem to look down on that experience, let me explain to them what the job involves. I guess a small-town mayor is sort of like a "community organizer," except that you have actual responsibilities. I might add that in small towns, we don't quite know what to make of a candidate who lavishes praise on working people when they are listening, and then talks about how bitterly they cling to their religion and guns when those people aren't listening.[18]

Obama's choices were dismissively juxtaposed against McCain's highly practical hands-on experiences in the military and Palin's elected executive, but also rural, "real" political positions. However, there is an expressed sense that urban, typically Eastern elites hit first—condescending to rural, western, former frontier citizens first. These rhetorical framing choices and reactions are not without consequence and typically not without intent. Existing geographic and demographic cleavages are highlighted and reinforced by the selection of preferred frames by candidates and in the frames media chose to highlight more than others.

In a September 3 *Wall Street Journal* article written immediately following the Palin vice presidential announcement, journalist Gerald Seib suggested her selection "was designed in part to put forth a vice presidential nominee whose profile—mother, hunting enthusiast with a blue-collar husband—would appeal to blue-collar Republicans, moderate Democrats and independents."[19] He went on to connect the dots across recent Republican candidates, suggesting that since Reagan's 1980 presidential victory, Republicans had employed a successful formula "emphasizing tough military and national-security views, cutting marginal tax rates, reforming the welfare bureaucracy, fighting crime and resisting affirmative action" that was grounded in these references and cues to voting constituencies.[20] The frontier frame is instrumental in drawing this connection in that it concisely builds and reinforces the messages of toughness, individuality, self-sufficiency, and law and order.

Sarah Palin's framing of herself as a Western frontier woman links her directly and intentionally to this particular brand of modern Republican candidate, with roots reaching back to a conservative movement galvanized during the Barry Goldwater presidential campaign of 1964. Palin's framing and its cues serve as familiar signposts indicative of the connection to this particular modern ideological standpoint. Others, including Robert Taft and William F. Buckley, Jr., could perhaps lay claim to intellectual or legislative fatherhood for modern American conservatism. But Barry Goldwater galvanized and gave early electoral credence to a conservative philosophy and movement within the Republican Party on a national presidential stage.[21]

Goldwater's 1964 contest for the Republican presidential nomination brought front and center the long-simmering tensions within the Republican Party itself between moderate liberal Eastern Seaboard Republicans, exemplified by Nelson Rockefeller, and Western conservative Republicans personified by Goldwater. During his legislative career, Goldwater had gone so far as to proclaim the country might benefit without the Eastern Seaboard of the country, telling a 1961 news conference that "sometimes I think this country would be better off if we could just saw off the Eastern Seaboard and let it float out to sea."[22] During the general election campaign between Senator Goldwater and Lyndon Johnson, a visual re-enactment of the Eastern tier of states being sawed off a map of the United States was incorporated into a Johnson advertisement to emphasize the statements Goldwater had made.

Interestingly, Goldwater's opponent in the presidential race in 1964, incumbent President Lyndon Johnson, successfully used this notion of extremism in an effective strategy that turned aspects of the frontier narrative against Goldwater. Instead of allowing Goldwater the image of a white hat, boot-wearing cowboy who defends order, justice, and morality, Johnson worked hard to suggest that Goldwater might be the force to fear in the cowboy myth—the black hat rather than the white one. His campaign characterized Goldwater as a dangerous gunslinger—quick on the trigger in a disagreement—an extremist. They frequently asked explicitly and implicitly "whose finger do you want on the nuclear trigger?" Goldwater did not reassure voters or anyone else in this regard. For instance, in his nomination acceptance speech at the Republican convention he reminded Americans that, in his view, "extremism in the defense of liberty is no vice ... and also that moderation in the pursuit of justice is no virtue."[23] Goldwater's stance was perhaps principled, but it was not very reassuring to millions living in Cold War-era America.

Johnson contrasted this view of Goldwater as one to take overly quick, irrational, and violent action (also from the Western myth) to his own constructed biography of steady experience, safety, fairness, decency, and reason. This tactic played out obviously and caustically in what became known as the Daisy ad, perhaps the most famous negative political advertisement ever created. While it was only aired once on broadcast television during the campaign, its impact was devastating.

The Daisy ad opens with a little girl standing in a meadow, picking petals from a flower as she counts them. When she reaches the number nine, a menacing voice begins counting down like a launch count in the background. As the girl turns toward something she sees behind her in the sky, the camera zooms in until her pupil fills the screen, blacking it out. When the countdown reaches zero, a flash occurs followed with a picture of a mushroom cloud, the result from a nuclear explosion. As the visual of a firestorm raged, a voiceover by Lyndon Johnson states:

> These are the stakes!
> To make a world in which all of God's children can live.
> Or to go into the dark.
> We must either love each other, or we must die.

The commercial ended with a final voiceover stating that "The stakes are too high for you to stay home." Johnson had successfully co-opted the cowboy narrative and used it to call Goldwater's temperament and suitability for office into question. As Jack Valenti, a close Johnson campaign advisor has suggested, Goldwater committed the most serious of campaign sins in allowing his image to be controlled by his competitor. The framing of his image worked to make his opponent's case, not his own.

Despite his resounding defeat in the 1964 presidential election, "Barry Goldwater and his brand of cowboy conservatism ... taught millions of Americans—white southern voters, in particular—how and why they were conservative Republicans."[24] At considerable electoral cost, Goldwater explained the conservative view that Americans were in danger from communism, at risk from liberal free spending and jeopardized by the limits liberals had placed on economic liberty. Goldwater set the stage for what was to come decades later. Columnist George Will has stated in multiple venues his view that Goldwater "won" the struggle in 1964; it just took 16 years (until the resounding Reagan presidential election) for the final vote count to come in and be recognized. "The Goldwater network, built from a multitude of single-issue organizations, nonpartisan conservative groups, and populist grassroots activists, became the other sixties movement."[25] Ronald Reagan's 1980 election can be viewed as the culmination of this movement begun by Barry Goldwater. Reagan adopted not just Goldwater's conservative philosophy, but also much of the frontier cowboy frame that accompanied it and he took both to the next level of success. He took the same playbook and, more effectively, executed the game plan.

Given his performer's instincts honed by years spent as an actor, Ronald Reagan embraced the cowboy imagery along with the conservative ideology he came to love. He served as a California co-chair for the 1964 Goldwater campaign and campaigned actively on Goldwater's behalf. Reagan's campaign activities, along with his broader political activism, selective reading, and study of economics and political philosophy, motivated him to enter politics on a large scale, espousing the conservative ideology. Along the way, historian David Farber suggests that Reagan made:

> conservatism popular and conservatives nationally electable. In the face of sixties leftist activists and then the hard times of the late 1970s, Reagan convincingly portrayed conservatism as a forward-looking, optimistic faith in the American way of life (as he defined it).[26]

Reagan reclaimed the narrative through his choice to marry optimism to the existing plan and to explain what conservatives were in favor of, not simply what liberals had done wrong. In part, he accomplished this by employing the frontier frame and its focus on clear moral choices—right versus wrong, good versus bad, the powerful versus those in need of protection. Conservative Republicans were protecting Americans—from communism, from moral decay, from unrestrained spending and a lack of disciplined limits, and from a lack of confidence the left had in the American way of life. Over his two terms in office, Reagan became an iconic figure for Republicans and conservatives everywhere. And clearly Sarah Palin's studied attitude and smile seem connected to the Reagan approach of positivity, down-home folksiness combined with a big picture vision and focus. Like Reagan, she was a patriotic, flag pin-wearing conservative with a confident smile (even if, at times, her smile morphed to a smirk).

During his campaigns and time in office, Reagan frequently visited his California ranch, eventually widely referenced as the Western White House. He was often photographed wearing denim shirts, and cowboy hats and boots—nearly always with a full sparkling smile. Michael E. Welsh has suggested that not since Theodore Roosevelt had a president so clearly embraced the myths of the American West.[27] Reagan confidently mounted horses. He chopped wood. Reagan projected an image of a man confidently, calmly in control of his environment. His background in film seemed to give him a sense that the visuals mattered. Imagery could be linked metaphorically to emotions and values in important ways. He consciously framed himself as the mythological strong, white hat-wearing cowboy who preserves law and order and protects the community from evil threats wherever they lie.

When Sarah Palin framed herself and adopted others' framing of her as a frontier woman, it was an effective way to not only reference the highly popular, iconic Reagan, in particular, but also the conservative ideology espoused by the earlier "cowboy conservative" Goldwater. The frontier frame connected her to an ideology focused on individual liberty and preserving traditional social order. What Sarah Palin shares with each of these men is a personality and lifestyle well suited to this type of appeal. She actually did spend her youth in rural America, much of it in Alaska. She and her family did embrace frontier life—hunting, fishing, snowmobiling, skiing. The Palins created their own small business in the face of economic and geographic hardship. Simply put, like many Americans, they just did what had to be done to make it on the frontier. Frames, to take hold, have to possess some element of truth or authenticity in the eyes of stakeholders.

In contrast to Palin's frontier credibility, when John Kerry tried to spontaneously take up bird hunting during the 2004 campaign, the attempt at reframing his candidacy encountered a tremendous level of amusement and outright resistance. The choice was inconsistent with other frames employed by him and others to organize and understand his candidacy up to that point. People viewed the approach as inauthentic at best, crass at worst. Instead of outdoorsy frontiersman, the frame that resulted from the effort was that Kerry was the classic Washington politician, desperate and willing to "do anything" for attention and votes.[28] Frames cannot be randomly employed; genuineness matters greatly in their success.

Gendered Aspects of the Frame

In 2008, Cindy McCain frequently began joint campaign appearances with Palin by introducing the governor as "a true Western *woman*."[29] Mrs. McCain's practiced introductions employing the frontier frame beg the question of what it means to be a woman on the frontier as opposed to the archetypical frontiersman—a Western woman as opposed to the Western man, a cowgirl rather than a cowboy. In this narrative, do Western women carry guns? Are they patriotic, hard-working, self-sufficient individualists as well? Or are they the ones who needed protecting in the narrative? Where do women fit into this picture and can they claim this frame successfully for themselves? For women candidates on a national stage, at a minimum the situation appeared significantly more complicated to succeed with this frame. Though complicated, Palin's path suggests a road women have navigated successfully in the past, one that provided political opportunities, not simply roadblocks.

Despite a long history of political men employing the frontier narrative in presidential politics, and modern conservative candidates polishing the appeal to near perfection going into 2008, there were no examples of past women candidates in national campaigns who might serve as reference points for comparison. Interestingly, Palin did not appear daunted by the challenge ahead of her or to question the fundamental equity of the task at hand. Instead, she looked to be having fun and laughing at it all just a bit, playful and competitive in her approach to the task.

Portrayed on the cover of *Newsweek* with a shotgun thrown jauntily over one shoulder, Palin seemed to be putting the men in the race on notice that "anything you can do, I can do better."[30] Palin was a veritable sharpshooting Annie Oakley in many portrayals from the campaign trail. Her speeches emphasized her sense of individualism, toughness, direction and vision, hard work, and a clear moral compass. As noted above, the visuals were focused on familiar frontier accoutrements—casual work clothing, active outdoor endeavors, guns, woods, parkas, and boots, although hats were infrequent. Palin clearly aspired to be the main character starring in the narrative—the Reaganesque cowboy who protects and boldly leads. Her challenge was to hold on to the benefits of the frontier frame with conservative voters while at the same time not threatening their relatively traditional views about women at work outside the home.

Here, Palin attempted a tightrope walk—adopting complementary frames focused on and emphasizing her sexual attractiveness and beauty queen past, her fertility and parenthood as a mother to five children, and her religious faith and religiously motivated positions on such charged issues as abortion right/rights of the unborn. Each of these complementary frames reinforced, rather than challenged, traditional notions of gender roles and the sharing of power between men and women in public and private spheres.

The real key in understanding Palin's challenge as a Republican woman in the 2008 campaign is in her navigation of the *paradox* of this wilderness tomboy frame with the feminine beauty and the All-American Mom. Could she be effective as the sharpshooter while wearing pencil skirts and balancing on high heels? Palin needed to demonstrate her capability to hold down the fort at home with aplomb while her husband was absent for weeks on the northern oil fields, while also proving she could join him in the physically demanding work of commercial fishing. Palin remained charmingly feminine, even while retaining her outdoorsy assertiveness. After all, Annie Oakley may have been able to beat Wild Bill Cody in a shooting competition, but she still wanted him to fall in love with her. Laura Browder suggests that "Oakley, who epitomized the 'civilization' that the Wild West shows set out to promote, was known for her trademark skip and pout ... just as Sarah Palin is known for her winks and nose wrinkles during her speeches."[31] Palin was a "guy's girl," the sexually attractive woman who shares a man's interests and hobbies without requiring any concessions to feminine qualities, pursuits, or "weaknesses." This plucky Western "gal" is:

> self-confident and in-charge, but not threatening. She likes to do the same things the boys like to do, to hunt, fish and play sports ... Palin represents the (symbolic) possibility of the perfect girlfriend or wife. "She brings home the bacon, cooks it, and will wear the sexy apron while serving it to your friends, who all want to sleep with her."[32]

In the September 6 *Wall Street Journal*, Peggy Noonan highlights just this contrast, while along the way invoking a nickname, "Baberham Lincoln," for Ms. Palin.[33] Noonan's article didn't question whether Sarah Palin was this generation's Honest Abe Lincoln or this generation's babe—rather, it seemed to accept Palin's attempt to be both. But can she? And if she can, is this a persona that helps win elections or builds confidence that she can govern effectively if called on?

Noonan's early view suggested optimism at the prospect as she pondered how Democrats would deal with the intersection of the Western narrative and a woman candidate. On the continuity of the conservative's past messages contrasted with the discontinuity in the messenger, Noonan suggested Democrats

> seemed like they were thinking, "I've seen this movie before and it doesn't end well." Actually, they haven't seen it before in that Palin is something new, but they have seen it before in terms of what she said.[34]

The 2008 Palin experience did not fully answer the question of whether or not the toughness implied by this frame translated into a voter-perceived ability to operate in this most traditional of "male" environments—the presidency. Palin's early fumbles in answering foreign policy questions called into doubt her suitability in that policy realm to such a large degree that we cannot be certain of how voters might have viewed this evaluation independently from the knowledge question. We are still left to question whether or not there are alternative frames that women candidates might employ in order to demonstrate the types of qualities men can certify—for instance, through military combat. We still wonder whether the ability to master the frontier might serve as a proxy for the ability to handle stressful life-and-death situations. This has remained one of the enduring doubts women candidates for the top political office have faced.

The early reaction to Palin's attempts suggested that her approach provided an opening of the playing field for other candidates, especially when one returns to the real frontier and asks what women in that context actually did politically. Sara Hayden suggests the settlement of the middle and far western territories coincided in time with the rising tide of calls for women's suffrage in the United States.[35] She argues that women who moved into the agrarian frontier confronted a different world than women living in the quickly urbanizing, industrializing society they left behind on the Eastern Seaboard. The distinction between private and public was far less apparent on the frontier as work was grounded in the same space as home. In the Eastern cities, the workplace was quickly moving outside the home to storefronts and factories. In these urban areas, men were quickly becoming producers while women were transformed primarily into consumers.

The frontier woman confronted a very different reality from the city woman. Limited population levels in the newly settled frontier lands meant an insufficient number of men to confront the "work." Out of necessity, if nothing else, women stepped up to do what needed to be done. The resulting blurring of traditional gender roles left women feeling entitled to the participation rights men were granted in society. Women worked on farms and ranches side by side with men. Even when women took on different tasks from men, the genders were interdependent. Everyone's work contributed to successful outcomes. Hard work was appreciated and valued. Along with contributing their labor, women were credited with bringing certain social competencies to the frontier. They were often viewed as agents of civilization—bringing order and structure to the expanding society. Calls for social justice and suffrage, in particular, were grounded in "how hard they worked." Women's claim to full citizenship came by virtue of their invested labor. In this way, their claim for suffrage rights did not threaten traditional notions of masculinity and femininity. Women accepted the burden of work that needed to be done in the absence of men, not out of simple desire of their own to seek these new roles and responsibilities. Instead, the political influence of women expanded on the frontier in a manner that did not overtly threaten the existing balance of gender roles and the existing hierarchy. Suffrage became a reward bestowed to women because of work and sacrifice, not as the result of demands and renunciation of an existing social order.

Examining a map of states where women had received suffrage prior to the adoption of the Nineteenth Amendment to the Constitution is telling. Women had full or presidential suffrage rights in nearly all states west of the Mississippi River prior to the adoption of the constitutional grant. Only Texas, Louisiana, Arkansas, and New Mexico did not grant women national voting rights; but even there, women exercised local and/or state suffrage. Along the East Coast, the situation was far different, with suffrage rights being the exception rather than the rule for women in these areas.

This connection of work and women's entitlement to political access and power can also be found in the narrative of 2008. In early September that year, a *Wall Street Journal* article examined the sudden appeal of Sarah Palin, particularly to women. The reporter identified common threads. The women interviewed suggested that "the angry, woman-as-victim" thing drove them nuts. They hated victimology. One woman told the interviewer: "The point is that across the ages women have been doing pretty much what Sarah Palin has been doing: bearing children, feeding families, bringing in an income, working to improve their communities."[36] In other words, they were getting Palin's point in framing herself this way. The women, like Palin, understood that most of the time, women were capable and self-sufficient, simply doing what needs to be done. Their access to power is grounded in doing the work of society. And women who without complaint, without whining, without much support or assistance can appeal in certain fashion to women on the historical frontier, perhaps differentially so. Women went on to say that Palin's "story reflects a more normal reality" of active women: "the harder you work, the luckier you get."[37] These women mentioned her grit, determination, and character. Palin's frontier woman frame was read as empowering in that it appreciated the struggle and contributions of women who get things done and who uphold the foundations of society on a regular basis.

Losing Control of the Frame

Finally, it is worth noting that Palin and her partisans were not completely in control of how this frame was employed and reproduced over the course of the campaign. While the McCain/Palin campaign tried to present Palin as a guy's girl—sharing masculine hobbies like hunting and not requiring concessions to her femininity (though remaining sexually attractive)—they could not control what others did with these same "frontier woman" cues of firearms and femininity. Nor were they completely in control of the balancing act across all of the intersecting frames surrounding her candidacy.

Frames are iterative in nature and audiences aren't passive observers, especially in the age of ubiquitous news and television coverage of candidates, viral clips on YouTube, Photoshop, and Facebook. Audiences interpret frames as well. They run with them in unpredictable ways. One notable example, a much-Googled photo of Palin, depicted her clad only in a skimpy red, white, and blue bikini, with a rifle draped seductively across her body. All the cues from the frontier frame are present to some degree—strength, confidence, patriotism, nature. But the controlled balance with gender-related frames is off. The femininity in this photo is neither subtle nor winking—it is overt and explicit. The popularity and supposed veracity of this pin-up pose (actually of another woman's body with Palin's head photoshopped onto it) speak to how easily this frame asserting feminine empowerment can become sexually objectified in ways not originally intended.

This frontier woman frame, as applied to and by Sarah Palin throughout 2008, captured racial and class issues floating just below the surface of American electoral politics as well. The notion of pioneer or frontier women conjures an image that is white and rural—as opposed to black and urban. And rural white votes were seen as a vitally important voting base to the Republican party, although one not necessarily energized by John McCain throughout his run for the Republican nomination

By contrast, as mentioned above, in her speech accepting the vice presidential nomination, she famously mocked Obama's experience as a community organizer. Journalist John Heileman suggests that this is "no wonder, given that occupation's urban (read black, read poor, read black poor) connotations."[38] In emphasizing her rural, even "backwoods," affinities, Palin's frontier woman frame may alienate some voters—even while evoking identification and approval from small-town white women (and men) who consider themselves down-to-earth, hard-working, patriotic folks not afraid to shoot a rifle, drink a beer, or get their hands dirty.

Perhaps the lack of control over this and all other narrative frames surrounding candidates is best exemplified by the relationship between Sarah Palin and *Saturday Night Live* regular guest star Tina Fey. In her ubiquitous impression of Ms. Palin presented in a series of skits on *Saturday Night Live* throughout the fall of 2008, comedienne Fey repeatedly satirized the details and behaviors referenced in the frontier frame. Dressed as Palin, Fey was seen cocking a shotgun in the background of a September skit where Amy Poehler (as Hillary Clinton) comments seriously on sexism in campaigns. Another skit brought Fey making cutesy shooting sounds in a childlike girlish voice and blowing smoke from the ends of her pretend guns in a skit skewering her poor performance during a *CBS Evening News* interview with Katie Couric. Fey's portrayal further mocked Palin's attempted intersection of femininity and gun-slinging—the cutesy and tough—suggesting a lack of seriousness, sincerity, or true conviction. In yet another skit replaying the 2008 vice presidential debate between Palin and Joe Biden, "Palin" was asked to clarify her recent statements about states where "real" Americans might reside. After coyly refusing at first to answer, Fey as Palin blissfully blurts a list including New York, New Jersey, Massachusetts, Connecticut, Delaware and California as states where you would find relatively few real Americans in residence. She continued suggesting that other states still had time to decide if they were real Americans or not. The relationship to Goldwater and his claims about the Eastern Seaboard jumps out from this example.

This frame, even in its iterative form, highlights the continuing geography of American electoral politics. Place remains, as it always has been in politics, an important variable given its intersection with other notable factors in elections such as race, education, or social class. We can observe an underlying geographical dimension to politics that can be activated through narrative references and allusions as much as an explicit reference to issue positions and particular stances staked out by political parties and candidates. Framing provides a mechanism by which players may converse covertly about politics when the overt is considered impossible or ill considered for some reason. Individuals can make race, class, or gender-based appeals without having to risk the full range of consequences for making them explicitly. Framing can also allow voters their pre-existing beliefs while still leveraging these types of cues. A wealth of data exists documenting Americans' strongly held belief that huge majorities of us are "middle class," that we hold few, if any, racist, sexist, classist beliefs. But leverage points are still accessible. Conversely, frames also allow citizens a way to criticize and condescend. We can laugh at the narrative while convincing ourselves that we are not condescending or unfairly judging real actors. Frames serve not only as shorthand through which we can convey information about candidates, but they also provide a means by which we can disguise from ourselves or others similar types of information.

3

POLITICAL OUTSIDER

Throughout the fall of 2008, Sarah Palin was framed as an outsider to mainstream national politics. In various forums, she characterized herself or was presented by others as a person from outside the Washington, D.C., Beltway (as an average citizen or as a woman candidate); outside the Republican Party mainstream (as a maverick reformer); or outside what she and other conservatives termed a liberal, elite insiders' club (as a proponent of religious faith, values, and country first). Palin was just like the proverbial "average Joe" in that she and her family worked regular jobs and, at times, struggled to make ends meet. Palin did not present herself or her family as perfect or as model citizens. They were flawed but they supported each other loyally. Palin was willing to stand up for her views regardless of what that meant in terms of personal consequences. Within this frame, Palin's allegiance was to what she believed was right—not necessarily to institutions or to individuals that might be more politically expedient.

As discussed above, frames are often developed strategically in response to the political environment and the best opportunities available to political actors at any point in time. The outsider frame was aptly selected for the state of public opinion in 2008. That fall, Americans continued a long pattern of tremendous ambivalence about men and women who make their careers in politics, especially those in elective office. We saw this reflected in public opinion polls where trust in government to do what is right was at historic low levels. The American National Election Study (ANES) index measuring trust in government reached a low point of 26 (out of 100 points possible) in 2008.[1] Public support for elected institutions measured at similarly low levels. Only 12 percent of Americans expressed "great" or "quite a lot" of confidence in Congress and an only slightly higher 26 percent in the presidency.[2]

Popular culture also provides interesting insights into the prevailing belief structure as well. In political narratives, innocent Davids routinely run up against corrupt, threatening Goliaths. In the iconic 1939 film *Mr. Smith Goes to Washington*, Jimmy Stewart played a naive young politician appointed to fill a vacant Senate seat who runs up against scheming careerists determined to stop his well-intentioned reform proposals.[3] The 1993 film *Dave* featured Kevin Kline in a dual role as a cheating, unethical president and a lookalike everyman who steps in to impersonate the president when he suffers a stroke. Dave and his accountant friend, Murray, manage to find $650 million in budget cuts to fund a homeless shelter in a single evening over a dinner of submarine sandwiches.[4] Like these illustrative films, popular culture more generally tends to reflect the widely shared view that longtime insiders are complacent, at best, corrupt, and dangerous at worst. Conversely, ordinary individuals with common sense can offer the decency and perspective needed to solve the challenges of the day. Much like the dichotomy captured by the frontier narrative between good and evil, this frame juxtaposes jaded Washington Beltway insiders against the decent, hard-working common men and women found beyond the confines of the Capitol.

Average American

Given this context, it is not surprising to see candidates frame themselves as outsiders to the mainstream political system. Sarah Palin's selection as John McCain's running mate was unabashedly focused on her status as an outsider to mainstream Washington, D.C., circles and effectively evoked this narrative. John McCain's announcement of her as his running mate set the tone:

> I've spent the last few months looking—looking for a running mate who can best help me shake up Washington and make it start working again for the people who are counting on us … I have found the right partner to help me stand up to those who value their privileges over their responsibilities, who put power over principle and put their interest before your needs … She's not from these parts, and she's not from Washington … She's exactly who I need, she's exactly who this country needs, to help me fight—to help me fight the same old Washington politics of me first and country second.[5]

At a December 2008 Annenberg Public Policy Center and FactCheck.org debrief discussion of the November presidential election, Nicole Wallace, senior advisor to the McCain/Palin campaign in 2008, suggested the strategic nature of the decision to choose Palin:

> it was a strategic imperative and I think, personally important to John McCain to remind voters of his record of standing up against entrenched

special interests and, probably more important, his own party ... He sought a running mate who had done some of the same things that he had done, had stood up to special interests, had stood up to her own party, had taken a stand against corruption and was a doer and a player on the national energy scene.[6]

The framing strategy goes beyond merely proclaiming outsider status. The underlying and not very subtle implication of the McCain/Palin approach is that as an outsider Palin would be a more legitimate representative of average people's interests than insiders who are often conceptualized as out of touch with "ordinary" Americans. As an outsider she is "just like us"—those of us who aren't members of Congress, vice presidents or other high office holders—often expressing disconnection and distrust of those who hold political power. Again, in his speech announcing his choice of Palin as his running mate, McCain described Palin as someone who "understands the problems, the hopes and the values of working people."[7] She pays a mortgage, belongs to a union, worries about healthcare. In this frame, Ms. Palin is qualified to lead because she is like the collective "us" and will therefore make decisions that average citizens would make under the same conditions. As she indicated in her nomination acceptance speech: "Our family has the same ups and downs as any other ... the same challenges and the same joys."[8] The clear intent is to build identification and connection between the average citizen and Palin. Palin epitomizes the ordinary person (unlike longstanding Washington insiders such as Joe Biden, whose speeches she has been listening to since she was in grade school). Given this affinity with normal Americans, Palin can better advocate their best interests than insiders who have grown distant from those whom they purport to represent.

Throughout the campaign, Palin talked at length of her small-town background and Main Street values with media coverage following suit. In early September, Daniel Henninger, writing in the *Wall Street Journal*, offered his view that Palin "didn't abandon her hometown for the big city. She stayed home, had babies, helped her snowmobiling husband with his commercial fishing business and with him, tried to assemble a life."[9]

Palin's self-presentation also reflects a more common, folksy flair. Her speech delivery is casual and unpretentious—she drops her g's ("our financial system needs some shakin' up and some fixin'"); "heck," "darn," "shoot," and "gee" are mixed in as well; she gestures enthusiastically and cutely as if we're all in on the joke here. She's the cool kid making subtle fun of the far less cool intellectual kids in this election contest—no overly cerebral phrasing or carefully detailed answers from her that might intimidate or alienate potential supporters. Sarah Palin aimed her remarks openly and directly to Joe Six Pack and Joe the Plumber—average, "real" men. This was even true in her family life—no formal "First Gentleman" title for her husband—he's the "First Dude" of Alaska. Tina Fey's portrayal of Palin on *Saturday Night Live* (*SNL*) was built around a humorous mocking of these mannerisms and colloquialisms. In the October 4, 2008, *SNL* parody of the recently held vice presidential debate, Tina Fey (as Governor Palin) states in response to a question posed by Queen Latifah (as Gwen Ifill):

> I'm, uh … I'm happy to be speaking directly to the American people to let them know that if you want an outsider who doesn't like politics as usual or pronouncin' the "g" at the end of the words she's sayin', I think you know who to vote for.[10]

Sarah Palin is hardly the first to adopt this narrative frame as part of her presentation of self. One need look no further than the man she ran for office with—John McCain—to see another. In fact, the outsider, "normal guy/gal" frame is far from uncommon in American politics, generally speaking. This often geographic, class-based frame has been around at least since Andrew Jackson ran for president on the platform of promoting the common man's involvement in America's political future. Since Jackson, politicians have periodically appealed to the notion that Western and rural interests might view themselves as outsiders, distant geographically, but also politically and socially from the urban coasts. These citizens might therefore be open to supporting candidates viewed as more in touch with "ordinary" lives and values. The strategy has morphed over time, but the undercurrent has long been a part of American political discourse.

In recent election cycles, Ronald Reagan ran openly against Washington—he pledged term limits for office holders and objected to pointy-headed entrenched bureaucrats. Democrats supported Bill Clinton, who may have been a Rhodes Scholar but also put on his jogging shorts and stopped by McDonald's for Big Mac meals on his way to the White House. Republicans nominated George W. Bush who, despite his status as the son of a former president and grandson of a senator, offered himself during his run for office as a downhome guy from west Texas who enjoyed spending time outdoors at the ranch.

Republicans, in particular, have employed the very effective targeted and oppositional strategy of appealing to average Joes and "Main Street" values. Again, the idea that somehow Main Street values are different from Washington or, more recently, Wall Street values is a longstanding American cultural motif and belief. In a 1981 speech, Ronald Reagan offered his hope that "the people on Wall Street will pay attention to the people on Main Street. If they do, they will see there is a rising tide of confidence in the future of America."[11] The Republicans' populist concept of Main Street references God, patriotism, hard work, and individualism in very particular ways that implied (as much as explicitly declared) a moral superiority to those Main Street folks outside Washington and New York. Palin demonstrated a keen ability to carry this message and be framed within this narrative. In a post-election evaluation of Palin's impact, Yuval Levin suggested that Palin was "something genuinely new in American politics: a lower-middle class woman who spoke the language of the country's ordinary voters and had a profound personal understanding of the hopes and worries of a vast swath of the public."[12] And Libby Copeland wondered: "Could central casting produce a more ideal messenger [than Sarah Palin] for the new Republican populism?"[13]

Levin insightfully observes that the Palin appeal generally "has much to do with the age-old tension between populism and elitism in our public life."[14] He elaborates, suggesting:

> The Republican Party has been the party of cultural populism and economic elitism, and the Democratic Party has been the party of cultural elitism and economic populism. Republicans tend to identify with traditional values, unabashedly patriotic, anti-cosmopolitan, non-nuanced Joe Sixpack, even as they pursue an economic policy that aims at elite investor-driven growth ... Both economic and cultural populism are politically potent, but in America, unlike in Europe, cultural populism has always been much more powerful. Americans do not resent the success of others, but they do resent arrogance, and especially intellectual arrogance ... It was this sense, this feeling, that Sarah Palin channeled so effectively ... Palin channeled these cultural energies more by what she was than by what she said or did.[15]

So when Sarah Palin chose this frame and used these reference points, it was in no way accidental or without meaning. These were appeals to carefully constructed images and ideas. Further, the frame reinforces aspects of the other framing choices discussed throughout the book. As noted earlier, there are both geographic and class-based roots to them. Much like Hillary Clinton in the closing weeks of her primary campaign, with this frame, McCain and Palin were in all likelihood aiming to connect with unhappy working-class white voters in the industrial Midwest and the South. These voters had been instrumental to winners in several recent presidential elections. Appeals focused on winning their support were not a surprise. However, as one reporter from the 2008 campaign trail concluded, "Like Clinton before her, Palin failed to straddle critical lines—between being enough of an insider to have credentials and enough of an outsider to bring about change. Between feminine and tough enough to be taken seriously."[16]

Clearly, as a woman, Palin already does not look like the traditional candidate for vice president. The "outsider" running against the status quo system has been a relatively common strategic frame employed by women running for political office. Grounded in the reality that there simply have not been many women in high-level national leadership positions, the frame attempts to turn a potential negative into a strategic advantage. Women candidates are almost inevitably viewed as outsiders in the American political process simply as a result of their status as "women." The strategy presents itself easily given the non-traditional paths women often have followed to candidacy and office, as well as the issues that drew them into politics initially. This is clearly the case with the Palin candidacy.

Like all strategic choices, adopting an outsider framing approach has the potential to cut in a variety of ways. However, the McCain/Palin campaign embraced the frame with enthusiasm and employed it as a perceived strength of not only Sarah Palin, but of McCain more centrally. In fact, presidency scholars have suggested this frame is a part of one of the defining paradoxes of the presidential office itself—the tension between citizens' desires for a superhuman president who is smarter, more capable, and therefore more "qualified" to lead versus their also very real desires for a president who is "just like us." Some candidates and presidents manage to balance these competing demands and expectations from the citizenry; but many are defeated by the double-edged sword of this paradox, either in failing to be "presidential" enough or by becoming "out of touch" with average Americans.[17]

The Maverick Reformer

Another aspect to the outsider frame was the notion that both John McCain and Sarah Palin were maverick reformers unafraid to take on entrenched interests even within their own political parties. McCain had embraced the label "maverick" in his aborted 2000 run for the Republican presidential nomination as a way to claim ownership of his willingness to work in a bipartisan way to pass reform legislation, including landmark campaign finance reforms. When McCain looked in the mirror he saw a fiercely principled, honest, unafraid warrior image looking back. His vocal and nearly unwavering support for President Bush's post-9/11 foreign policy, however, had left him vulnerable to claims that he was no longer the partisan maverick he had once been. Following discussions with a McCain advisor immediately after the announcement that Sarah Palin would serve as McCain's running mate, *New York Times* editorial writers Bumiller and Cooper recounted that "Mr. McCain was betting ... that she [Palin] would help him reclaim the mantle of maverick that he had lost this year."[18] Cooper and Bumiller later added that the McCain campaign viewed Ms. Palin as a kindred spirit to Mr. McCain, "particularly in her history of taking heat from fellow Republicans for bucking them on issues and spotlighting their ethical failings."[19]

The McCain campaign also perceived that this anti-establishment story and imagery would appeal to 2008 voters who were in a decidedly anti-incumbent, throw-the-rascals-out type of mood. *New York Times* writer Matthew Continetti argued that the "only way for [McCain] to win this election is to break with the national Republican Party. Mr. McCain needs to recast the party in his own image: anticorruption, pro-reform and fiscally and socially conservative."[20] As Sarah Palin reiterated multiple times, she and McCain were the ones who wouldn't blink when facing down challenges or hard decisions (wink maybe, but never blink). In his consideration of the Palin candidacy, Levin suggested that:

> Palin was an uncanny match for John McCain. Her political style and priorities resembled McCain's in a way that no other senior Republican

elected officials did. Her conservatism, like McCain's, was more an attitude than an ideology: it was a kind of moralistic anti-corruptionism, obsessed with honest dealing and powerfully allergic to excess and waste ... she shared what he often stressed most about himself, and what he most wanted to run on: she was, as the public would soon be informed *ad nauseam*, a reforming maverick.[21]

These aspects were prominently on display, especially in the early weeks of Sarah Palin's entry onto the Republican ticket. In her nomination acceptance speech, she proclaimed proudly that she had told the Congress: "Thanks, but no thanks" to the Bridge to Nowhere.[22] Early articles about Palin centered around how as a mayor, state board member, and governor she had fought her own entrenched partisans, sold the state plane on eBay, and fired the personal chef employed by the outgoing (Republican) governor. Palin drove herself to work each day, and served as a whistle-blower when she observed ethically questionable behavior—a giant killer. She had pushed for transparency in one of the least transparent state governmental systems in the United States by advocating for open bidding for oil contracts where there had been none in the past. She was often described as a breath of fresh air—a politician who calls them as she sees them. It is not a tremendous surprise that she appealed to a man who ran the Straight Talk Express or to an electorate hungry for change in Washington.

Another central aspect to this frame is the willingness to fight the principled fight and "fight to win." Palin and McCain proudly embraced her image as an ultra-competitive sportswoman: she was "Sarah Barracuda" on the basketball court. In her Republican convention speech she introduced her vision of what it meant to be a "hockey mom" with the amusing (unscripted and over-quoted) question: what's the difference between a pit bull and a hockey mom? (Answer: lipstick). Along with the earlier discussed aspects of this anecdote, its use was also designed to signal voters she was tough and tenacious—a fighter. "She's a woman who doesn't back down."[23] She spent her years as governor "in combat with oil executives, lobbyists and politicians comfortable with the status quo."[24] In her nomination acceptance speech, Palin explained to voters how she and McCain were tied together in this understanding that some battles must be waged when she reverently described John McCain as a "leader who's not looking for a fight but is not afraid of one either."[25] *New York Times* columnist David Brooks argued that "The Palin pick allows McCain to run the way he wants to—not as the old goat running against the fresh upstart, but as the crusader for virtue against the forces of selfishness. It allows him to make cleaning out the Augean stables of Washington the major issue of his campaign."[26]

If the past is any indication of the future, the maverick-reformer piece of the outsider frame should have worked effectively for Sarah Palin and John McCain. Both have long careers focused on the theme of reform. Both had framed themselves and been framed by others over time as reformers. They had each worn this mantle in past election campaigns and been very successful with it. They knew the narrative well and it suited their candidacies and personas. Republicans, in general, had successfully capitalized on the frame's impact for decades. And yet it did not really work well in 2008, especially as the campaign wore on throughout the fall.

This case highlights the degree to which the political context influences the strategic impact of each narrative frame. The framing process does not occur in a vacuum: the narrative plays out within a particular set of conditions and events. McCain in 2000 easily wore the mantle of maverick reformer and political outsider. Palin herself easily adopted the frame in her stands and runs against the Murkowski machine in Alaska. In spite of the fact that the individual candidates and the factual record were largely the same, the frame was perceived differently because of the new context and fresh competition. Economic conditions were different, the political times were different, and the opponent was different.

Perhaps the narrative frame's impact was muted because the Obama campaign effectively took ownership of the "change" mantle early. We have noted that frames are nearly always relational in their interpretation and the McCain/Palin campaign faced a formidable fight over which candidate best embodied a change from the status quo. The Obama campaign effectively countered the claims that McCain and Palin were reformers or had bucked their own party (particularly McCain) by providing evidence to the contrary in advertisements and appearances. The frame's positive features were lost once the drum beat of "McCain is the same as Bush" really took hold. Political communications scholar Kathleen Hall Jamieson noted that:

> Although McCain painted himself as a maverick, the Democratic forces succeeded in casting him as either Bush's kin or clone. As a result, our survey data from the beginning of period one to election eve show an upward trend in the belief that McCain equals Bush. We take this to mean that communication strengthened the relationship between McCain and Bush. At campaign's end, McCain is seen as McSame in part because the Democrats scraped the maverick label from him and melded his identity to that of the star-crossed incumbent … His handling of the economic crisis did nothing to improve this read of him as more of the same or to turn the tables on Obama.[27]

Also, if women have been outsiders to the political process, people of color have been to the same or even larger degree. The automatic "outsider" or "reformer" points do not automatically accrue to Palin in this mix of individuals in the way they likely did in others. And the Obama campaign organization was one of the most professionally competent ever constructed—they worked hard to brand the McCain/Palin campaign as "more of the same."

Of all the frames employed during the campaign, this is perhaps the one that lost the most focus and depth with observers—the meaning of the term maverick and what it meant in practice about McCain and Palin did not come through all that clearly in 2008. This was perhaps best illustrated in the widely viewed impersonations of Palin by Tina Fey on *Saturday Night Live*. In one widely circulated clip of *SNL's* vice presidential debate skit, Fey's Governor Palin is asked how she and John McCain will solve the financial crisis:

> *Ms. Fey (as Sarah Palin):* Ya know, John McCain and I, we're a couple of mavericks. And gosh darn it, we're gonna take that maverick energy right to Washington, and we're gonna use it to fix this financial crisis and everything else that's plaguin' this great country of ours.
> *Queen Latifah (as Gwen Ifill, moderator):* How will you solve the financial crisis by being a maverick?
> *Ms. Fey (as Palin):* You know, we're gonna take every aspect of the crisis and look at it, and then we're going to ask ourselves, what would a maverick do in this situation? And then, you know, we'll do that.[28]

Much like another frame we will discuss—the sexy puritan/beauty queen—this aspect of the outsider frame became emblematic of a candidacy perceived to lack intellectual seriousness or depth. By the end of the campaign, no one was quite sure what being a maverick meant anymore: it was a phrase and a concept without impact or solid cultural reference points. And the blame seemed to be placed more squarely on Palin's shoulders.

Pop culture has become a central part of presidential contests; but never before had there been anything quite like the reception received by Sarah Palin. By the time she went on *SNL* in person, the definitional war over her persona had divided into camps. She retained the ardor and loyalty of her fans, who continued to turn out for her, root for her, and defend her. But in the eyes of the broader public—and even more so those of the national media and political establishments—any traces of her image as a maverick reformer had been erased. For them, Palin had been reduced to nothing more than a hick on a high wire.[29]

The McCain/Palin campaign largely responded to the negative commentary and comedic interest through the lens of the outsider frame, suggesting that in a predictable fashion, the mainstream media and cultural elites were attacking Palin unfairly and treating her differently than other candidates. Levin maintained that the campaign's response reflected the long held belief of conservatives that they had been "shut out of mainstream institutions such as the mass media and universities."[30] Palin "became the 2008 poster child for the longstanding conservative grudge against the mainstream media."[31]

Palin's defiant response to what she believed was condescending and unjustified criticism from the liberal mainstream media has long been reflected in popular culture as well. Here the political geography that underlies the cultural discussion becomes clear as rural folks fight back against the attitude they believe arrogant elites have about them. They firmly stake their ground in defense of their way of life and its accompanying pleasures; no one will look down their noses at these proud people. At a campaign appearance, Sarah Palin met country music artist Gretchen Wilson, best known for her hit song "Redneck Woman". Wilson's song invites its audience to join in claiming and celebrating the redneck label, rather than accepting it as an insult from more sophisticated and cosmopolitan types who look down on them. Wilson's redneck women "don't give a rip" what these folks think. They look sexy wearing Wal-Mart lingerie and happily party to Charlie Daniels, Kid Rock and George Straight songs. They metaphorically thumb their noses at an elite culture they believe judges them and finds them lacking. At their joint campaign appearance, Palin told Wilson she loved her song. "Someone called me a 'Redneck Woman.' I told them, 'Thank you— that's a compliment.'"[32] The whole cultural conversation seemed to echo the early 1970s musical conversation between Neil Young and the band Lynyrd Skynyrd. Young's song "Southern Man" strongly criticized the historical racism of the South. Lynyrd Skynyrd replied in "Sweet Home Alabama" that they'd heard what Mr. Young had to say about the South and a Southern man "don't need him around anyhow."

In her speech accepting the vice presidential nomination, Palin famously mocked Obama's experience as a community organizer: "no wonder, given that occupation's urban (read black, read poor, read black poor) connotations."[33] In emphasizing her rural, even "backwoods," affinities in her speeches and in her musical choices, Palin's framing may have alienated some voters—even while evoking identification and approval from small-town white women (and men) who considered themselves down-to-earth, hard-working, patriotic folks not afraid to shoot a rifle, drink a beer, or get their hands dirty. These geographic and cultural differences illustrate fundamental differences among American citizens regarding the competencies and qualities that qualify one person over another for leadership. For some, "Palin's failure to speak the language and to share the common points of reference of the educated upper tier of American society essentially rendered her unfit for high office."[34] Others favor "a very different notion of politics, in which sound instincts and valuable life experiences are considered sources of knowledge at least the equal of book learning … where physical prowess and moral constancy are given a higher place than intellectual achievement."[35]

Faith, Values, and Country First

Sarah Palin also defined herself as outside a cultural elite that in her view rejected many of the values and issues that have energized the "Christian right" as a crucial component of the Republican Party's electoral base. White evangelicals' political mobilization and realignment is one of the most important factors in modern American electoral politics. Evangelicals moved from being white, rural, working-class folks with relatively low voter turnout who leaned Democratic during most of the twentieth century, to a rising tide of "values voters" motivated since the

1980s by church/state, racial, and sexual politics. While nineteenth-century evangelical Protestants were active in political movements such as temperance reform, after the modernist controversies of the early twentieth century (exemplified by the 1925 Scopes Monkey Trial regarding evolution) and the rise of the "social gospel" in mainline Protestant denominations, evangelicals "remained largely quiescent."[36] The Southern Baptist Convention is the largest evangelical denomination, and Southern evangelicals were generally Democrats, like the rest of the Southern electorate prior to the 1960s; Northern evangelicals were split between the parties, but less wealthy and Republican than Christians in mainline denominations (such as Episcopalians, Presbyterians, Lutherans, and United Methodists).[37]

Several events in the 1960s began the slow but seismic realignment of evangelical Christians, and white Southerners generally, to the Republican Party. Some historians credit Supreme Court decisions that eliminated prayer in the public schools and, in 1973, legalized abortion with mobilizing the religious right in opposition.[38] Others focus on a 1978 Internal Revenue Service (IRS) decision that denied tax exemption to the white Christian prep schools that had sprung up in resistance to racial integration in Southern schools, infuriating white Southern Christians.[39] Issues such as busing to achieve racial integration, women's liberation, gay rights, divorce, and affirmative action troubled religious conservatives, leading Baptist pastor Jerry Falwell to found the Moral Majority in 1979, Pat Robertson to start the Christian Broadcasting Network in 1977, and psychologist James Dobson to found Focus on the Family in 1977.[40] Daniel K. Williams traces the evangelicals' alliance with the Republican Party back to the 1940s, when conservative Protestants identified the GOP (or the Grand Old Party) as the party of anti-communism and moral order.[41] During the 1960s, culture wars replaced the Cold War as the focus; evangelicals began to feel that the Christian identity and moral core of the nation were being lost.[42] Seeing an electoral opportunity, Republicans became "adept at framing party identity with the story of moral threat," and evangelicals came to recognize "moral values" as a Republican brand label.[43]

As the Civil Rights movement pushed northern Democrats in a more liberal direction, particularly on questions of race, Republican presidential candidate Richard Nixon adopted his "Southern Strategy" to win votes in the one-party Democratic South. Using phrases such as "law and order," the GOP appealed to socially conservative Democrats who did not favor integration and felt ending Jim Crow would lead to racial violence. The two parties began an ideological polarization that has continued to the present, in which moderate and socially liberal Republicans have all but disappeared, leaving primarily conservatives in the GOP; and conservative Democrats have realigned, leaving the Democratic Party considerably more homogenous and liberal. Most importantly, white Southerners who had been longtime Democratic partisans began to feel more and more out of touch with their own party's stances on social issues of race, sexual politics, and "family values." By 1980, Ronald Reagan was able to win the votes of many blue-collar and Southern Democrats—several of them socially conservative Catholics and evangelicals. Reagan won 67 percent of the white evangelical vote in 1980, and 74 percent in 1984—13 percent higher than the rest of the white population in both elections.[44] In 1988, they voted 81 percent for Republican George H. W. Bush, becoming a solid and reliable voting bloc in the GOP coalition.

The growth of the Sunbelt during the 1980s to 1990s and the concentration of a majority of evangelicals in the South only increased their enormous electoral importance in the Republican base.[45] By 2004, white evangelicals made up a full quarter of the American electorate; they provided George W. Bush with 40 percent of his votes in 2004, and John McCain with 40 percent of his in 2008.[46] This was a huge increase from the 1970s, when evangelicals accounted for only 22 percent of GOP presidential votes.[47] In the past 30 years, they have doubled in size and importance to the Republican coalition. Just as African Americans are the most reliable base for Democratic candidates (supporting John Kerry 83 percent in 2004, and Barack Obama 93 percent in 2008), white evangelicals are the most solid constituency for Republicans, voting for Bush 77 percent in 2004 and 76 percent for McCain in 2008 (a much higher rate than McCain's overall 45.7 percent of the popular vote).[48] In addition, religion and politics scholars have discovered that simply classifying voters by their denomination or religious tradition does not fully explain how faith is influencing electoral politics. Religiosity—how often a person actually attends church, how important faith is in one's everyday life, and adherence to theological orthodoxy in one's own worship tradition—explains a great deal, and usually pushes people in a more conservative political direction. For example, white Catholics have recently been swing voters in American elections, cross-pressured by conservative and pro-life social views but more liberal, New Deal blue-collar economic interests. In 2008, this group's votes were split: 53 percent for Obama and 47 percent for McCain (very close to their overall popular vote totals of 52.9 and 45.7 percent). But "traditionalist Catholics"—those who attend mass frequently and hold theological positions closely aligned with the church—supported McCain 71 percent.[49] Traditionalist Catholics and evangelicals may have more in common, electorally, than they do with less-committed members of their own churches. Frequent church attending evangelicals, those most likely to be mobilized by their pastors or church-going friends, are the most supportive of Republican presidential candidates. In both 2004 and 2008, 85 percent of them voted Republican—an overwhelming majority, and one the party has come to rely on electorally.[50] Thus, energizing and securing that base is crucial to Republican victories in gaining the White House.

During the past three decades, Republican presidential candidates have appealed to social conservatives, but once in the White House, their issues have been given relatively little emphasis. In the 2008 primaries, religious conservatives were suspicious and unenthusiastic about John McCain; while they could appreciate him as a war hero and maverick reformer, they were wary of stories about his marital unfaithfulness and divorce, his outbursts of temper, and his nominal religious faith. In contrast, Sarah Palin was embraced by many of those frustrated or disappointed religious right voters as one of them: she grew up attending a Pentecostal church and was comfortable being prayed over and using evangelical language in the campaign. Both in her introduction in Dayton and her speech at the Republican National Convention, Palin specifically inserted a line that would resonate with evangelicals: "No one expects us to agree on everything. But we are expected to govern with integrity, good will, clear convictions, and *a servant's heart* [italics added]."[51]

The idea of a "servant's heart" is a familiar trope in the evangelical subculture. Mega-church pastor Rick Warren used the phrase is his 2002 best-seller *The Purpose-Driven Life*.[52] Charles Swindoll's classic *Improving Your Serve* has been popularizing the idea of "servant leadership" among evangelicals since the early 1980s.[53] Swindoll based the imperative to lead not by command, but by serving others as Jesus Christ did, using New Testament text Matthew 23:11-12: "But the greatest among you shall be your servant. Whoever exalts himself shall be humbled; and whoever humbles himself shall be exalted." The allusion signaled to evangelical voters that Palin was "one of them," sharing the same idioms and values. Palin was certainly not the first to do this. For example, in George W. Bush's 2003 State of the Union speech, he referred to the "power—wonder-working power—in the goodness, and idealism, and faith of the American people" to encourage Congress to fund faith-based initiatives that provide social services.[54] Evangelicals immediately heard the cadence of Lewis Jones's 1899 gospel hymn "Power in the Blood," a camp meeting staple with the refrain: "There is pow'r, pow'r, wonder-working pow'r/In the precious blood of the Lamb." Using such phraseology seemed to signify that the president was steeped in the language and rhythms of evangelical life.

One of the things that excited social conservatives most about the Palin pick was her strong opposition to abortion. Not only was she pro-life in her issue positions, she "walked the walk:" she carried her Down syndrome baby to term, and supported her unwed teenage daughter's decision not to have an abortion. "It is almost impossible to exaggerate how important that is to the conservative faith community. They're beyond ecstatic," said Ralph Reed, former head of the Christian Coalition.[55] James Dobson, then head of the family values organization Focus on the Family, had proclaimed that he would not vote for McCain, but quickly reversed his position and called Palin an "outstanding choice" that gave conservative voters confidence regarding the kinds of Supreme Court justices their administration would appoint.[56] Matthew Staver, dean of Liberty University School of Law (founded by Jerry Falwell), called Palin an "absolutely brilliant" choice who has "electrified conservatives."[57]

Roberta Combs, president of the Christian Coalition, also praised Palin as "a reformer not afraid to shake up the establishment;" Wendy Wright, president of Concerned Women for America, applauded her "admirable record of confronting corruption and living her pro-life values;" and Pentecostal blogger and editor

J. Lee Grady warned the media not to underestimate "this woman's Christian faith, which has shaped her anti-corruption policies, her pro-life convictions and her refreshingly humble servant-leadership style."[58] Social conservatives were attracted to her reformer résumé and saw her as a woman of integrity, honesty, and principles. Grady likened her to Deborah, the Old Testament prophet "who rallied God's people to victory at a time when ancient Israel was being terrorized by foreign invaders. Deborah's gender didn't stop her from amassing an army; she inspired the people in a way no man could."[59] The Christian Broadcasting Network's David Brody blogged in early September: "The McCain camp may want to play her as the reformer maverick, but it's really her Christian warrior spirit that has brought McCain and his team the jolt they've needed."[60]

The campaign itself downplayed her faith: when asked by CNN specifically about Palin's religious beliefs, spokeswoman Meghan Stapleton merely said that the governor had "deep religious convictions," and Palin described herself simply as a "Bible-believing Christian," perhaps to avoid controversy over her Pentecostal roots.[61] Just as Barack Obama had to deal with controversy over a video of his former pastor, Reverend Jeremiah Wright, seeming to damn America for its persistent racism, Palin was criticized when a videotape surfaced of her at a 2005 service at the Wasilla Assembly of God Church, the congregation in which she had grown up, being prayed over by a visiting African pastor who asked God to protect her "from every form of witchcraft."[62] Questions about religious extremism and a mindset of spiritual warfare were raised again when a YouTube video showed her asking worshippers at Wasilla Assembly of God to pray that leaders were sending U.S. soldiers to Iraq "on a mission from God."[63]

Palin clearly did have deep roots in evangelical and Pentecostal religion. She regularly attended the Assemblies of God Church, was baptized at age 12, and "was the leader of the Fellowship of Christian Athletes at her high school … she used to sign her yearbook with Bible verses."[64] But a mid-September article on Palin's faith in *Newsweek* speculated that the greatest impact her faith had on her political career might not be opposition to abortion and same-sex marriage, or her willingness to teach creationism in public schools; rather, it was "her sense of personal mission" and unblinking confidence:

> She was raised in a tradition that tended to emphasize an intimate connection with God, through the Holy Spirit—a tradition that puts the believer at the center of the spiritual drama, in direct communion with the Lord. Formed in such a milieu, it is not surprising that someone like Palin would have a heightened sense of self, and of the possibilities of self, for she was taught from her earliest days that she could be directly moved by God.[65]

Indeed, one narrative about Palin that seemed to resonate with evangelical Republican voters was that of Queen Esther from the Old Testament. A *New York Times* article from early September relates the story of Palin emailing her former Assemblies of God pastor, Paul Riley, shortly after becoming governor of Alaska in 2006, for spiritual advice on how to do her new job. She asked him for biblical examples of people who were great leaders and the secret of their leadership. Reverend Riley recalls telling her she should reread "the story of Esther, a beauty queen who became a real one, gaining the king's ear to avert the slaughter of the Jews and vanquish their enemies. When Esther is called to serve, God grants her a strength she never knew she had."[66] Esther is an unlikely heroine, able to save her people through a serendipitous course of events as well as her own bravery and ability to persuade her husband with her charms. Riley saw Palin as a modern-day Esther, whom God had placed in a position of power "for such a time as this."[67] That phrase from the book of Esther, "for such a time as this," resonated with evangelicals, and began appearing on homemade signs at Palin rallies. An evangelical hagiography of Palin, published by Christian press Zondervan and with a foreword by evangelical leader Charles Colson, came out in October 2008 and emphasized the Esther story.[68] Like Esther, Palin was a beauty queen; like her, Palin had come from obscure political beginnings to sudden prominence on the national stage, poised to make a difference in the fate of the nation. Like her, religious-right voters hoped, Palin would govern not in her own interests, but righteously and on behalf of others. The Esther narrative wove together important elements across the Palin frames: the beautiful woman using power in a feminine way, the unlikely person chosen to be used by God for his purposes, the outsider possessing courage and integrity. Evangelical voters could relate to Sarah Palin's embodiment of pro-life values, and the fall-and-redemption subtext of her daughter Bristol's pregnancy. Palin's nationalism, her prayers for "God's plan" for America, and her own bold certainty that she was "chosen" by God for leadership all tap into a narrative of patriotism, populism, and faithful certainty shared by evangelical voters.

There are potential risks to using this frame. At what point does the outsider frame cross the line into "fringe"? Can outsiders govern effectively in a culture of insiders? This highlights the degree to which electoral politics has become divorced from discussions or considerations of how best to govern. Those who employ the frame, in conclusion, can be seen as "lunatic fringe" or opponents can attempt to position them as such.

Figure 1 Palin's "outsider" narrative made racial and class appeals to a rural, white, working-class base in the electorate. These supporters reacted to the pejorative, dismissive label "redneck" by reclaiming it as a proud identity they saw as shared by Palin. *(Source: Douglas Graham/Roll Call/Getty Images)*

Figure 2 Palin reinforced her femininity, even as she broke barriers for women with young children on the national political stage, by appearing frequently with her infant son Trig on the campaign trail. By highlighting her motherhood, Palin appealed to pro-life forces and set off "The Mommy Wars: Special Campaign Edition." *(Source: Win McNamee/Getty Images)*

Figure 3 Palin was framed by the media as a sexy and attractive woman, which both added to her appeal and undermined her seriousness as a candidate. The novelty of her high heels on the campaign trail prompted many photos like this one. *(Source: Robyn Beck/AFP/Getty Images)*

Figure 4 An early profile of Palin featured this photo of the governor in her Alaska statehouse office, juxtaposing her femininity with the fierceness of the bear in an example of the frontier woman frame. *(Source: Stephen Nowers/Anchorage Daily News/ MCT via Getty Images)*

Figure 5 Winking at the cameras during the vice presidential debate, Palin seemed to embrace and make use of her framing as a sexually attractive woman. Palin did not downplay her sex appeal, as conventional wisdom advised women candidates to do in order to be taken seriously, but used it in powerful and ironic ways. *(Source: Robyn Beck/AFP/Getty Images)*

Figure 6 Palin's joke about pit bulls and lipstick reinforced the tough but girly message of the "hockey mom" narrative. The frame resonated with women at campaign rallies, who held up their lipstick in response to Palin's appearance. *(Source: Max Whittaker/Getty Images)*

Figure 7 Was Palin a post-feminist role model or a victim of sexist media coverage? This photo, taken at an October campaign rally, objectifies her by using only parts of her body (her shapely high-heeled calves) and framing the rapt young man suggestively between her legs. It demonstrates the overt sexual framing of Palin, which allowed *Saturday Night Live* to refer to her as a MILF, and CNBC commentator Donny Deutsch to opine: "Men want a sexy woman [candidate] … I want [Palin] lying next to me in bed." *(Source: Reuters/Carlos Barria)*

PART II

Contested Frames: Gender Narratives

4

HOCKEY MOM

Palin was framed by the campaign and media as a "hockey mom," drawing on maternal traditions used by women in politics, and transforming them to appeal to diverse groups in the electorate (such as working moms, social conservatives, and white blue-collar workers). By asking voters to understand her as "just your average hockey mom," the Palin campaign invited working women to see her as representing their gendered views and experiences. Her staunch pro-life position, demonstrated not only in her own decision to give birth to Trig but also in the views she expressed about her daughter's unwed pregnancy, underscored a commitment to mothering as one of women's primary roles, appealing to conservatives. Importantly, Palin described herself as a "hockey mom"—evoking a pit bull-with-lipstick toughness with a more working-class appeal than the suburban soccer mom. Through these narratives, voters could relate to Sarah Palin as an everymom, admire her as a supermom, applaud her maternal values, or judge her parenting choices, even while reinforcing her conservative, white, working-class appeal.

There is almost nothing as familiar to the story of American women's lives as the narrative of motherhood. For most adult women in the United States, it is a lived reality: the US Census Bureau reports that in 2008, 82 percent of women who had reached the ages of 40 to 44 were mothers. (That number is down from 90 percent in 1976, when motherhood was an even more ubiquitous role!)[1] Certainly, there are many options for women in the twenty-first century that may not include motherhood. But even as we see parenthood as less normative for all women—and as experiences of motherhood vary widely across different cultures, economic classes, racial, and ethnic groups, and family types—being a mom is something that many American women still choose and aspire to. Indeed, the image we have of mothers and mother-love is still seen by many as American as apple pie.

The McCain campaign, and Sarah Palin herself, made motherhood a central feature of her potential political appeal. When McCain announced that he had chosen her as his running mate, Palin introduced herself to the crowd (and the nation) as "just your average hockey mom from Alaska." She pointed out her husband, Todd, and five children even before explaining her own political biography or issue stances, foregrounding her identity as a mother in her first moments on the national stage. Her large family accompanied her on the campaign trail throughout the fall, and she often ended her speeches at campaign rallies waving to the crowds while holding her infant son Trig. Early in the campaign, a *Time* cover story included a two-page photo spread with the caption "Baby on Board." The picture showed Palin sitting around a table on the "Straight Talk Express," McCain's campaign bus, with the senator, his wife, and advisor Steve Schmidt. Scattered amidst the cell phones, briefing books, and soda cans on the table is a baby bottle. Everyone is frowning, appearing deep in conversation about campaign strategy. Yet, Palin is cradling a sleepy four-month-old Trig in her arms and, without looking down at him, waving a baby rattle to keep him occupied.[2] The story itself opened by describing Palin as a down-to-earth suburban mom: the first paragraphs recounted how she has remained friends with the same group of new mothers she practiced yoga with in the early 1990s, and who still hold an ornament exchange each Christmas.[3]

As Palin burst unknown onto the national landscape, many news stories led with this framing of her as "Governor Mom," to quote a headline from *The Washington Post*.[4] Reporter Lois Romano noted: "An accomplished—even glamorous—working mother, projecting to the world that she can and does have it all … the facts of life for Alaska Gov. Sarah Palin are fascinating and seem, frankly, exhausting."[5] Indeed, while the frame of "average hockey mom" may have been a narrative that seemed relatable to many voters, Sarah Palin's motherhood also became a source of questions and debate. Controversy swirled as news of her teenage daughter's pregnancy hit the media during the first weekend of the campaign, fueled by internet rumors that Palin was perhaps not the biological mother of her youngest child. Was Palin, a supermom of five, able to run a large family and a state? Or was she an irresponsible mother, not paying enough attention at home to keep her daughter from an unintended pregnancy and using her Down syndrome baby as a campaign prop? Was she a hypocrite for advocating for abstinence-only sex education while her own daughter had sex with her high school boyfriend, and for "choosing life" when her adamantly anti-abortion stance would not permit others to make a "choice"? Were her policy stances friendly to other working moms, or antithetical to their needs? The hockey mom narrative brought Palin a lot of attention, particularly from women voters and commentators. The admiration, and the scrutiny, opened a national conversation in which they reflected not only on Palin's choices, but their own.

Like many women in politics, Sarah Palin attributed the start of her political career not to deliberate ambition, but to her identity as a mother. As she explained on August 29, 2008, in Dayton, Ohio, when McCain made his surprise announcement:

> I was just your average "hockey mom" in Alaska. We were busy raising our kids. I was serving as the team mom and coaching some basketball on the side. I got involved in the PTA and then was elected to the City Council and then elected mayor of my hometown, where my agenda was to stop wasteful spending and cut property taxes and put the people first.[6]

A few days later, introducing herself to millions of Americans in her acceptance speech at the Republican National Convention in St. Paul, Minnesota, she told a similar story of how she became involved in politics: "I was just your average hockey mom, and signed up for the PTA because I wanted to make my kids' public education better."[7]

Motherhood as a motivation for political activity is not unique to Sarah Palin. In evoking the narrative of motherhood, Palin drew on a *schema* familiar to women in political life. Since the earliest days of the new nation, women in the United States have used maternity to create a political role for themselves. While separate spheres ideology kept colonial women in domestic space and out of conventional politics, the notion of "Republican Motherhood" constructed an empowered role and public influence for American women based on their maternal identity.[8] Men played a direct political role as citizens that women could not fully share. But a democratic republic that relied on citizens to govern themselves needed those citizens to be loyal, courageous, judicious, and committed to participating in electoral and political life. Women, as mothers, were entrusted with developing those civic virtues in the next generation. By raising patriotic citizens, mothers played a vital and important—if indirect—political role in the first decades of American nationhood.

By the end of the nineteenth century, motherhood became the basis for more direct involvement in politics. Historian Suzanne Lebsock points out that progressive women based their reform activities and calls for female suffrage on the "Politics of the Mother Heart."[9] They drew on the notion of a superior maternal morality to "clean up" corrupt political machines and solve social ills caused by urbanization and industrialization. "Social housekeeping" did not challenge separate spheres ideology directly, but extended women's domestic and moral concerns into public arenas, legitimizing their political activities.[10] Traditional femininity was reaffirmed even as reformers campaigned for pure food and drugs, temperance, public sanitation, ending child labor, and public education. At the dawn of the twentieth century, American suffrage rhetoric based on motherhood and the "special" qualities of woman's nature became almost universal. For example, Jane Addams, founder of urban settlement houses, made an impassioned plea for women to gain the vote based on her maternal responsibilities:

> A woman's simplest duty, one would say, is to keep her house clean and wholesome and to feed her children properly. Yet if she lives in a tenement house, as so many of my neighbors do, she cannot fulfill these simple obligations by her own efforts because she is utterly dependent upon the city administration for the conditions which render decent living possible ... if the street is not cleaned by the city authorities, no amount of private sweeping will keep the tenement free from grime; if the garbage is not properly collected and destroyed a tenement house mother may see her children sicken and die of diseases from which she alone is powerless to shield them, although her tenderness and devotion are unbounded. She cannot even secure untainted meat for her household, she cannot provide fresh fruit, unless the meat has been inspected by city officials, and the decayed fruit, which is so often placed upon sale in the tenement districts, has been destroyed in the interests of public health ... If woman would fulfill her traditional responsibility to her own children; if she would educate and protect from danger factory children who must find their recreation on the street; if she would bring the cultural forces to bear upon our materialistic civilization; and if she would do it all with the dignity and directness fitting one who carries on her immemorial duties, then she must bring herself to the use of the ballot—that latest implement for self-government. May we not fairly say that American women need this implement in order to preserve the home?[11]

Suffragists marched with brooms, and were depicted in pamphlets with shovels, ready and willing to clean up the cutthroat, masculine realm of politics; one postcard contained the picture of a baby drinking a bottle with the text "Votes for Mothers: Politics governs even the purity of the milk supply. It is not outside the home but *inside the baby*."[12] While suffragists made many arguments for women deserving the right to vote, including those that emphasized fairness and equality for female citizens, maternal rhetoric based on traditional gender differences was popular and effective. Putting children first has been a shrewd rhetorical strategy deployed by women social welfare activists over the past century, taking advantage of romanticized notions of motherhood to influence and benefit from public policy.[13]

Recently, as women have entered the electoral arena more frequently as candidates themselves, they have drawn on maternal identities to connect with and appeal to voters. Although she tried to project an image of "toughness" typical of Texas politics, Ann Richards relied heavily on references to her granddaughter Lily in her successful 1990 campaign for governor in order to convey the pragmatic-yet-caring style she would bring to problem-solving.[14] In 1992, the so-called "Year of the Woman" in American electoral politics, Patty Murray self-consciously cultivated the image of a "mom in tennis shoes." Women busy with everyday problems had grown impatient with levels of inefficiency in government that would throw the households they themselves managed into chaos and bankruptcy. Murray propelled herself into the United States Senate by emphasizing a commonsense approach to political dilemmas that voters could relate to. A *Newsweek* cover story ran photos of Senator Dianne Feinstein nuzzling her baby granddaughter, resplendent in a frilly pink dress, and of Patty Murray and her two children lounging on the family room floor in their Nikes and Reeboks. *Redbook*'s "Who's Who: The New Women of Congress" listed not only standard political information—the name, party affiliation, state, and age—of each freshman female legislator, but her marital status, the number of children she had, and their ages as well. *Vogue* magazine credited swift passage of the Family and Medical Leave Act in 1993 to the new members' "personal as [well as] powerful" rhetorical style, noting that the women spoke "not only as legislators but as working mothers—mothers with 67 children, all told."[15]

These female politicians themselves credited motives springing from motherhood for their political success. When Murray's speech on family leave drew such reactions as: "I have never heard anybody talk like that before," she was dumbfounded. "All I did was talk about my very own personal experience" of having to quit her job 17 years earleir because maternity leave was unavailable.[16] When Congresswoman Karan English's children back in Arizona said they missed her, she told reporters that she was reminded of "my goals in coming here in the first place. I'm driven by maternal instinct. I'm trying to do what's best for my children, my community, and the whole country." Much like Sarah Palin crediting her initial political involvement to the PTA and making her children's education better, Senator Barbara Boxer recalled that as a young mother in the late 1960s, her initial interest in political activity was "about saving our country for our families and the families of the future."[17] As she rose in leadership in the Democratic Party (to become the first woman speaker of the House of Representatives), Nancy Pelosi presented herself and her leadership style as distinctly maternal: "I'm a mother of five. I have five grandchildren. And I always say: Think of a lioness. Think of a mother bear. You come anywhere near our cubs, you're dead. And so, in terms of any threat to our country, people have to know we'll be there to strike."[18] Women candidates are more likely to explain their political motives altruistically as mothers improving society for their children and others. This can be an appealing strategy, but makes it difficult for women to articulate their own political ambition and acknowledge their own desire to lead.[19] It may remain harder for women to claim their fair share of elected offices or policy agenda space if they cannot do it straightforwardly, acting for themselves and their interests, but instead must legitimize their political efforts as acting only on behalf of others.

This narrative of sacrificial, nurturing, sentimental motherhood remains a familiar one in American culture. In a 1976 article aptly titled "The Motherhood Mandate," sociologist Nancy Felipe Russo described how the idea of motherhood was central to society's definition of adult females, and how social and cultural forces pushed women toward becoming mothers.[20] Over three decades later, despite sweeping changes that opened up a wide variety of options for women's lives, "cultural discourses of femininity still centre on motherhood."[21] Researchers JaneMaree Maher and Lise Saugeres report finding "great resonance in the 'good mother' ideal and her key attributes of selflessness and all-encompassing commitment to motherhood."[22] Cultural norms attributing emotional warmth, self-sacrifice, and total personal fulfillment to mothering are commonly found in popular culture as well. From movies such as *Baby Boom* to *Raising Helen*, *No Reservations*, and even the raucous comedy *Knocked Up*, female protagonists are rescued from heartless careers and emotionally sterile lives by the unexpected arrival of children to care for, bringing them true happiness and recapturing them into (blissful) domestic space. Motherhood is naturalized as feminine destiny.

Just as features of motherhood served as the basis for urging women to join political movements, from suffrage to temperance, motherhood has also been used politically to appeal to women as a voting bloc. In every presidential election since 1980, scholars of American elections have observed the presence of a "gender gap," in which female voters have been significantly more likely to support Democratic candidates than male voters.[23] Greater support among women for social programs such as education, healthcare, and welfare seem to drive the gap, as well as lower support for military action and spending. The gap is especially pronounced among single, urban, and African American women, who are most likely to choose Democratic candidates, while other subgroups of women are somewhat split between the parties.[24] In the 1990s, pollsters coined the phrase "soccer moms" to identify a group of women (married, suburban women) who were particularly important swing voters. Bill Clinton aimed at gaining their support with his pragmatic policies of family medical leave, reforming welfare (but not eliminating it), and putting more police on the streets. In 1996 and 2000, both parties also tried to appeal to the so-called "NASCAR dads," working-class white males who liked the peace and prosperity of the Clinton years, but who could also become "angry white males" in resenting affirmative action or the decline of manufacturing jobs with the rise of free trade and global outsourcing. After the September 11, 2001 terrorist attacks, George Bush's 2004 reelection campaign focused on winning over "security moms," those same soccer moms who might be fearful for their children's future and more appreciative of the Republican president's war on terror. Even in 2004, the gender gap persisted in the Democrats' favor.[25] But women voters are not monolithic, and not all women tend to support Democratic candidates. While Gallup polls in the spring and summer of 2004 showed a five-point gender gap favoring Democrat John Kerry

(50 to 45 percent), married women actually favored Republican George W. Bush by 13 percentage points (54 to 41 percent).[26] Single women, on the other hand, leaned strongly Democratic (60 to 35 percent). This "marriage gap" exists among both men and women, pushing both in a more conservative direction, and has been present in U.S. presidential elections for the past three decades. Interest groups such as Women's Voices Women Vote see the mobilization of single women, who register and vote at lower rates than married women, as a potential untapped base of strong support for Democrats in national elections.[27] Republican strategist Matthew Dowd noted that married women who do not work outside the home are a solid base for the Republicans, but working wives and mothers are a key target for the party: a "persuadable group" that reliably votes, sometimes for Democrats, and could be swung over to the GOP.[28]

By the 2008 campaign, the Republican Party was well aware of its need to combat, or at least chip away at, the perennial gender gap in order to win the presidential election. As their nominee, John McCain personified much of the problem in appealing to women voters *en masse*. He was older, with documented health issues and partially disabled from his time as a prisoner of war. He was a war hero, steeped in military honor, but also tended to be a hawk when it came to war policy, strongly in favor of the troop surge in Iraq. He was known for having a temper. Little about his biography countered the "angry white male" image of the Republican Party. Then he chose Sarah Palin as his running mate.

Palin showed a dramatically different face of the Republican Party. She was young and attractive, with a ready smile and wink. Standing next to McCain, she radiated youth, charm, and charisma. In tailored suits that showed off her trim figure and her high heels, she exuded femininity. To top it all off, she stood on the public stage holding her four month-old baby, surrounded by her other children. Palin evoked a narrative of femininity and motherhood that was instantly recognizable to American women voters. It was a narrative that appealed to traditional roles and norms, while at the same time breaking boundaries for women in politics.

Not only was Palin the first woman on the Republican presidential ticket, but she was also unusual as a mother of young children in such a prominent political role. Women with small children were still a novelty in politics. In 1972, Patricia Schroeder was the first woman elected to Congress with children still at home, and in 1974 Yvonne Brathwaite became the first congresswoman to give birth while in office. Blanche Lincoln chose not to run for re-election to her congressional seat when she became pregnant with twins in 1996 (although she returned to successfully run for the U.S. Senate two years later). Kay Bailey Hutchison, senator from Texas, adopted two children after winning her seat. Although there are now more women in Congress with young children, balancing motherhood with a national political career remains a challenge. Kathleen Hall Jamieson notes that political women face the "double bind" of womb versus mind. If seen as smart and strong, women may gain political credibility but lose their "femininity," becoming frightening, unnatural women. On the other hand, if appropriately feminine or maternal, they become reduced to their bodies, without the rationality to be leaders in the public sphere.[29] This impossible choice leaves motherhood and politics as incompatible. Women also enter electoral politics later, often not running for office until their children are older.[30] They are criticized in the media, with questions about who will be taking care of their children if they are not at home—questions rarely, if ever, posed to male candidates with small children.[31] It may be particularly difficult for women in executive office, as opposed to legislative service, given the stereotypes and perceptions voters have of those different roles. Some of the desired qualities in a legislator, such as listening to and caring for constituents, or being able to work collegially with others to solve problems, or communicating well with colleagues, may seem similar to characteristics developed in mothering. But the decisive, aggressive qualities valued in an executive may seem more masculine to voters and less compatible with the warmth, emotional attunement, and collaboration attributed to women-as-mothers.[32] Women candidates with children who aspire to executive office may face an especially daunting set of expectations and challenges.

Republican Jane Swift was widely criticized in the press for being pregnant on the campaign trail when she successfully ran for lieutenant governor in Massachusetts in 1998. That scrutiny intensified when, after she became acting governor in 2001, she subsequently became pregnant with twins. Even feminist columnists wondered how she could manage a state and an expanding family at the same time.[33] In examining the tone of narratives surrounding Swift, researchers found that 78 percent of the quotes in *The Boston Globe* and *New York Times* stories in 2001 about Jane Swift running for governor and being a mom were negative, while only 22 percent were favorable.[34] A typical letter to the editor in *The Boston Globe* declared: "There's no way, despite the amount of help she has, that Jane Swift can be both a competent governor and an adequate mother." An article by reporter Brian McGrory used the structure of a simple children's book to mock Swift, while at the same time underscoring the connection with children as the more appropriate sphere for her: "See Jane run from the governorship to motherhood and back again. See Jane run from Boston to Williamstown several times a week to be with her three young children. See Jane run until she can barely tell yesterday from tomorrow, until her physical and mental health deteriorate, and until the state and its government are probably better off without her."[35] While Swift did face credible ethical questions about her use of gubernatorial staff to help care for her children, the resistance to her efforts to balance motherhood with governing was remarkably strong and unrelenting, so forceful that she eventually quit the race. Swift's pregnancies made her female body particularly obvious and problematic: "Pregnancy makes the differences between men and women apparent; it 'otherizes' the woman, and can serve a subjugating role in putting woman back in her place" in the private sphere, outside of politics.[36] Reduced to her (pregnant) body, Swift faced Jamieson's "double bind" of womb versus mind, finding it impossible to bridge the public–private sphere divide. Swift's example raises the question: are beliefs about women's domestic roles as impediments to governing still salient?

In contrast to Swift, Alaska governor Sarah Palin got less critical, more sympathetic press treatment regarding motherhood. Perhaps this was because she always constructed herself first as a mom, then as governor, keeping in place traditional ideological gender roles; or because the masculinity of her oil-sloper husband Todd was not in question (unlike Jane Swift's spouse Chuck, a stay-at-home dad).[37] Perhaps she learned a lesson from Swift, hiding her latest pregnancy well into her sixth month to avoid being reduced to mere spectacle as a pregnant female body. Perhaps it was because her son was born with Down syndrome, making the media more reluctant to attack a special-needs child or its mother. Whatever the reasons, Palin was initially framed in the 2008 campaign as an ordinary mom, one the Republican party hoped voters—particularly women voters—would relate to as someone they trusted and admired. As Republican consultant Leslie Sanchez opined in the early days after her selection, Palin presented herself as Everymom:

> She takes the kids to practice … she knows what it is to meet a budget— not just for a state with $11 million in income and expenditures or her state's seventh-biggest city, but for a family of seven. She knows what it's like to be a mother, and a wife, and to care for aging parents, and pay for the groceries, and the heat, and the mortgage, and to make the car payment … Truth is, we all know a Sarah Palin.[38]

Some voters responded positively to this framing of Palin's maternal qualities and experiences as particularly relevant. *Newsweek* quoted one as saying, "I'm voting for Sarah because she's a mom. She knows what it's like to be a mom."[39] Women's magazine *Redbook* ran a story on Palin entitled "The Debut of the Hockey Mom."[40] It described her "rise from hockey mom and PTA member to mayor, governor, and now only the second woman on a major-party ticket in our country's history" and "her five fresh-faced children," and left the author and reader wondering "if this all-American mom, someone a lot of us recognize as much like ourselves, might be the breath of fresh air politics needs." The story framed her explicitly as the mom-next-door:

> Many of the 37 million viewers watching [Palin's acceptance speech] on TV at home (or at least the female ones) thought, *Huh. That could be me up there.* As the countdown to Election Day intensifies, REDBOOK asks: How much does it matter that we feel like we *know* Sarah Palin—that it seems like she could be our neighbor, our girlfriend—and how will (or won't) this affect the big decision each one of us will make alone in the voting booth on November 4?[41]

In response, 42-year-old mother of three Leanne Keirstead is quoted as saying: "Finally, here's someone I can identify with, someone who isn't afraid to call the 'big boys' out, and someone who will serve our country with honor. How will she handle the Vice Presidency, Capitol Hill, and a family? Please! Multi-tasking is God's gift to women!"[42] Similarly, on September 23, 2008, the "ParentDish" parenting website posted its "Red Mom, Blue Mom" pair of columns, in which an ideologically conservative and liberal woman each debated the Palin nomination, but less in terms of policy and more in terms of how much the Alaska governor was a "regular mom" with whom they could identify.

Throughout the campaign, Palin was often pictured surrounded by her husband and five children; she was shown countless times onstage after a speech or rally tenderly cradling her infant son, Trig. It was the first time a vice presidential debate showed a candidate holding her baby as she received congratulations afterward, highlighting the juxtaposition of motherhood with political life at the highest level to a national television audience. Having her new motherhood very much on display worked to affirm how young, fresh, and different Sarah Palin was as a vice presidential candidate. It reinforced her outsider status, making an overture to other ordinary moms who saw themselves embodied and reflected on the road to the White House in a way they never had before.

The narrative of Palin as mother also worked powerfully at a policy level, reinforcing the Republican Party's platform opposing abortion. She embodied a specific, conservative, pro-life view that places a high value on motherhood. In her later autobiography, Palin herself commented on the centrality of motherhood to her life, stating that "On April 20, 1989, my life truly began. I became a mom."[43] By choosing not to terminate her most recent pregnancy after discovering the fetus she was carrying had Downs syndrome, and by featuring her infant son prominently in speeches and photos, Palin became something of a heroine to anti-abortion forces. Head of the conservative, "pro-family," and anti-choice organization Focus on the Family, James Dobson hailed her selection as McCain's running mate. Dobson called her an "outstanding choice" and rescinded his vehement refusal to vote for John McCain, urging his followers to support the ticket with Palin onboard.[44] Opponents of *Roe vs. Wade* applauded the fact that she "walked the walk, not just talked the talk" of "choosing life" when faced with an unexpected and complicated pregnancy. Her staunch pro-life position was demonstrated not only in her own decision to give birth to Trig, but also in the views she expressed supporting her 17-year-old daughter's unwed pregnancy. J. Lee Grady, editor of *Charisma* magazine, a publication aimed at Pentecostal Christians, proclaimed on his blog: "What excites me most is the fact that she is a working mom with solid Christian values. We are way overdue for a conservative mother's touch in the White House," especially one who was "the embodiment" of "pro-life values America desperately needs ... sometimes it takes a true mother to rally the troops."[45] In fact, a political cartoon by Matt Wuerker on September 3, 2008, captured the way in which the mothering narrative overlapped with traditional Republican issues and constituencies. It depicted a huge poster of Sarah Palin, a baby in one arm and a rifle slung over the other shoulder, in an Uncle Sam top hat with a cross painted on it, with the slogan, "I WANT YOU to bear arms and bear children." John McCain, arms folded, surveyed the poster and said: "This just might work!" In this cartoon, Palin's frontier, gun-toting image converged with narratives about patriotism, Christianity, and motherhood.

Some critics wondered why social conservatives who had fought against the Equal Rights Amendment in the 1970s, disapproved of day care, and urged women to stay home with young children rather than pursuing careers were now embracing this 44-year-old woman with a new baby who was seeking such a demanding job and public role. Indeed, earlier in 2008 a Pew Research Group survey revealed that Republicans were far less likely to support a candidate who was female with small children, preferring a childless woman or, most ideal, a man with a family.[46] Yet, suddenly conservative Republicans were defending Palin's candidacy, holding her up as a strong, successful woman worth emulating, despite her many children at home. Was this support for a working mother hypocrisy, or crass partisanship trumping the idealism of social values?

Many "family values" conservatives remain committed to an ideal of gender roles reflecting Victorian separate spheres division of labor. They see men and women as having different essential natures, best suited for different tasks in the family and the wider world. This assertion of gender difference as valuable and important was used to refute 1970s notions of gender constructivism and androgyny. For example, Eagle Forum founder Phyllis Schlafly claimed that the Equal Rights Amendment (ERA) would deny recognition of any sex differences, requiring unisex public restrooms and women to serve in combat, and allowing men to shirk financial support of their wives. This rhetoric was powerful in mobilizing opposition to the ERA and preventing its ratification.[47] Although the culture wars continued to rage throughout the 1980s and 1990s, with Marilyn Quayle famously arguing at the 1988 Republican National Convention that "women do not want to be liberated from their essential natures," much about gender roles in the United States has changed.[48] As Maria Shriver pointed out in her 2010 report *A Woman's Nation*, women have made huge gains in education and employment.[49] More women than men earn college degrees each year, and they have infiltrated many formerly male-dominated occupations. Many of the changes Schlafly feared have happened: women soldiers are captured, wounded, and killed in our new style of warfare without a traditional frontline, and few divorced women receive alimony anymore, as judges consider both former spouses capable of supporting themselves financially. In fact, most women contribute significantly to their household's income, without assuming a male breadwinner can and should support them. In 2009, nearly four in ten working wives out-earned their husbands, and a growing number of single moms are the sole financial supporters of their families.[50]

As the economy has changed, making it harder for working- and middle-class families to rely on a single male provider, so have evangelical and conservative families: many of them have working mothers now. While being a stay-at-home-mother may be the preferred option for some women, it may be more an aspiration than a practical reality. As a result, certain political issues and stances may take on greater gender role symbolism, as sociologist Kristin Luker found in her interviews with abortion activists. For those involved in abortion politics, being pro-life was not simply about reproductive choice; it was an important way to signal commitment to traditional gender roles, women's feminine nature, and the institution of family.[51] If pro-choice advocates have argued for women's need to control fertility in order to compete equally with men in pursuing their educations, professions, and other life goals, opponents of abortion have countered that those arguments seem individualistic and selfish. Pro-life advocates see motherhood not as an oppressive burden to women, but as a God-given privilege and powerful responsibility. To reject motherhood by terminating a pregnancy is akin to rejecting the divine order of creation and the destiny women were made to find fulfilling, with their feminine, emotional natures and boundless mother-love.

Thus, Palin's strong pro-life stance communicates a reassuring message to social conservatives. It is a symbol of commitment to traditional family and gender roles, especially in private life (home and church), even if those roles are somewhat more flexible in the public sphere (in the workplace). Even if motherhood is not a woman's *only* role, it is still her *most important* role. Women can and do work outside the home; even women who would shun the label "feminist" agree that mothers often need to be able to help support their families, and that women in the workplace should be treated fairly and paid equally to their male colleagues. But within the charged symbolism of abortion politics, this view of the marketplace does not necessarily challenge a more patriarchal conception of differentiated gender roles within the family. And when women do participate in a leadership role such as politics, like Schlafly or Beverly LaHaye, founder of Concerned Women for America, it is often in defense of the family and traditional, maternal femininity.

Albert Mohler, president of Southern Baptist Theological Seminary and member of the Council on Biblical Manhood and Womanhood, rejects ordaining women to the ministry and is an influential advocate for male headship and female submission as appropriate Christian practice. His endorsement of Palin surprised some commentators, such as Sally Quinn, who asked in her "On Faith" blog: "Women can be presidents but not pastors? I don't understand."[52] His carefully parsed response in support of Palin asserted that women must be submissive in the church and home to male headship, but deserve equality in the public world and workplace:

> The Bible states that women are not to hold the office of teaching authority in the church, and sets forth a portrait of different but complementary

roles for men and women in the home and in the church … [But] our confession of faith does not speak to the appropriateness of women serving in public office. It does speak to the priority of motherhood and responsibilities in the home, but it does not specify any public role that is closed to women … When Gov. Palin was announced as Sen. John McCain's choice as running mate I was elated about her pro-life commitments.[53]

Mohler made it clear he was still not supportive of women's leadership in all spheres of life, and that as a Christian, he believed most women would be most fulfilled at home, raising children. But, technically, Sarah Palin was not breaking any biblical norms (as long as she didn't usurp Todd's authority at home or neglect her children). Because Palin cast herself as "chosen," not seeking the vice presidential nomination, but instead accepting that God had placed her in that position "for such a time as this," like the biblical Esther, her rise to power did not directly threaten notions of biblical womanhood. Rather, she could be used to spread a pro-life message upholding the value of motherhood.

Not all conservative Christians agreed. One *Charisma* magazine reader reacted in dismay to favorable coverage of Palin in Christian media. Karen Parrish's November 2008 letter to the editor read:

> Sarah Palin's candidacy is a sure sign of God's judgment on this nation. We must continue to uphold the biblical, traditional roles of women who are wives and mothers. Unless we do this we will proceed into darkness and apostasy. I believe God has been trying to chasten His daughter Sarah Palin. Her greatest hour is ahead—when she returns to her family sphere, honors her husband and publicly renounces her despising of her place as a wife and mother. I will not join with the wicked who think they are in control by casting their votes for John McCain.[54]

Christian dominionists Anna Sofia and Elizabeth Botkin warned: "Sarah Palin's example poses a more serious threat to Christian womanhood than more liberal feminist icons such as Hillary Clinton … Palin's example tells young women that it can be conservative and 'Christian' to neglect children and family… Despite Todd Palin's traditional, manly-man image and Sarah's traditional, womanly one, we believe they are undermining biblical marriage relationships and gender roles," and that Palin is "biblically unqualified" to hold political office because she is a woman.[55]

But many evangelicals did seem to have accepted the rationale of different roles for different spheres.[56] As Molly Worthen explains in a feature article called "Housewives of God," some conservative evangelical women have even become well-paid, popular public speakers and Bible teachers—which is fine as long as they do not call their teaching "preaching," and "submit" to their husbands' decision-making, even when they split household chores and childcare in a fairly equal manner.[57] Palin's political career reflected an everyday reality in many Christian households, in which women worked both inside and outside the home, and men sought to be good fathers as well as successful breadwinners, without disturbing traditional gender rhetoric. Palin's emphatic pro-life, Christian stance trumped her working motherhood as a credential of traditional femininity. She might have been active and accomplished outside the home, in that most masculine of realms: politics; but her large family, her faith, and her pro-life credibility established that her motherhood was more important to her narrative than political power. The large family she was juggling along with her high-powered political career seemed to underscore a commitment to mothering as one of women's primary roles or duties. She might have *added* an ambitious profession; but she had not given up, or downplayed, her role as wife and mother in exchange for it.

In fact, one of Palin's initial charms was how effortlessly she seemed to embody not just Everymom, but Supermom. Women journalists described themselves as "intrigued" and "delighted" when McCain first picked Palin, seeing her as the personification of the successful working mother. Sarah Palin "seemed to have achieved what so many of us were struggling for: an enviable balance between career and family ... She was running a state and breast-feeding a newborn and yet, amazingly did not seem exhausted. There was something inspiring about seeing a woman so at ease with her choices."[58] Palin reinforced this image of being able to "do it all" with her (in)famous quote in an early *People* magazine interview: "What I've had to do, though, is in the middle of the night, put down the BlackBerries and pick up the breast pump. Do a couple of things different and still get it all done."[59] In September, a *Newsweek* cover story on Palin claimed that white women, energized by Palin's can-do attitude and embrace of the hockey mom label, began shifting toward the Republican ticket once she was added to it (53 percent in support, up from 44 percent in July, with one in three saying they were more likely to vote for McCain because of his vice presidential pick).[60] The article suggested that she both represented and inspired ordinary working mothers: "This is her great skill: she works extraordinary hours but appears ordinary, thereby validating all moms and what they do each day—and what they might be capable of ... She validates motherhood by reviving the archetype of the impossibly confident Supermother, simultaneously managing teenagers, teething and the trials of a vice presidential campaign. No wonder she drinks Red Bull."[61]

As most initial profiles of Palin led with information about her multitasking motherhood, a few details were mentioned over and over: she had no nanny or full-time babysitter, but did keep a crib in the governor's office. She was down to earth, getting rid of the governor's chef because she didn't want her children to get used to having someone serve them. She gave birth to her third daughter, Piper, on a Monday and was back at work on Tuesday. She carried on making a political speech in Texas even as her amniotic fluid was leaking, then boarded a plane to fly all the way back to Alaska so that Trig would be born there. From these anecdotes, voters could fill in the rest of the supermom frame for themselves. "She is not weak or overwhelmed ... To many mothers she is empowering; she wields motherhood with pride, as something that doesn't diminish ability but enhances it—a sign of competence, indeed a qualification to speak on a national platform," *Newsweek* summed up.[62]

Yet just as quickly as Palin was "presented as a magnet for female votes, the epitome of everymom appeal," in the words of a *New York Times* story, her parenting became the target of fierce criticism. Over the weekend after her candidacy was announced, word began appearing on the internet, television, and newspapers that Palin's 17-year-old daughter Bristol, an unmarried high school student, was pregnant. Suddenly, reporters, bloggers, commentators, and voters were debating whether or not Sarah Palin was really a good mother.[63] Some of the criticism accused Palin of hypocrisy, noting her insistence on "abstinence-only" sexual norms and education for teens. Would the news of an out-of-wedlock pregnancy hurt Palin with her evangelical Christian base? Interestingly, evangelical leaders reacted with support for the Palins, not outrage and horror. Richard Land, a Southern Baptist leader, exclaimed: "Those who criticize the Palin family don't understand that we don't see babies as a punishment, but as a blessing ... This is the pro-life choice."[64] When Bristol appeared, visibly pregnant and engaged to be married, at the Republican convention, evangelicals saw it as more evidence that Sarah Palin and her family lived out their pro-life values rather than just paying them lip service. Another advocate of strict sexual morality, then head of Focus on the Family's James Dobson, noted that his ministry had offered prayer, counseling, and help to thousands of families facing unplanned pregnancies;

> We have always encouraged the parents to love and support their children and always advised the girls to see their pregnancies through, even though there will of course be challenges along the way. That is what the Palins are doing, and they should be commended once again for not just talking about their pro-life and pro-family values, but living them out even in the midst of trying circumstances. Being a Christian does not mean you're perfect ... but it does mean there is forgiveness and restoration when we confess our imperfections to the Lord.[65]

Dobson attacked "the media" for trying to spin Bristol's pregnancy as evidence of hypocrisy. Rather, he explained, it simply meant that she and her family were human, and he vowed to keep them in his prayers.[66] The narrative of sin and redemption was a familiar one to these Christians. The evangelical gospel message is, at its heart, the story of a fall from grace and God's forgiveness. Palin could have been judged harshly for the drama unfolding in her family, but instead it was framed as making her more relatable. Indeed, Hanna Rosin explained on

Slate.com that Bristol's pregnancy was a situation many American families, including evangelicals, were quite familiar with. Despite their idealistic rhetoric around sex and marriage, evangelical Christians—for reasons intertwined with socio-economic class—were now more likely to get divorced than "coastal elites" with college degrees, and just as likely to live together, have children out of wedlock, and for teenage girls, have sex at a younger age than other Americans.[67] Bristol's pregnancy became "just another one of the Palin's impeccable working-class credentials—salmon fisherman, union member, DWI [driving while intoxicated], hockey mom, soldier son, pregnant teenage daughter."[68]

Within a mere two hours of Bristol's pregnancy being reported on *The Washington Post*'s website, more than 1000 people had weighed in, arguing about whether Sarah Palin was placing political ambition above the needs of her family. Questions ran rampant, with John Roberts on CNN wondering: "Children with Downs syndrome require an awful lot of attention. The role of vice president, it seems to me, would take up an awful lot of her time, and it raises the issue of how much time will she have to dedicate to her child?"[69] Similarly, *The Washington Post*'s Sally Quinn opined that "Palin is a bright, attractive, impressive person," but questioned, "is she prepared for the all-consuming nature of the job? Her first priority has to be her children. When the phone rings at 3 in the morning and one of her children is really sick, what choice will she make?"[70]

Gender and language expert Deborah Tannen called those queries unfair, asserting: "What we're dealing with now, there's nothing subtle about it. We're dealing with the assumption that childrearing is the job of women and not men. Is it sexist? Yes."[71] But many writers, voters, and mothers shared those concerns. Could she do the "big job" and still take care of all those kids, especially a special-needs baby? Was her daughter's unwed pregnancy proof that she was a neglectful or absent mother? Would a good mother subject her pregnant teen to the scrutiny of a presidential race? Was the fact that she went back to work three days after giving birth admirable, or ludicrous and horrifying? If she could do it all, did that mean all the rest of us moms, stretched too thin and doing a double day, were supposed to somehow do it all too—without "whining" for policies that support working families?[72] Can women do it all—and do they even want to? As columnist Michelle Cottle noted, pitching "Palin's Supermom-of-five status as one of her chief assets has opened yet another front in the endless and endlessly counterproductive Mommy Wars."[73]

Indeed, "The Mommy Wars: Special Campaign Edition," was the subject of a front-page, above-the-fold story in the *New York Times* on Tuesday, September 2. Reporters Jodi Kantor and Rachel Swarns documented the fierce arguments among women about whether there were enough hours in the day for Palin to take on the vice presidency, and whether she was right to even try. They noted that motherhood blogs were flooded over that first weekend after Palin's nomination, with comments questioning Palin's judgment in going back to work when Trig was three days old, affirming how she put her pro-life values into practice by not terminating the pregnancy, or asserting it would be harder to juggle a BlackBerry and breast pump in the vice presidency.[74] Even more than evaluating Palin, this framing led women to wonder how her candidacy would affect their own careers, and the effect it would have on how working mothers are seen and supported in American society.

The same day, *Slate* ran a story entitled "Questions for a Superhuman Mom." Columnists Emily Bazelon and Dahlia Lithwick discussed the controversy over Palin's work–life choices and how that translates into large policy implications. They defended her right to run for vice president and make the choice to have her special needs child:

> But oh how we wish we didn't have to hear about her pulling off all these feats without household help—and without, or so she's determined to make it appear, breaking a sweat or gaining a pound … Does this woman sleep? Do conservative feminists really have to be the kind of larger-than-life working mothers who make every pro-family policy or job-based concession the rest of us require, and have finally demanded, seem like self-indulgence?[75]

Palin's example of running a state without a babysitter could imply no need for childcare subsidies or universal preschool for other families; and family leave laws seem unnecessary if even the governor can go back to work just a few days after giving birth. They also wondered if Palin has the right to haul her children into the spotlight in order to appeal to voters as supermom, but then make one of them—the pregnant Bristol—off limits to the press. "The Sarah Palin candidacy could have been a moment for women to celebrate, in glass-ceiling terms if not policy advances. But it never should have stood for the notion that the only way a woman is going to make it to the White House is if she's the best mom in America first."[76]

The mom narrative, and its double-edged nature, was everywhere. Two days later, *Slate* hosted an online chat with readers about Palin's acceptance speech at the Republican National Convention. Questions ranged from whether or not Palin had time to care for a newborn and serve as vice president, to the possible hypocrisy of her abstinence-only position regarding sex education when her own unmarried daughter had now become pregnant. Was it even fair to ask questions about her family? Yet how could it not be, when she made her maternal competence and family values such a key part of her résumé? One blogger observed that it was mostly other women judging Palin's work–life choices. Did men just not care?[77] A few days later, National Public Radio aired a chat with the Mocha Moms support group of young mothers, in which nearly identical issues were raised. The next week, Nancy Gibbs wrote a column in *Time* which used the Palin phenomenon to continue exploring contemporary work–life issues entitled "Parent Trap: Sarah Palin's Complicated Life Story Speaks to the Agonizing

Choices that Women Face."[78] A letter to *Newsweek* from Houston's Ximena Tagle exemplified much of the tenor of the conversation:

> If I had a friend with five kids, including a newborn with Down syndrome and an unmarried, pregnant teen, plus a demanding job and legal problems, I wouldn't ask her to so much as bring cookies to a PTA meeting! What was John McCain thinking when he asked Sarah Palin to take on the responsibility of being one heartbeat away from the presidency? I am a feminist and all for breaking glass ceilings, but not at the expense of the family.[79]

Or as Karen Tumulty succinctly phrased it in the title of her late September article on Palin, perhaps the hockey mom narrative had veered from appealing Everymom to "Maxed-Out Moms."[80]

In addition to being "Everymom" or Supermom, Sarah Palin was also importantly framed as a "celebrity mom." During the first week of September, Palin appeared on the cover of several decidedly non-public affairs magazines: grocery store tabloids and celebrity gossip magazines. *US Weekly* had a shot of Palin holding infant Trig with the headline, "John McCain's Vice President Sarah Palin: BABIES, LIES & SCANDAL," while *OK* ran the same picture under a banner screaming, "Sarah Palin's Baby Scandal: A MOTHER'S PAINFUL CHOICE." *People* announced: "Sarah Palin's FAMILY DRAMA," picturing her again holding the baby, but this time accompanied by daughter Piper. The ubiquity of these images may reflect not only her own positioning of herself as a "mom," but also the sheer novelty that a mother with so many young children running for such high office presented to the media. Pictures of Palin with her children appeared in all sorts of press coverage and media outlets, but these types of shots seemed particularly popular with more entertainment-oriented publications such as *US Weekly* and *People* magazine. These images allowed her to be "contained" within the norms of traditional femininity, situated in a narrative of "celebrity mom," similar to musicians or movie stars with babies who fascinate the public. Indeed, one online commentator bemoaned that "this election cycle could turn from one that was electrifying and energizing for women into one that situates their political prospects firmly back in the feminized territory of sex scandals, babies and mothering."[81]

Finally, Palin is, importantly, a "hockey mom"—not a soccer mom. Beginning with the 1996 presidential race, the "soccer mom" demographic has been identified as an important swing vote in American elections.[82] Soccer moms, as defined by scholars of gender and politics, tend to be white, married, middle-class suburban women with school-age children.[83] Their lives—and their politics—are defined largely by those kids they are ferrying to soccer practice in their minivans or SUVs; in 2004, Republican strategists appealed to their fears about terrorism to turn "soccer moms" into "security moms." As Minnesota blogger Jay Weiner pointed out, the addition of "hockey moms" to the political lexicon in 2008 lent a slightly different connotation. Hockey moms describe themselves as more "tough," "competitive," and "aggressive" than soccer moms, able to deal with the pre-dawn practices, freezing rinks, and broken teeth that go along with the sport.[84] There is also a class component to the distinction. While hockey is actually a less affordable sport (it requires more expensive equipment and is played by those with a median household income of $99,000 per year, twice the national average), the image of hockey moms is more working class.[85] As Tina Kelley explained it, soccer moms are married to doctors or lawyers and drink wine; hockey moms' husbands are ironworkers or fishermen, and they drink beer.[86] As a self-proclaimed "hockey mom," Palin makes a geographically based, blue-collar appeal: here is a rural gal from Alaska or Minnesota, not an elitist Ivy League grad raising her kids in the suburbs of Westchester, Connecticut.

Palin reinforced her toughness and down-to-earth qualities in the most-quoted line of her vice presidential nomination acceptance speech: "You know the difference between a hockey mom and a pit bull? Lipstick." No fragile, swooning, Victorian lady here—this female politician framed herself as tenacious and direct as a pit bull. But we should pay attention to how she also reasserted her femininity. She might be tough, but she also cared about being pretty. She was still a woman, and she wore the lipstick to prove it. With this pithy one-liner, Palin uses her definition of motherhood to position herself again as that juxtaposition of *both* a tough candidate to be reckoned with and utterly feminine.

Frames matter not only in the story they tell about the candidates, but also in the context of other frames and the issues of that particular election. The "lipstick" joke drew a stark contrast with one of the other women characters prominent in the 2008 election season, Senator Hillary Clinton. Whereas candidate Clinton strove to be taken seriously as "one of the boys"—with her dark pantsuits and mastery of policy detail, resisting focus on her clothes, hair, or other "frivolous" distractions—Palin wryly, fearlessly referenced a girlish accoutrement like lipstick. She offered an alternative femininity to that of Clinton, who was caricatured as scary, too powerful, and emasculating in the national imagination for the past 16 years. While Clinton may have had a "likability problem," Palin was described with adjectives such as perky, feisty, winsome, and cute.

The "hockey mom" also stands as a frame that contrasts with another prominent woman on the 2008 campaign trail, Democratic nominee Barack Obama's wife Michelle. Controversy erupted in February 2008 when Michelle Obama remarked: "For the first time in my adult life, I feel really proud of my country, because it feels like hope is finally making a comeback."[87] While the Obamas tried to explain that she simply meant she was proud that people were coming out to participate in the primaries in record numbers, Cindy McCain shot back that she had always been proud of her country—evoking a comparison of the patriotic military wife to the angry black woman.[88] Later that summer, the cover of the July 21 issue of *The New Yorker* garnered significant comment and debate over its depiction of Michelle and Barack Obama. She was shown with an Afro, fatigues, and an AK-47 machine gun, like a revolutionary Angela Davis, fist-bumping her husband, who was in a turban and robes. The connotations to terrorism are evident in the portrait of Osama Bin Laden on the wall and American flag burning in the fireplace of the Oval Office. While the cartoon cover was meant by its illustrator as satire, it seemed in bad taste to many commentators, and it certainly drew on a frame that Michelle Obama might be seen by some voters as an angry black woman. A tall, muscular woman with a no-nonsense way of speaking, particularly about her husband, Michelle Obama was "softened" at the Democratic convention as she talked about her ordinary working-class roots, her first dates with her husband, and her devotion to her adorable daughters, who joined her on stage. She made it clear in numerous interviews both before and after the election that she sought to be the "Mom-in-Chief" of the Obama administration—not an emasculating black matriarch, or a bitter Black Panther—which were American cultural stereotypes that one could assume needed to be deliberately avoided. In contrast, Sarah Palin's sunny suburban mom image, with its fierce pit bull protectiveness but its feminine lipstick, was a frame that drew on a very different set of white working-class schemas.

As an ordinary, yet extraordinary, hockey mom, Palin was framed in ways that many American women might relate to. Married mothers of young children and conservative women saw a new face on the political stage, one that looked like them and spoke about things that were familiar to their lives. Those women were energized by her presence and performance. The hockey mom frame also became a lens through which all American women could discuss what defined a "good mother." This narrative provided one way for Palin to be dismissed as merely a celebrity mom, repositioned in the female, domestic space of tabloids and family; but it also provided a frame through which a host of gender politics was debated, from work versus family concerns to reproductive rights. Palin as hockey mom created space to revalue mothering, making it more visible and potentially useful in the political realm. Yet in juxtaposition with the narratives of other women in the 2008 electoral context, it also resituated her as traditionally feminine, with a white, rural, working-class and socially conservative appeal. The maternal narrative allows Palin to be tough and feminine, and to break boundaries (like the political glass ceiling) while not shattering traditional gender norms.

5

BEAUTY QUEEN

From the beginning of her involvement on the national political stage, Sarah Palin's looks and style have been central focal points in our collective experience of her persona. Even before the vice presidential campaign, in a July 2007 *Weekly Standard* article that introduced Palin as a rising Republican star, Fred Barnes made mention of her previous beauty pageant involvement. He noted that Palin had won the Miss Wasilla beauty contest in 1984, was named Miss Congeniality, and later competed in the Miss Alaska competition.[1] A *Wall Street Journal* profile made early mention of her Miss Wasilla title, as well as the fact that she was "featured in a photo spread in *Vogue*."[2] Sometimes admiring, sometimes scornful, references to Palin's youth and sexual attractiveness were ubiquitous. Pollster Dave Dittman described Palin as "young and pretty," Rush Limbaugh referred to her as a "babe," Tina Fey invoked the off-color term "MILF" (a sexually attractive middle-aged woman) on *SNL*, and blogger Cintra Wilson mocked her as "the White House bunny." Countless others commented on her hair, her eyeglasses, her skirts, and her shoes.

It was not just her attractive looks that were part of the image—it was her overall style and approach. Former Miss America Kate Shindle suggested "there's a touch of pageant world to Palin's voice, to her careful adherence to sound bytes, and that 'cheerful aggressiveness' [that is] part cheerleader, part news anchor and part drill sergeant."[3] Media commentator Troy Patterson, analyzing her television image during the first week of the campaign, declared: "The key is her smile, the blue-ribbon-and-collar smile of a red-state pageant queen, a smile like a confident handshake."[4] The frame did not go unnoticed by observers. Columnist Maureen Dowd, for one, commented that "Instead of going home and watching *Miss Congeniality* with Sandra Bullock, I get to stay here and watch *Miss Congeniality* with Sarah Palin ... She has a beehive and sexy shoes, and the day she's named she goes shopping with McCain in Ohio for a cheerleader outfit for her daughter."[5]

The narrative framing Palin as merely a pretty pageant queen draws on a familiar feminine trope in American popular culture. From "blonde jokes" to cheerleader tropes, the stereotype is that attractive girls are not very smart; beauty is not accompanied by brains. Beauty queens are to be looked at, not listened to. The idea that a pretty girl is also a bimbo is reinforced in movies such as *Miss Congeniality* (2000), in which FBI agent Gracie Hart initially mocks pageant contestants. Unconcerned with feminine appearance and just wanting to be taken seriously by her male FBI colleagues, Gracie (played by Sandra Bullock) has rumpled clothes, unkempt frizzy hair, and bad table manners. When she is asked to go undercover as a contestant in the Miss United States pageant, Gracie immediately refuses: "I'm not going to parade around in a swimsuit like some airhead bimbo that goes by the name of Gracie Lou Freebush, and all she wants is world peace." Finally convinced to take the assignment, Gracie prepares by watching tapes of former contestants. Though the sound is muted, both Gracie and the movie audience watch on screen as a pageant contestant's name is announced as the winner and a crown is placed on her head. The young woman gasps in delighted shock and tears up, emotion overwhelming her. Unimpressed, Gracie mutters, "Look, she's gonna cry again," and then, in a higher register, as if giving voice to the beauty queen on stage: "If I only had a brain."

Indeed, the Miss America pageant began in 1921 as a "bathing beauty" contest on the boardwalk in Atlantic City. During the 1920s, it not only served as a marketing scheme to keep tourists in Atlantic City over Labor Day weekend, but the type of girls crowned the winners stood in contrast to the "new woman" images of suffragettes and flappers.[6] By the mid-twentieth century it was watched on live television by millions and cemented its place in popular culture as a display of wholesome ideal American womanhood. Bert Parks, a previous host of the Miss America pageant, sang to each newly crowned Miss America for decades:

> There she is, Miss America
> There she is, your ideal
> The dream of a million girls who are more than pretty
> Can come true in Atlantic City
> For she may turn out to be the Queen of femininity.

Even though the pageant evolved from mere beauty contest into a major source of college scholarship money in the 1940s, Miss America still retained the image of women being primarily pure and pretty.[7] The baton-twirling, swimsuit-with-high-heels-wearing, evening-gowned contestants embodied a demure, sweet, and girlish version of American femininity that was also decidedly white and middle class. It was no coincidence that the emerging Women's Liberation Movement chose the 1968 Miss America pageant as the site of their first widely publicized protest. On the boardwalk outside the convention hall, feminist protesters threw bras, girdles, curlers, wigs, and fashion magazines into a "Freedom Trash Can" and crowned a sheep Miss America.[8] (Contrary to popular lore, no bras were actually burned, although that had been the original plan. Local authorities informed protestors they could not set the trash can alight because of fire danger to the wooden boardwalk.[9]) Women's Liberation activists chose the Miss America pageant as a perfect target because it was such a symbol of male-defined femininity: it displayed woman as spectacle, woman as object, and woman as consumer, in need of products like those thrown in the trash can to create an artificial image of beauty.[10] These early second-wave feminist protesters saw the beauty queen as the antithesis of liberated women, who sought to have a voice, power, and autonomy. As Christine Yano points out, there is an inherent lack of power in the beauty queen role: "Beauty queens, like other contemporary celebrities, hold symbolic prestige in representing the group, but no actual power in controlling that group or shaping its future."[11] Smiling serenely from her throne, the beauty queen attracts admiration and attention. Yet she is not expected to have much to say, and her understanding of a complex world is superficial at best: all she wants is "world peace." Sarah Palin framed in this way drew a lot of attention, but it also lowered expectations of her political acumen, and created assumptions that the girl with the brilliant pageant smile was perhaps lacking in intelligence and authority.

From Miss America to the queen of the local county fair, there are also connotations of race, class, and nationalism that fit the beauty pageant image and that are important to notice as they fit the narrative of Sarah Palin's candidacy. Strong implicit notions of beauty as white are embedded in the Miss America pageant, which did not crown a woman of color until 1984.[12] Even then, the first few African American winners were critiqued for being light-skinned and reinforcing white notions of beauty.[13] Beauty pageants are also a very middle-class phenomenon. Historically, Victorian standards of decorum dictated that upper-class women should not display themselves in public, except in exclusive events such as a debutante ball. Beauty pageants as a phenomenon are a way for lower- or middle-class girls, aspiring to those upper-class ideals of privileged femininity, to "emulate some of the performance idioms of putatively upper-class debdom."[14] Here was a way for non-elite girls to appropriate the gloves, gowns, and tiaras of the debutante. The fact that they are copying these practices from the exclusive society they would never actually be able to participate in marks pageants themselves as solidly middle-class affairs.[15] The practices and accoutrements of pageants not only refer to upper-class cotillions; they can be seen as aspiring to nobility and royalty as well. To wear the crown—at a pageant or prom, homecoming dance or county fair—was to be "queen for a day." The gowns and sparkling tiaras allude to the charmed existence of princesses in fairy tales, with the promise of "happily ever after" and most privileged status. Yet, the prom queen or county fair princess was chosen by peers or judges: there is an element of the meritocracy to this American pageantry. Even the lowliest girl, if possessing beauty, charm, talent, and grace, could rise to be the queen of all. Given Sarah Palin's framing of herself as an ordinary citizen, not an elite, there is something consonant with her framing as this sort of beauty queen: a middle-class "girl next door" who just happens to be beautiful and worthy of rising to the top.

Beauty pageants have also been successful venues for fusing ideals of nationalism and femininity: the "Miss America" or "Miss USA" titles imply both ideal femininity *and* ideal patriotism, embodying and representing the nation. During World War II, the Miss America organization explicitly embraced patriotic activities, sending the winners of the crown to sell war bonds and entertain the troops with the United Service Organization (USO). Miss America 1943, Jean Bartel, sold over $2.5 million Series E bonds during a three-month tour across the country, selling more bonds than any other single person that year.[16] Venus Raney, Miss America 1944, was given a Special Citation from the US Treasury Department for her efforts in selling war bonds, and her likeness was painted on the nosecone of a B-17 bomber stationed in Italy, as "the pageant allowed men to know what they were fighting for."[17] Miss Americas have continued to embrace and encourage national pride, entertaining troops around the world with the USO and visiting veterans' hospitals as part of their reign.

The beauty queen narrative provides a specific example of a larger theme of politicized American femininity in the postwar years. Images of American women were juxtaposed against those of Soviet women as evidence of US superiority in the Cold War (see Elaine Tyler May's *Homeward Bound* for an in-depth and fascinating discussion of postwar femininity and its political meaning). Rather than drab, androgynous Communist "comrades," American women were portrayed as warm, appealing, and curvaceous in Dior's "New Look." These lovely pin-up-worthy girls were indeed what red-blooded American men had been fighting for, and the new feminine ideal encouraged women to leave their wartime jobs for white picket fences and contribute to the baby boom. As postwar prosperity expanded the middle class, fueled by the GI Bill, suburbanization, and consumerism, women were seen as the beneficiaries of labor-saving homemaking devices that allowed them to be even more devoted wives and mothers. The beauty and leisure of American women became important symbols of democracy and patriotism. The ideals of femininity in popular culture no longer resembled the spunky, clever, fast-talking heroines of 1930s and 1940s screwball comedies. They were replaced by the cool, quiet beauty of Grace Kelly and the voluptuous, breathy sexuality of Marilyn Monroe. Hyper-feminine beauty and mannerisms were reified, as well, in the spectacle of beauty contests. The popularity of beauty pageants from mid-twentieth century on can be seen as another example of the idealization of women's physical appearance and sex appeal, made patriotic and accessible to mainstream American culture. Those white, middle-class, patriotic implications are tapped into by Palin and underscore her appeal.

When John McCain announced that Sarah Palin was his choice to be his running mate on August 29, 2008, most of the press coverage introducing her to the

American public emphasized her reformer credentials in Alaska, her social conservatism, and her large family. Some included a sentence, almost a throwaway line, mentioning that she was Miss Wasilla 1984. It seemed at first just one more novelty of her biography, like the fact that her husband raced snow machines or that she'd played high school basketball. A few mentioned her inclusion in a photo shoot by *Vogue* magazine, profiling political women. However, comments about her looks and narratives framing her as sex object soon became more prevalent. Internet researcher Bill Tancer noted on the *Time* magazine website on September 2 that in just two days, US internet searches for "Sarah Palin" spiked higher than searches for any other political personality in the preceding three years. Searches for Palin were almost four times as popular as those for Barack Obama, who had just become the first African American to accept a major party's presidential nomination.[18] Not surprisingly, many people were curious about this woman they had not heard of before, who was now running for vice president. The number one search term was simply "Sarah Palin." But the next three most popular were "*Vogue* magazine," "Photos," and "Beauty Pageant," with "Hot" coming in at number ten. Tancer found that "one of the most commonly entered search topics surrounding Palin was 'hot photos,'" with "Sarah Palin Bikini Photos" and "Sarah Palin Naked" other common queries. "I doubt that any of us have ever considered any of our past vice-presidential candidates a sex symbol," he mused, "But that may be changing."[19] In fact, the campaign itself may have wanted to play up this angle of Palin's candidacy. One report noted that the McCain campaign purchased the URL www.votefortheMILF.com within 36 hours of picking Palin as a running mate, and visitors to the site were redirected to a video message from Governor Palin on the official McCain website.[20]

An online chat about the Palin pick on the *Slate* website led to comments like this one, regarding the upcoming vice presidential debate: Joe Biden "should be working on that smile of his, because hers is a killer."[21] Also on *Slate*, editor David Plotz's September 9 headline enquired: "I Dream about Sarah Palin. Do You?" In a move that was surely unprecedented, Plotz asked readers to send in stories about dreams they had that featured the vice presidential nominee. He noted that "a couple of conservative men I know" told him they had sexual fantasies about the Alaska governor, adding slyly, "I'm sure they're not alone."[22] Stunningly, the website received nearly 500 responses to this query, and published their 20 favorites three days later.[23]

Newsweek framed Palin as a beauty queen in the opening paragraph of its cover story on McCain's choice of Palin as his running mate, disingenuously refuting the charge of being sexy instead of serious even as it raised it. Here is how the newsmagazine introduced its readers to the possible Republican vice president: "Sarah Palin posed for a photo spread in *Vogue*," the story opened, then quickly insisted, "but that's about as far as the glamour goes."[24] (Ironically, in the February 2008 *Vogue* story, Palin appeared in a heavy parka and boots, leaning against a seaplane and striding across the tundra, so the allusion to the *Vogue* shoot as glamorous was inaccurate. But the implication that there was a sexy *fashionista* side to Palin was already made.) *Newsweek* mentioned that Palin was once a beauty queen, winning the title of Miss Wasilla 1984, then quoted Palin's father from the *Vogue* profile as saying: "We were really surprised when she wanted to do it. That wasn't her thing," and noted that Palin herself "regretted the whole beauty pageant experience." The *Newsweek* story then interjected a quote from Palin herself about competing in the Miss Alaska pageant. On the one hand, it demonstrates her chagrin and refusal to be objectified; on the other hand, it undermines her indignation and reinforces in the minds of the electorate the most prevalent stereotype of beauty pageants and their contestants. "'They made us line up in bathing suits and turn our backs so the male judges could look at our butts. I couldn't believe it!' she told *Vogue*."[25] The article went on to detail how she "*charmed* a fierce contrarian like John McCain" into picking her as his running mate, under the headline "McCain's Mrs. Right."[26] Though the story spent several more pages detailing her political background and accomplishments, it framed her initially in ways that were girlish and sexualized.

One of the most memorable and influential vehicles for framing Sarah Palin as a beauty queen was the popular late-night television comedy show *Saturday Night Live*, with Tina Fey performing as the vice presidential candidate. Fey bore a striking resemblance to Palin and appeared on the *SNL* season opener on September 13, 2008, as the Alaska governor, in a sketch that also featured Amy Poehler as Hillary Clinton. As the two candidates Palin and Clinton, Fey and Poehler held a press conference discussing the issue of sexism in the 2008 campaign and their respective paths toward the White House. This sketch was powerful in creating a popular narrative for Palin, as it occurred just two weeks after Palin burst on the national scene and marked the widely anticipated debut of Fey impersonating her. (*SNL* has a long history of political and presidential impersonations, including Chevy Chase's clumsy Gerald Ford, Dana Carvey's George H. W. Bush, and Will Ferrell's George W. Bush.) Fey played Palin as flirtatious and ditsy. Two days earlier, the first major interview of Palin had aired on ABC News. Palin was panned for stumbling over a question about the "Bush Doctrine" on foreign policy; she was also interrogated over her claim that she had national security credentials simply because Alaska shared a narrow maritime border with Russia, in such proximity that Russian territory could be seen from an Alaskan island. On *SNL*, Fey translated the gaffes into memorable lines that cemented a public image of Palin as shallow, silly, and unprepared for national office. When Poehler's Clinton declared her opposition to the Bush Doctrine, Fey's Palin giggled and admitted coyly: "I don't know what that is." Poehler asserted the importance of diplomacy, and Fey uttered the line that became indelibly connected to the public's image of Palin: "And I can see Russia from my house!"

The heart of the sketch was both women critiquing sexist treatment of them in the campaign, making the point by contrasting the divergent but demeaning public images of each of the candidates. While Poehler asked that people stop saying Clinton had "cankles" or call her a "flurge"—unflattering and unfeminine terms—Fey asked slyly that people not manipulate digital images of Palin's head onto sexy bikini photos or call her a "MILF." Both women demanded the media stop using "words that diminish us:" "harpy, shrew, boner-shrinker" for Clinton, but "pretty, attractive, beautiful" for Palin. Fey delivered the requests with smiling gusto that belied her protests. The audience got the joke: the gendered lens through which Palin was being described was not really unacceptable to her as long it gave her the advantage. While Poehler continued talking, Fey did a pageant wave and posed with a side profile to show off her bust. Finally, Poehler's Clinton exploded in utter frustration that her ambition for the White House has been thwarted: "I scratched and clawed through mud and barbed wire, and you just glided in on a dog sled wearing your pageant sash and Tina Fey glasses!"

In the next few weeks, the characterization of Palin as a bimbo was heightened. On September 27, *SNL* did a sendup of Palin's disastrous interview with Katie Couric. Much of the sketch used lines from the actual interview transcript, which made the skewering even more sharp and effective. At one point, the Couric character (played by Amy Poehler) asked Palin (played by Fey) about her recent meeting with world leaders at the United Nations. Fey responded: "They embraced me, Katie! Both figuratively and—a couple of them Pakistani guys—literally," highlighting her sex appeal. The portrayal situated Palin as more at home in the realm of pop culture than world politics, as she called U2 singer Bono "the King of Ireland." When asked a difficult question about Iraq, she requested to use one of her "lifelines" and "phone a friend," as if she were on the game show *Who Wants to Be a Millionaire?* instead of running for vice president.

On October 4, *SNL* did a sketch recapping the vice presidential debate, with debate moderator Gwen Ifill (played by Queen Latifah) drily noting the "historically low expectations of Governor Palin." If she simply did not cry, faint, run out of the building, or vomit, viewers were advised to consider the debate a tie. In the actual debate, Palin had (oddly) winked at the audience several times as she spoke. Fey mimicked and exaggerated Palin's winking, and added other flirtatious mannerisms. She also repeated the word "maverick" several times in a circular fashion, demonstrating its lack of any meaningful substance and her own superficiality. For example, when asked how she and McCain would deal with the implosion of Wall Street and the housing market, Fey's Palin replied breezily: "You know, we're gonna take every aspect of the crisis and look at it and then we're gonna ask ourselves, 'What would a maverick do in this situation?' And then, you know, we'll do that [winks coyly]!" The Palin character told the audience she had enjoyed the opportunity to answer questions directly during the debate, without reporters' pesky follow-up questions, fact-checking, or "incessant need to figure out what your words mean or why you put them in that order." *SNL* connected this airheaded image directly back to the beauty queen stereotype. When asked for a closing statement, Fey looked startled and asked:

"Oh, are we not doing the talent portion?" She then held up a flute, played a few bars, and winked again.

On October 18, Sarah Palin herself appeared on *Saturday Night Live* as a guest. To open the show, Tina Fey appeared dressed as Palin, pretending to hold a press conference. She returned immediately to the pageant queen narrative, saying, "And now, I'd like to entertain everybody with some fancy pageant walkin'" As Fey strutted and winked, the audience saw the real Sarah Palin watching this performance on a monitor in the studio hallway with the show's executive producer, Lorne Michaels. The guest host of *SNL* for that week, Alec Baldwin, joined them. Mistaking Palin for Fey, Baldwin began to mock her, saying Palin went against everything the show stood for: "What do they call her again, Tina?" Palin responded wryly, "Uh, that'd be Caribou Barbie." When Baldwin finally realized his error, and that the woman he was making fun of was actually standing right in front of him, he did not apologize. Rather, he leered at her for a moment and then stammered admiringly, "YOU are way hotter in person." Instead of objecting to the crude appraisal, Palin demurely replied, "Why, thank you."

Palin's appearance on *SNL* on October 18, 2008, garnered the show its highest ratings since 1994.[27] A Nate Beeler editorial cartoon in the *Washington Examiner* on October 3, 2008, poked fun at the conflation in viewers' minds between Governor Palin and Tina Fey's depictions of her. The power the show had commanded in successfully shaping the public's widespread understanding of Palin is demonstrated in the cartoon. A reporter was shown with tape recorder and notebook, asking an ordinary-looking citizen in jeans and ball-cap: "Who would you say was the winner of the vice-presidential debate?" The man replied simply: "Tina Fey." The performance and the candidate blurred into one another inextricably. As Fey highlighted the beauty queen elements of Palin's performance on the campaign trail, the beauty queen narrative seemed an increasingly appropriate frame in which to understand her.

Political cartoons are another way to distill what the public's impressions of a candidate are. To be humorous, a comedy sketch or cartoon needs to capture something that seems true and resonates with the audience, as well as exaggerating or lampooning it. In early September 2008, editorial cartoonists were still trying to figure out who Sarah Palin was, and what image or narrative would ring true with the electorate. By early October, particularly after the Couric interview and little chance for other media to interact with her, an image of Palin as ditsy and incompetent seemed to have taken hold. Rob Rogers's cartoon on October 2 in the *Pittsburgh Post-Gazette* depicted Palin preparing for the vice presidential debate by shaking a Magic Eight Ball for answers. That same day, Joel Pett (syndicated for the *New York Times*) drew Palin behind a debate podium, with McCain advising her that all she had to do was walk and chew gum, albeit "top-secret commander-in-chief material gum!" Palin blows a gigantic bubble, which pops all over both their faces, and McCain sighs, "OK, just walking may do it." Signe Wilkinson's October 6 cartoon, syndicated for the Washington Post Writers

Group, shows Palin in a cheerleader outfit, shaking her pom-poms for a small McCain figure with a deflating football of "Bush policies." Off to the side of the panel are two ordinary citizens. One remarks to the other: "At least he's got the hottest cheerleader."

An October 14 cartoon by Clay Bennett, also for the Washington Post Writers Group, depicted a middle-aged woman in an optometrist's shop. She is admiring herself in rimless glasses in a mirror, while a sign behind the optometrist proclaims that Sarah Palin glasses are now in stock. The caption read: "Not only will they make you look more qualified than you really are, but they'll also let you see the world however you want." This cartoon underscored the perception that Palin lacked intelligence and depth, but possessed a cheerful, confident ignorance—much like a pageant contestant who smilingly insists on the likelihood of world peace. This cartoon also highlighted another aspect of the "Palin effect:" her impact upon the world of fashion and style.

Within just a few days of her nomination, Palin's glasses had become a coveted fashion item. *USA Today* and Good Morning America reported her rimless designer glasses were sought after by women all over the country.[28] The US distributor was being flooded with calls from dealers wanting to stock the $375 Kazuo Kawasaki frames, and the national sales manager said few celebrities in glasses had ever set off this kind of frenzy.[29] By mid-September, orders for the frames had quadrupled and the manufacturer was trying to keep up, shifting production to a round-the-clock assembly line.[30] News stories also reported that people were requesting her hairstyle at salons and debating exactly what shade and brand of lipstick she wore during her convention speech.[31] Like many political women before her, her appearance was intensely scrutinized. What seemed novel was the way in which women wanted to copy her look; numerous feature stories devoted to her fashion and beauty choices seemed to resituate her in the realm of celebrity women such as music and movie stars, whose haircuts, makeup, and dress are intended to inspire imitation by their fans. The time and energy spent on finding her glasses or lipstick could be seen as undermining her political gravitas and shifting the narrative back to Palin as beauty queen or celebrity model to be copied. Palin's footwear also drew a lot of attention during the campaign. She favored peep-toe heels, often red or with some sparkle, and tall, black high-heeled boots worn with above-the-knee skirts. The online sales of the "Naughty Monkey" red peep-toe pumps with 3½-inch heels she wore when McCain introduced her as his running mate shot up 50 percent in the next two weeks, selling out in four sizes.[32] Brand director Jay Randhawa noted that it caught him by surprise that the 40-something governor was spotted wearing Naughty Monkey shoes: "It's a very edgy, very hip, very street brand" usually marketed to women in their early to mid-20s "who go clubbing," he explained.[33] The sexy heels and motorcycle boots Palin wore at campaign stops were a more risky, playful look than most female politicians typically sported. They seemed to invite voters to see her first and foremost as a sexually attractive woman, not as political candidate who just happened to be a woman (and perhaps, like Hillary Clinton in her ubiquitous black pantsuits, just wanted to blend in and be taken seriously).

In past election cycles, this open and direct talk of traditional femininity and attractiveness, sexiness, and wardrobe might have all been viewed as just the type of objectification that women candidates for office had experienced in the past. Feminist critics have commented on how these variables have been used to call into question the seriousness, readiness, or qualifications of women candidates and to disadvantage them with voters in some way. As the classic study *Running as a Woman* points out, women candidates have had to consider how they dressed "to be taken seriously, not sexually; how then to overcome the stereotype of women as frilly, fussy beings; how next to assume the authority granted men virtually as their birthright and be, in camouflage if not reality, one of the boys."[34] The authors quote Congresswoman Louise Slaughter recalling being "told to wear black so that she would look more serious" and Senator Barbara Boxer noting that she was told to "tone down the California brightness."[35] As political consultant Mary Matalin told *Vogue* magazine in November 1991, "Women in politics who look chic are perceived as frivolous. If you're pulled together that means you've been shopping … instead of laboring over papers … fifteen hours a day. Besides, every woman who looks good gets hit on, and after a while they just don't want the hassle."[36] The conventional wisdom of campaign advisers was that being stylish or sexy was not an asset for a woman candidate; instead, they undermined her competence and credibility.

Women candidates have had to battle this recurring stereotype of femininity and frivolity, even when running for president. A quantitative study comparing newspaper coverage of Elizabeth Dole during her bid for the Republican presidential nomination in the fall of 1999 to coverage of male GOP rivals Steve Forbes, George W. Bush, and John McCain found that, predictably, Dole received less issue coverage than the men, but more coverage of her appearance and personality.[37] In their study of the political rhetoric surrounding women officeholders, one of the primary "codes" or narratives Karrin Vasby Anderson and Kristina Horn Sheeler have found typically applied to female politicians is that of the hostess/beauty queen. Calling it one of the most traditional and recognizable stereotypes in media accounts of political women, they describe how the "beauty queen" rhetoric praises them for filling proper feminine roles and focuses on their appearance, but limits their power.[38]

Yet Palin seemed quite comfortable, almost amused, with this imagery and framing—even empowered by it. *The Washington Post* reporter Libby Copeland noted that this "traditional feminine warmth" is what set her in direct opposition to Hillary Clinton, who took the more common approach of projecting great strength and demonstrating experience.[39] Rather than respond by confronting and contradicting the stereotypical focus on her appearance, the McCain/Palin camp instead responded by trying to reframe the discussion altogether and turn the focus to their advantage. Palin herself seemed to embody an argument that women could be strong without threatening traditional social values and practices, particularly men's sense of masculinity. She could handle it all—happily and prettily. One news story evaluating Palin's appeal put it this way: "For many Palin supporters, her attractiveness does not weaken her appeal—rather, it balances those tales of valor on the tundra. Supporters have charged her critics with sexism but at the same time, at the GOP convention, delegates wore buttons that said 'Hottest VP from the Coolest State.'"[40] The simultaneous narrative of the frontier woman complicates the beauty queen frame, keeping her strong as well as feminine. Through this frame Palin could be seen as less defensive and shrill, and more authentic as a candidate. Republican speechwriter Landon Parvin suggested that "She's not a woman trying to deliver a speech like a man, and there is an integrity to that."[41] Or as one observer told a reporter: "She's a different kind of feminist … a strong woman who can wear a skirt and be proud of it."[42]

In fact, one of the other popular culture tropes that Palin seemed to evoke with this framing was the "sexy librarian:" the woman who surprises with both beauty and brains. Like prim and proper Marian the Librarian in the 1957 Tony award-winning musical *The Music Man*, Palin chose—with her glasses instead of contact lenses, and her dark hair contained in a neat bun—a look that seemed serious and bookish. The power of the sexy librarian is the smoldering sexuality under the plain looks and intelligence, a sultry femininity unleashed when the glasses come off and the hair comes tumbling down. In *The Music Man*, prim and proper Iowa librarian Marian Paroo is a self-proclaimed spinster, and the only one in River City smart enough to see through the scheme of con man Harold Hill. By the end of the musical, Hill is responsible for bringing Marian's socially awkward brother out of his shell, and Marian has fallen in love with him. She realizes that being a stickler for honesty and propriety has led her to overlook larger emotional truths. Reclaimed by romance, the musical ends with Marian falling into the arms of the man she loves. This pop culture image may also refer back to the 1946 movie *The Big Sleep*, a film noir thriller that featured a seductive scene between Humphrey Bogart (as detective Philip Marlowe) and Dorothy Malone (as the proprietress of the Acme Book Shop). Questioned by Bogart, the plain and proper Malone gives him some information pertinent to his investigation and displays a deep knowledge about rare books. When Bogart lingers, waiting for the object of his investigation to appear across the street from her store, Malone suggestively closes up shop early, takes off her glasses and loosens her pinned-back hair. Bogart does a double-take and almost wolf-whistles as he murmurs: "Hel-looo." Glancing up at him from seductively lowered eyes, Malone replies with a smile: "Hello," and the screen fades to black, leaving the rest of their steamy encounter to the viewer's imagination.

Elements of Palin's appearance and mannerisms—the glasses, the hair, the surprisingly provocative footwear under the serious suits—evoked this smart-but-sexy trope. The online entertainment news site Zimbio published a post entitled "U.S. Public Stupified by Palin's 'Sexy Librarian' Look" on September 9, 2008, referring to the allure of Palin's glasses and pulled up hair.[43] The *Newsweek* cover story also described "strands of hair [falling] from her librarian's bun" during an interview with Palin. "She seemed unfazed" by the constant buzzing of her two BlackBerrys and a cell phone, it noted, "as she deftly executed an intricate 'don't drop the BlackBerry while fixing the bobby pin' maneuver, several times."[44] Here the narrative captured both the competence of a governor multitasking and the not-quite-contained femininity of a sexually attractive woman. There was a lot of potential appeal in that barely contained, hinted-at sexuality. Conservative talking heads such as Rush Limbaugh and Newt Gingrich seemed to gloat repeatedly that their side had the "babe," the "attractive" woman candidate, as opposed to Hillary Clinton, who had been mocked throughout the election year as old and unappealing, even emasculating. Tucker Carlson referred to Clinton as a castrating woman on MSNBC on July 16, 2007, saying: "when she comes on TV, I involuntarily cross my legs." Just after Palin's acceptance speech, Donny Deutsch appeared on CNBC decrying Palin as "the new feminist ideal" of a woman in power. "Before you can sell the candidate ... you gotta first sell her as a woman," Deutsch proclaimed, saying: "Men want a sexy woman ... Hillary Clinton didn't figure it out. She didn't put a skirt on." Palin was different, he asserted, because while "women want to be her, men want to mate with her ... I want her lying next to me in bed."[45]

Even as she was being ogled and sexualized, Palin was held up as a symbol for social conservativism. While she seemed to encourage, or at least tolerate, all the attention her attractiveness brought her, she espoused positions on family, sexual abstinence, and abortion that were more associated with a buttoned-up conservative agenda. Tom Perotta, in his article "The Sexy Puritan," suggests that Sarah Palin embodies the most recent representation of a particular type of woman—the Sexy Puritan—that has become a familiar and potent figure in the ongoing culture wars between right and left in American politics. His analysis suggests:

> Sexy Puritans engage the culture wars on two levels—not simply by advocating conservative positions on hot-button social issues but by embodying nonthreatening mainstream standards of female beauty and behavior at the same time. The net result is a paradox, a bit of cognitive dissonance very useful to the cultural right: You get a little thrill along with your traditional values, a wink along with the wagging finger ... The right has understood for a long time that harsh social messages seem a lot more palatable coming from an attractive young woman than a glowering old man.[46]

Palin as "sexy Puritan" makes use of her sexuality as a powerful tool. Her flirtatious teasing of the electorate, in her stilettos and sexy librarian bun, modernizes and twists the socially conservative positions she espouses. Winking and playful, this archetypal "hot" conservative woman undermines the conventional wisdom that these views on abortion, abstinence, and homosexuality reflect repression, prudishness, or lack of libido. By having an attractive woman embrace this message, it refutes charges that these issue positions merely oppress women and allow men to retain control. Palin's sexiness is appealing and useful. It titillates and teases, but doesn't go too far; the sexuality is on display, but still under (conservative/male) control. In fact, this strategy may reposition the conservative viewpoints on sexuality as consonant with feminism (or post-feminism), chosen freely by women as a mark of self-respect and empowerment.

However, much like the other frames, this one had potentially negative aspects and features that had to be confronted over the course of the fall campaign. Without the careful balancing of other narrative frames (such as the frontier woman and the maverick), the focus on traditional femininity and appearance had the potential to convey girlishness and a lack of seriousness and preparedness. Some would argue that over time the balance was lost and that this danger was realized both in the real political world and in satirical portrayals of Palin, particularly those appearing on *SNL*. Near the end of the campaign when it appeared clear that the McCain campaign was not going to prevail over Obama and Biden, the McCain campaign operatives who embraced the positive aspects of Palin's traditional femininity were quick to leak "negative" stories about her shopping habits and diva-like qualities when the results turned against them in November. This seemed an easy criticism, more easily received and believed because of the earlier decision to present Palin through this frame.

After an initial flurry of interest in Palin's shoes, glasses, and hairstyle, scrutiny turned to her experience and preparedness. After her acceptance speech, she was shielded from the press and gave very few interviews for nearly three weeks. When her performance in the much-anticipated, nationally televised Katie Couric interview that aired on September 24 and 25 was widely seen as a disappointment, even some of her early supporters began to turn against her. Conservative commentator Kathleen Parker wrote of her growing doubts in an article entitled "Palin Problem" on September 26.[47] "She's clearly out of her league," Parker wrote on the *National Review* website, not demonstrating enough knowledge of economics and foreign policy to make Americans feel comfortable with a possible Palin presidency. While Parker had initially been excited by the Palin nomination and had wanted her to "perform brilliantly," she now publicly advised Palin to "bow out" of the race and spend more time with her newborn, off of the national stage.[48] On the *Slate* website, Dahlia Lithwick voiced her frustration with Palin's lack of substance (albeit with visual style). Since she had held no press conferences, spoken to just three television reporters (including Couric and ABC's Charlie Gibson), and done no informal interviews in the first month of her candidacy, "a nation is permitted to know her almost exclusively through photo ops in fabulous shoes" that smack of empty tokenism, Lithwick complained.[49] The blog post summed up the way in which Palin was seen as going beyond a feminine candidate with girly shoes, to mere fashion accessory herself: "John McCain has mastered the fine art of turning women into campaign accessories, a flag pin with nice calves."[50]

The beauty queen narrative became synonymous with Palin in popular culture. A brief item about an Israeli woman candidate for prime minister in the October 6 issue of *Newsweek* compared her to Palin, noting that a common label for Palin was "a ditzy cheerleader."[51] In addition to the photo-shopped bikini pictures of Sarah Palin flooding the internet, other political kitsch played on her sexy image and undermined her political credibility. A toy company called Hero Builders began selling Palin action figure dolls. The choice of outfits included, among others, the "schoolgirl" with a tiny plaid miniskirt, midriff-baring white blouse and peekaboo red bra, or the "superhero" ensemble (which looked vaguely like a dominatrix) featuring a long black trench coat over white miniskirt and gun strapped to her bare leg.[52] Hustler shot a porn video, "Nailin' Paylin," which starred a Sarah Palin lookalike and was advertised for release on November 4, 2008.

With just two weeks to go before election day, *Politico* broke the news that the Republican National Committee (RNC) had spent $150,000 to dress Palin and her family for the Republican National Convention and the campaign trail.[53] The story spread like wildfire in the media and on blogs; it seemed irresistible, in part, because it fit the narrative about Palin as a beauty queen, the kind of girl who could be dressed up like a Barbie doll. The political gossip blog *Gawker* immediately criticized her "fashion spree" as "profligate;" Salon.com called her a "$150,000 fashionista;" National Public Radio's Day to Day show labeled it a "makeover" (remarking that it cost more than a Porsche); and celebrity gossip magazine *People* noted that the campaign also spent over $4700 on hair and makeup for Palin in September 2008.[54] David Letterman made it the subject of his "Top Ten" list on his late night comedy show on October 27, 2008. Among the "Top 10 Sarah Palin Excuses for Spending $150,000 on Clothes" were "Need to look good for the Russians who can see me in Alaska," "In addition to every newspaper and magazine, I also read every catalog," and "Wanting to impress the American voters in the evening gown competition."[55] The terminology and jokes underscored the frivolous, superficial image of Palin as a bubble-headed beauty queen.

Some saw the typical double standard facing women candidates playing out yet again. Campbell Brown, on her eponymous show on CNN, defended Palin, noting that not much attention was being paid to Barack Obama's $1,500 suits or John McCain's expensive Italian shoes.[56] "Women are judged far, far more based on their appearance," Brown explained, noting the amount of email she herself received when she wore a "bad outfit" on the air compared to the unimportance of a bad tie or lack of makeup for her male colleagues like Wolf Blitzer or Anderson Cooper. She acknowledged that "for women, appearance is part of the job," and that it was legitimate for the RNC to have paid for Palin's new campaign trail wardrobe as a necessary piece of the job they had picked her for; but Brown concluded by trying to shift the focus away from Palin as fashion plate:

> I think, in this campaign, with so much at stake, this is a peripheral issue. I myself have raised plenty of questions about Sarah Palin, much to the annoyance of the McCain campaign. But those questions have been about her qualifications and experience, never her appearance. Let's keep the focus on what really matters here.[57]

By objecting to controversy and refusing to pile on in criticizing Palin for being a frivolous clothes horse, Brown's move was similar to the many political women who have protested the double standard and pushed to be taken seriously for their competent leadership and issue positions. Downplaying gender difference was a way to level the political playing field for a debate about being qualified, not pretty. But the narrative that had situated Palin as hyper-feminine in the popular imagination made it easy for this controversy to become emblematic of her campaign. As Kate Betts wrote for *Time*: "It's an all-too-familiar fairy tale: small-town girl gets big gig—and the clothing to go with it."[58]

The Republican presidential ticket was loudly criticized for spending so much money on new clothes. Much of the negative press focused on the contradiction between Palin's anti-elite message and the news that most of these shopping trips took place at high-end retailers such as Neiman Marcus, Bloomingdales, and Saks Fifth Avenue. "After $150,000 Makeover, Sarah Palin Has an Image Problem," declared the headline in *The Washington Post*. The story questioned Palin and the campaign's judgment for what seemed like "luxury consumption" as the country's economy was imploding, and as Palin was trying to present herself as a no-frills hockey mom who hunted her own moose meat.[59] "It's hypocritical to say you're a hockey mom and then spend $70,000 at Neiman's," a Target-shopping voter told the *Los Angeles Times*.[60] The huge dollar amount and the choice of expensive stores undercut Palin's "ordinary citizen" image. As Joy Behar joked on the daytime talk show *The View* the day after the story broke, "I don't think Joe the Plumber wears Manolo Blahniks."[61] One fashion writer analyzed the clothes themselves, dismissing the conservative-if-expensive skirts and jackets as "a waste" that looked like they could have been bought at Ann Taylor; for the kind of money Palin spent, she should have chosen clothes that were much more "remarkable" and stylish, opined the fashion critic.[62] But most of the coverage stuck to the storyline of Palin's hypocrisy in hammering away at "cultural elites" while dressing like one herself. One story drew a contrast between the price of Palin's new togs and the $148 Donna Ricco dress Michelle Obama had recently worn on national television, making the point that in the climate of economic meltdown, fashion could be clever and appropriate without breaking the bank.[63] Palin complained that the stories misrepresented her. She claimed to be frugal, not a *fashionista*, and cited a consignment store as her favorite place to shop back in Anchorage.[64] But those protests did not fit the narrative. In an election year where being an outsider was important to voters, and "change" had emerged as a key theme, *Newsweek*'s headline "Not the Change They Wanted" summed up the public perception: Palin's "transformation from low couture to haute couture isn't the kind of change that voters had in mind."[65]

Even *SNL* referred to the shopping controversy as it reinforced the sexy, girlish image of Palin. A special edition of *SNL*, featuring a variety of political sketches, aired in primetime about ten days before the election. Will Ferrell appeared, reprising his role as former President George W. Bush, ostensibly to give the McCain/Palin ticket his endorsement. As the sketch opened, Ferrell's Bush referred to Palin as "the hot lady" (running against "the Tiger Woods guy," Barack Obama).[66] Tina Fey, playing Palin, perched on the edge of his desk in the Oval Office for a photo opportunity, hiking up her skirt to show more leg and giving a beauty pose. Palin then told the former president that she had been busy traveling around the country, "talkin' about change and doin' a little shoppin'!" When Ferrell's Bush said to her admiringly: "My God, you are folksy!" Fey's Palin replied with a wink and a smile: "Why, thank you, Mr. President. I like to think I'm one part practiced folksy, one part sassy, and a little dash of high school bitchy." Indeed, the narrative of folksy, flirty girl had begun to morph into that of a diva and "mean girl." As the campaign neared its end, with poll numbers showing the McCain/Palin ticket unlikely to win the election, recriminations for what went wrong began. The $150,000 shopping spree stories gave way to additional characterizations of Palin as difficult, self-centered, and manipulative. Unnamed McCain advisors blamed Palin for "going rogue" and not being a good running mate, telling political blogs: "She's a diva. She takes no advice from anyone ... she is playing for her own future and sees herself as the next leader of the party."[67] Her self-assurance and cheerful confidence became (gendered) flaws, not assets: "Remember: divas trust only unto themselves as they themselves as the beginning and end of all wisdom."[68]

Three days before the election, John McCain appeared as himself on *SNL*. With Tina Fey again doing a dead-on impersonation of his running mate, he participated in a sketch in which he sold campaign-themed merchandise on the home shopping channel QVC. As McCain lamely grinned and peddled "McCain Fine Gold" jewelry, Fey turned to a side camera and whispered: "OK, listen up everybody, I am goin' rogue right now, so keep your voices down."[69] Holding up a "Palin 2012" tee shirt for sale, she asked voters to wait until after Tuesday's election to begin wearing it, "because I am not goin' anywhere! And I'm certainly not goin' back to Alaska! If I'm not goin' to the White House, I'm either runnin' in four years or I'm gonna be a white Oprah, so ... you know, I'm good either way!" McCain suddenly asked: "What's going on over there, Sarah?" Fey's Palin winked slyly at the camera, then smiled angelically and said in a raised voice: "Ohhhh, just talkin' about taxes."[70] Weeks earlier, Amy Poehler's Katie

Couric had accused Palin of using her ability to be "increasingly adorable" as a way of evading tough questions. Now, Palin's cuteness was being portrayed not merely as a defense for being ditzy or unprepared, but as manipulative and shrewd. In the QVC skit, her bright smile and wide eyed exuberance for campaign talking points were shown to hide an underhanded mean streak, willing to undermine McCain to further her own ambitions. The electorate was left to wonder if Palin's beauty and femininity concealed a ruthlessness sometimes suspected of "mean girls" in popular culture, who use their looks and polite manners to fool adults and bully peers.

The framing of Sarah Palin as a beauty queen relies on familiar tropes about women and femininity. While former and current generations of female politicians have tried to minimize attention to their looks or characterizations of themselves as particularly girlish, Palin's persona and own biography seemed to invite this framing. Certainly the way in which she positioned herself as ordinary and middle class, albeit with higher aspirations, lent itself to the beauty pageant narrative. Being rural and white fit into this narrative as well, as the trope of the local "Miss County Fair" has not been one of urban sophistication, elite wealth, or ethnic diversity. Palin's perceived lack of intellectual depth, fostered not only by the evasions and gaffes of the Couric interview but also by her own positioning of herself as "ordinary" and unconcerned about the preoccupations of the "liberal elite media," fit into the frame of beauty queen as airheaded bimbo. Her sexiness belied her conservative social issue positions, and created the image of a woman who was powerful but not challenging traditional notions of femininity and masculinity. Ultimately, while the sexy girl narrative brought her enormous attention and even admiration, it also undercut her claims to credible leadership. The shopping stories, Tina Fey's "fancy pageant walkin'," and the leers of male pundits framed Palin in ways that emphasized her femininity over her political experience. Certainly, Palin embraced "running as a woman" in ways that few female candidates have before. But the beauty queen narrative minimized her potential to redefine power in a woman's voice, and left her trapped in feminine tropes that allowed many voters to dismiss her as frivolous, silly, and sly.

6

POST-FEMINIST ROLE MODEL OR VICTIM OF SEXISM?

Sarah Palin did achieve a historic milestone in becoming the first Republican woman to gain the vice presidential nomination of her party. But whether or not this was a victory for gender equality remained a controversial question. Was Palin a feminist role model—younger, with a more expansive and less doctrinaire definition of empowerment—or an anti-feminist throwback? Was she a victim of sexism during the campaign, or a beneficiary of John McCain's chivalrous protection? Framing Palin in terms of feminism involved highly contested narratives throughout the election season.

From the moment she publicly accepted John McCain's invitation to be his running mate, Sarah Palin touted herself as an empowered role model for women. She invoked the first wave of American feminism in her first speech that day in Dayton, casting her nomination as the fruition of the suffrage movement and an extension of gains made by other women in politics: "It's fitting that this trust has been given to me 88 years almost to the day after the women of America first gained the right to vote. I can't begin this great effort without honoring the achievements of Geraldine Ferraro in 1984, and, of course, Senator Hillary Clinton, who showed such determination and grace in her presidential campaign." After noting Senator Clinton's historic achievement in garnering 18 million votes in presidential primaries, Palin deftly cast herself as heir apparent to Clinton's mantle, asserting: "It turns out the women of America aren't finished yet, and we can shatter that glass ceiling once and for all."[1] In her September 30, 2008 interview with Katie Couric, Palin described herself as "a feminist who believes in equal rights."[2] Independent Women's Forum president Michelle Bernard agreed with that label: to her, Palin "really represents what early generations of women fought for, which was the right to do whatever you want to do with your career ... Regardless of whether or not you agree with her political ideology, she really is a good representation of what the women's rights movement was about."[3]

Other women vehemently disagreed, seeing the Palin pick as "cynical tokenism" on the part of the McCain camp.[4] They rejected this narrative of a feminist role model: "To try to suggest Sarah Palin might garner the Hillary Clinton vote, that one woman is just the same as another, that biology trumps ideology, is the ultimate evidence of sexism."[5] Palin's supposed feminism was called into question by her absolutist anti-abortion position, her support for abstinence-only sex education, her lack of advocacy for equal pay, flextime, healthcare reform, or childcare policies, and her free market, "no whining" opposition to policies that might support women and children. Critics wondered if it was hypocritical of her to talk about her daughter's "choice" to have the baby when she would like to outlaw that choice, or of "family values" Republicans to praise Bristol's decision not to have an abortion while conveniently ignoring the issue of teenage sex. Some cringed at Palin's willingness to use her looks or flirtatious charm as a political asset, and were appalled by tabloid-style headlines shrieking "Babies, Lies & Scandal" and "Palin's Family Drama."[6] Outraged feminist Katha Pollitt summed up what she viewed as Palin's cooptation of feminist rhetoric:

> What can you say after you've said that her career shows that even right-wing fundamentalist women have taken in feminism's message of empowerment and that's good, but that Palin's example suggests women can do it all without support from society and that's bad? Count me as a feminist who never believed that being PTA president meant you could be, well, President. The more time we spend on dippy ruminations—how does she do it? Queen Bee on steroids or hockey mom next door? How hot is Todd, anyway?—the less focus there will be on the kind of queries that should come first with any vice presidential candidate, and certainly would if Palin were a man.[7]

How to read Palin—as the fruition of a long feminist struggle for women to reach the highest levels of politics, or as the antithesis of the feminist ideal—opened up a debate not just about this particular candidate, but about the very definition of feminism itself. Palin's persona, and her appropriation of the feminist label, could be read as embodying a larger argument in the evolution of American feminism. Some of the issues and tactics of second-wave feminism, the women's movements of the 1960s and 1970s that were sparked by Betty Friedan's *The Feminine Mystique*, and New Left activism for racial equality, peace, and free speech were by the 1990s being challenged. A "third wave" of feminist activism and writing was characterized by a postmodern sensibility and individualistic, ironic approach to culture and politics. As third-wave feminism has evolved, several themes have emerged: a recognition of the importance of diversity among women; the inclusion of multiple voices; the notion that identity is multifaceted, not unified and singular; and a reputation for sexiness, playfulness, and frivolity, especially in reclaiming elements of feminine culture.[8] As Rebecca Walker explains in her anthology *To Be Real*, third-wave feminism is about accepting and respecting differences between women, and "being real" by "refusing to be bound by a feminist ideal not of [our] own making."[9] If second-wave feminism had revolutionized gender relations by insisting that "the personal is political," third-wave feminists rejected the notion that there was one politically correct, feminist way to live one's personal life. Gina Dent labeled her perception that there was a rigidity and religious orthodoxy to feminist activism, "missionary feminism," which "puts forward its program so stridently, guards its borders so closely, and legislates its behavior so fervently that many are afraid to declare its name."[10] Particularly limiting and unappealing, according to Dent, were definitions of a "correct" position on sex and women's pleasure, premised on the notion that women are victims of sexual violence and exploitation who need to be saved, even from their own agency. Dent encouraged young women to think critically "about how to take the religion out of feminism, how to break down the illusion that we comprise a community that has agreed upon its rules of existence ... If we continue to operate in [feminism] as if it is a religion, we lose our ability to translate its pleasures and joys to future generations."[11]

Examples of third-wave feminist theorizing were anthologies of personal essays, such as Rebecca Walker's *To Be Real*, Barbara Findlen's *Listen Up*, and Daisy Hernandez and Bushra Rehman's *Colonize This!*, that attempted to capture those pleasures and joys of feminism in the complexities of diverse women's lives. Sensitive to critiques of second-wave feminism as exclusively white and middle class, many of the third-wave theorists were women of color, and these anthologies strove for greater inclusion of multiple racial and ethnic perspectives. While rejecting the notion that there was one right way to be a feminist, these essays did insist that the personal was political in another sense. By claiming feminism for themselves, in all of the diversity of their lifestyles and identities, these young women were reshaping feminism to include them in its definition. "This is what a feminist looks like," these essays declared, without obvious similarities to unite them. The essayists included women who were straight, bisexual, lesbian, married, mothers, obese, anorexic, HIV positive, a corporate businesswoman, a sex worker, Christian, Jewish, black, Filipina, Indian, Bahamian, a hip-hop artist, an aerobics instructor, and a supermodel.[12] Rather than try to erase racial or sexual differences, third-wave feminism was more likely to revel in the paradox and contradiction.[13]

Definitions of feminism were being challenged and changed. Nineteenth-century feminism had seemed focused on women's legal rights (to vote, own property, and be educated). Twentieth-century feminism had made "the personal political" in raising questions of reproductive rights and security from rape, domestic violence, or sexual harassment; women protested being reduced to sexual objects, and demanded equal pay and opportunity. Twenty-first century feminism grappled with the challenges posed by postmodernism and post-structuralism, shifting from a focus on equality to the idea of difference, and abandoning totalizing theory in favor of giving voice to the local, marginal, indigenous, and postcolonial.[14] Third-wave feminism seemed to build on—or take for granted—the progress and potential that women had gained, while reclaiming sexual agency, playfulness, and an ironic stance toward femininity. If the iconography of late twentieth-century feminism was a businesswoman in a power suit, briefcase in one hand and baby in the other, who could "have it all," then twenty-first century feminism might get rid of the suit and don a miniskirt and heels instead, or dump the briefcase and build an entrepreneurial empire based on organic cooking or home decorating. Reclaiming traditional femininity or domestic, nurturing tasks—with an empowered twist—could become the new "having it all," without having to adopt more masculine behaviors, dress, careers, or lifestyles.

While inclusivity and multiple voices are important hallmarks of third-wave feminism, another distinctive feature is its engagement with popular culture and its willingness to play with femininity. While second-wave feminism was often critical of the media, and its limited or sexist portrayals of women, third-wave feminism was more open to the ways in which film, television, and music could be subversive and ironic in dealing with gender issues. Similarly, third-wave feminists do not summarily reject beauty culture and femininity. Aware of the powerful feminist critiques of the beauty, fashion, and sex industries previously made, young feminists opted to incorporate them into strategic uses of beauty, sex, and power.[15] Third-wave feminism seems to insist that feminism does not require rejecting femininity. As Jennifer Baumgardner and Amy Richards observe in *Manifesta*, the emergence of "girlie culture" in third-wave feminism reclaims feminine desires (such as high heels, makeup, fashion, and Barbies), declaring that women are not merely co-opted or duped into participating in femininity.[16] Playing with fashion, dressing provocatively, wearing makeup or stilettos: all of this is "a rebellion against the false impression that since women don't want to be sexually exploited, they don't want to be sexual," or that women have to be masculine or androgynous to be powerful.[17] "Girlie culture" replaces protective culture rules with equality, letting women use their beauty and sexuality for power by putting the former tools of patriarchy into women's own hands.[18] Without reclaiming femininity and reveling in one's sexual power, Baumgardner and Richards argue, women might find themselves in the same unhappy dilemma as Anastasia Higginbotham, a 28-year-old writer and feminist: she is "divided against herself, worrying that her desire to wear sexy clothes or to have attention is the result of brainwashing and destined to set her up for punishment; but, deep down, she knows that her need for sexual expression is real and hungry. She shouldn't have to starve herself of these desires, but she does, in an attempt to be safe [from rape or attack] rather than sorry, and typically feminist rather than typi-cally feminine."[19] Similarly, third-wave feminist culture has reclaimed traditional female activities, such as knitting circles, but recast with attitude as "Stitch and Bitch" gatherings. Rosalind Gill posits such traditional femininity as a "guilty pleasure" that transgresses the boundaries of second-wave feminist ideologies, offering women the pleasures of domesticity as "the return of the repressed."[20]

This new style of feminism is reflected in several popular Hollywood movies. *Miss Congeniality* (2000), starring Sandra Bullock, begins with the opposition of traditional femininity and feminism. FBI agent Gracie Hart is a successful, respected professional in a male-dominated field, who pays no attention to feminine mores. The film opens with images of her sparring with a punching bag in her apartment, snorting in unladylike laughter, and chewing with her mouth open. When a young woman comes into the FBI office to interview agents for a college paper she is writing on law enforcement, she sweetly asks if she can talk to Gracie: "I'd love to get a woman's point of view." The male agents guffaw in response, telling the college student: "Oh, no, no, no, you're barking up the wrong tree, right, Hart?" Though they treat Gracie like "one of the guys," the male agents flirt with the attractive coed and offer to answer more of her questions. Observing the girl's feminine appearance and her positive response to the male agents' attention, Gracie mutters darkly: "Bye, hope you have a good time at the mall."

When asked to go undercover at the "Miss United States" pageant to catch a serial killer who has made a terrorist threat regarding the beauty contest, Gracie adamantly refuses: "I don't even own a dress. I don't even own a brush!" Eventually, as it becomes obvious that she is the only female agent available for the job, she reluctantly agrees. A large part of the humor of the film comes from watching the tremendous effort put in to transform the unkempt, uncouth Gracie into a plausible pageant contestant. Pageant consultant Victor Melling (played with exuberant snobbishness by Michael Caine) says it is impossible, but then uses what resembles a SWAT team of beauty professionals for waxing, teeth whitening, hair highlighting, and styling. At the end of two days, an unrecognizably glamorous Gracie emerges in heels and mini-dress to the amazement of her FBI co-workers (though she immediately trips in the heels and falls down, still the same graceless girl under all the glitz). Gracie is still contemptuous of the beauty contest, however. She can't understand why any self-respecting woman would enter a beauty pageant, remarking that it's like feminism never happened, catering to a misogynistic Neanderthal ideal. She rolls her eyes when the pageant director insists that the competition is "not a beauty pageant—it's a *scholarship competition.*" Told that the interview portion of the pageant is worth 30 percent of the total score, she scoffs: "What's the other 30 percent? Cleavage?" When the other contestants compete in the talent portion of the competition by tap dancing while playing the flute, making balloon animals and baton twirling, she protests: "I am an FBI agent, not a dancing monkey in heels." Entering the pageant welcome breakfast, she demonstrates her dim view of the other contestants by muttering "Welcome to Barbie town."

Thus the film has starkly and humorously set up the contrast between the archetypes of contemporary, intelligent, professional women, enlightened by feminist progress, and anachronistic, unenlightened women still willing to objectify themselves, value their physical appearance as their most important quality, and use their feminine charms. The bulk of the movie, however, is the evolution in Gracie's thinking as she comes to know the other contestants and see beyond the superficial "beauty queen" image. When the FBI (wrongly) believes they have solved the case and leaves, taking Gracie's pageant consultant with them and leaving her with no idea how to get through the competition, the other contestants immediately jump in to help her with her dress, hair, and makeup. She suspects the sweet, naive demeanor of Miss Rhode Island to be false, but discovers that the young woman is genuine and generous, and encourages her to have more self-confidence. By the end of the pageant, Gracie has foiled the terrorist plot and saved the other contestants' lives. In the final interview question of the televised competition, she is asked what she would say to those who view the "Miss United States" pageant as outdated and antifeminist. Gracie replies:

> I'd have to say I used to be one of them. And then I came here and I realized that these women are smart, terrific people who are just trying to make a difference in the world. And we've become really good friends … for me, this experience has been one of the most rewarding and liberating of my life.

While she initially viewed the pageant—and traditional femininity, in general—as regressive and negative, Gracie has come to realize that beauty and brains are not mutually exclusive. She no longer views other women as passive dupes of a patriarchal culture, but values the care and camaraderie of female friendships. During the pageant, due to her more womanly and attractive appearance, the male FBI agent she has a crush on (played by Benjamin Bratt) finally notices her for more than her work and asks her out on a date. Delighted, Gracie realizes the power of her femininity. In the logic of the film, especially due to the fact that she alone figures out the criminal plot and is able to stop it, Gracie does not give up any of her intelligence and competence. But with her new-found femininity, she gains female friends and male attention. Her personality is rounded out into an expanded confidence, able to win the love of the man she wants as well as the admiration of her colleagues and peers for her brave and clever actions. The feminized pageant experience is "liberating" because it makes her even more wise and powerful. She has left behind her narrow view, rejecting womanhood as limiting, and come to the conclusion that femininity can be empowering. Gracie no longer wants to be "just one of the guys;" she wants to be respected and loved, smart and beautiful. The arc of the film encapsulates a kind of third-wave feminist argument: that feminism does not necessitate rejecting femininity and downplaying female difference. Women do not have to become like men in order to be taken seriously. Equality does not have to mean sameness; women can be different from one another without engaging in competitiveness and cat-fights, and women can revel in their differences from men without wanting subordinate status. This popular movie argues for embracing femininity and equality, sexiness and feminism—not choosing one at the expense of the other. "Having it all" takes on an entirely different cast, a connotation that will become relevant in the narrative Sarah Palin tells about her own feminism that is also utterly feminine.

Elle Woods, the protagonist of the 2001 film *Legally Blonde* (whose popularity spawned a sequel and a Broadway musical), is another pop culture precursor to Sarah Palin and her brand of (post-)feminism. In this Hollywood comedy, Elle is a blonde southern California sorority queen who seems shallow and superficial, a Barbie doll come to life. The opening shots of the film establish not only the sorority house setting but Elle's character, as viewers see stacks of fashion maga-zines, manicures being done, cheerleading practice, and Elle putting on makeup and donning high-heeled, pink rhinestone sandals in a pink room surrounded by girlish stuffed animals and Prada shopping bags. She is engaged in a phone con-versation about shopping and celebrity restaurant sightings. Her Chihuahua, a constant accessory, is dressed in a pink dog sweater. The drama begins with her boyfriend breaking up with her as he gets ready to head off to law school because, as he explains, "If I'm going to be a senator [someday], I need to marry a Jackie, not a Marilyn ... I need someone serious." The scene not only establishes the sexy, brainless blonde characterization of Elle; it also re-establishes a categoriza-tion scheme for women that is dichotomous and mutually exclusive. There are the classy, educated, cultured, and respectable "Jackie Kennedys," who are legit-imate marriage material, and then there are the trashy, superficial, breathy, glitzy "Marilyn Monroes," who are fun to use as girlfriends or sex partners.

However, the audience quickly learns that appearances can be deceiving, and that Elle may not be as dumb as she looks. The film also argues that the Jackie/Marilyn dichotomy sells women short, and that true empowerment for women lies in resisting that simplistic categorization and competition for men. Devastated by the unexpected breakup, Elle resolves to get into Harvard Law School to win her ex-boyfriend Warner back. Though this ambition confounds her friends and family, fashion-merchandising major Elle crams hard for the LSAT and earns admission to Harvard Law. Much of the comedy of the film comes from her "fish out of water" experience in landing in Cambridge. When she pulls up to her dorm in a convertible, wearing a pink leather suit, high-heeled boots and sun-glasses, a guy calls from his window: "Hey Brad, check out Malibu Barbie!" "Look at the way she walks," murmurs another onlooker in the stunned crowd in Harvard Yard. Elle is initially confused by the dearth of mixers and social events, and is shunned by her fellow law students. Maliciously, one of them invites her to a party, telling her it's a costume event. Elle shows up in a Playboy bunny outfit, complete with ears and fishnet stockings, while everyone else is dressed casually in jeans and sweaters. She is humiliated when they mock her, of course; but the outfit represents perfectly not only the view her classmates have of her, but the way she perceives herself as fun, playful, and sexy. She doesn't view dressing up as a Playboy bunny as degrading; she sees it as a way to show off her curves and her sense of humor, to be witty, sexy, and in control of her own image.

Warner, astonished that Elle has followed him to Harvard, tells her he is engaged to the smart, preppy Vivian (also a law student), and scoffs at Elle for thinking she might be smart enough to get a coveted legal internship. Elle realizes that Warner is never going to think she's good enough for him, and resolves to show him just how smart and valuable she is. She has found no solace in other women. A female professor throws her out of class on the first day, Vivian snubs her, and another disdainful female student, Enid Wexler, is set up as the archetypal feminist foil to Elle: with her glasses, curly brown hair, and casual hooded sweatshirt, she has a Ph.D. in Women's Studies from Berkeley, where she organized a march of lesbians against drunk driving. But sisterhood is far from powerful. These successful feminist women see Elle as a throwback or a threat. The only places Elle finds encouragement and support are from a young lawyer, Emmett, who works with one of the law professors in his practice and is attracted to her romantically (refuting any feminist argument that men are oppressive or not to be trusted); and at a local beauty salon, populated by working-class beauticians who are about as far from the elites at Harvard Law as one can imagine. Though Elle is wealthy, the film plays up the perceived distinctions in class and culture between southern California and the East Coast. Los Angeles is depicted as flashy, focused on consumer and celebrity culture; Harvard is the home of elites, Ivy-League intellectuals looking down their noses at Elle's bubbly persona. When Elle ultimately triumphs, the Harvard-trained lawyers and her snobbish ex-boyfriend get their comeuppance. Much like in the geographic narratives invoked by Sarah Palin, here the condescending, urban, Eastern Seaboard elites compare unfavorably to the populist kindness of Elle, a more "ordinary" girl who likes getting her nails done and celebrity gossip.

Elle takes refuge in going to the salon and studying hard. She refuses to give up her sparkly, pink style, but she does demonstrate diligence and intelligence, showing that femininity and brains are not incompatible. She earns the internship after an impressive answer in class, despite her pink, scented résumé. She also demonstrates a genuine kindness and lack of snobbishness when she helps her beautician, Paulette, get her dog back from an abusive ex-boyfriend. Elle does not look down on the less-educated Paulette, but considers her a true friend; she does not have a mean bone in her body, but is genuinely surprised and hurt when Vivian and her friends mock and ostracize her. In the end, Elle becomes the true (post-)feminist heroine of the tale. The legal interns are asked to aid in the defense of Brooke Windham, a young trophy wife accused of murdering her wealthy husband. The case looks hopeless, but Elle is able to successfully defend Brooke and expose the true murderer, thanks to her knowledge of "frivolous" feminine practices. She believes Brooke's pleas of innocence, noting that she is a famous aerobics teacher who spends her time making best-selling fitness videos. "Exercise gives you endorphins, and endorphins make you happy. Happy people don't shoot their husbands," Elle reasons. When the prosecution accuses Brooke of having an affair with the pool boy, offering that as a motive for the murder, Elle refutes the charge by revealing that the pool boy is gay; she figures that out when he notices her last-season Prada shoes, something she feels sure no straight man would know. In the dramatic climax of the trial, she questions Brooke's jealous stepdaughter on the stand and proves that she is the real killer. The stepdaughter's alibi that she was washing her hair during the shooting could not be true, because she had just gotten a perm. Elle's knowledge of hair care helps her to recognize what neither the judge nor other lawyers pick up on: the stepdaughter's hair is still curly, and she is lying about having been in the shower.

Elle's success in defending Brooke happens *because* of her hyper-femininity, and not in spite of it. Much like in Susan Glaspell's 1916 play *Trifles*, in which men overlook the important evidence of a crime and cannot solve a murder because they ignore the "trifles" of women's work (like quilting and canning) where the evidence resides, Brooke Windham's defense rests on knowledge about cosmetology, fashion, and exercise. It is exactly Elle's more "girly" pursuits that aid her in being a good lawyer. She wins her client's trust, and obtains important information about the case, because of their shared sorority sisterhood and because Elle thoughtfully brings her hair care products and *Cosmopolitan* magazine in jail. When Elle is harassed by a male supervisor in the middle of the case, she wants to quit, discouraged that she is not being taken seriously but sexually objectified as "a joke, just a piece of ass." Significantly, it is not in the masculine space of the law firm, but in the feminine space of the beauty salon that her complaint is overheard by a senior woman law professor, who encourages her not to let one sexist man ruin her life and to persevere. When Elle does return to court, she has given up her dark suits and sleek pulled-back hairstyle, reverting to her "true," more feminine sense of self. She wears a low-cut hot pink dress, rhinestone sandals with a pink pedicure, and long, loose blonde curls as she wins the case. She also wins her ex-boyfriend Warner back, but rejects his declaration of love as insincere and pathetic. Her desperation has been replaced by self-confidence and empowerment. The film ends by fast-forwarding to Elle's law school graduation, at which the audience learns she has a job offer from a prestigious law firm *and* gets the guy: Emmett, the supportive young lawyer, is about to propose marriage. The logic of *Legally Blonde* is that women can be smart and sexy, powerful and playful, feminist and feminine, all at the same time. The "new feminism" does not dictate that women give up their pink miniskirts or facials to be serious and successful; equality does not have to be achieved at the expense of frills, fashion, or domesticity. Perhaps real power is "girl power;" perhaps feminism's triumph is being able to choose whatever version of femininity one wants, without giving up any respect or authority. Certainly, just as Elle

Woods raises this question of contemporary feminism in the movies, Sarah Palin—in her red peep-toe heels and hockey-mom lipstick, with baby Trig in her arms—raises it on the political campaign stage.

For some, Palin was a marker of women's progress: the first woman vice presidential nominee in history for the Republican Party, and only the second (after Democrat Geraldine Ferraro in 1984) on a major party ticket. The fact that she was a conservative woman only seemed to prove that norms and beliefs about women's roles had changed dramatically over the past 40 years. Now, it seemed not only liberals would support more independent and powerful leadership positions for women; many conservatives saw nothing unremarkable or problematic about a woman in politics, running for the second-highest office in the land, instead of staying at home in the private sphere. Surely this indicated widespread support across the ideological spectrum for the basic tenets of liberal feminism: equal opportunity, equal pay, non-discrimination, and respect in the workplace. For some women, even those not inclined to vote for Republicans or endorse conservative policy positions, the nomination of Sarah Palin was still an indicator of feminist success. Increasing numbers of women candidates, across ideologies and in ever-higher positions on the political ladder, meant more power, prestige, and status for women generally. Kathleen Deveny confessed in *Newsweek*: "I really like Sarah Palin" despite their ideological differences on abortion and creationism. Labeling Palin "a thoroughly modern ass-kicker ... the political bad girl," Deveny notes:

> Like many former Hillary supporters, I would not step over *Roe v. Wade* to vote for anyone ... But I'm mostly just happy that there's another woman on the national political stage. I think it's good for my 8-year-old daughter, who has called Hillary Clinton her idol. She doesn't love Hillary because of her health-care policy or pro-choice stance: she loves Hillary because she thinks girls rule. The more powerful women there are on the national stage, the better it is for all women, because this is a game of numbers ... when there are enough women in our political life, maybe we will be able to judge them as individuals, rather than as representatives of all things uterine.[21]

The question of whether or not American women were moving into a "post-feminist" era or new wave of feminism, in which they have achieved equality of opportunity and can be treated as individuals, rather than as members of a victimized group, was raised in many arenas by Palin's nomination. Conservative talk show host Laura Ingraham, a Palin supporter, declared during the GOP convention that "Sarah Palin represents a new feminism," and National Public Radio's "All Things Considered" devoted an interview with feminist historian Estelle Freedman in early September to considering whether or not Palin could be "the new face of feminism."[22] The former president of the Los Angeles chapter of the

National Organization for Women, Tammy Bruce, wrote a column in the *San Francisco Chronicle* explaining why she was "thrilled" with McCain's pick of Palin for vice presidential nominee: Palin is "a woman who represents everything the feminist movement claimed it stood for. Women can have a family and a career. We can be whatever we choose, on our own terms."[23] Bruce argued that the Democratic Party has taken women for granted and become misogynistic. She noted that the unchecked sexist treatment of Hillary Clinton in the primary process, with a "Bros before Hos" attitude displayed by party leaders in supporting Barack Obama at Clinton's expense, should compel feminists to "look to the right" to put more women into power.[24]

Indeed, the McCain campaign attempted to use Palin's gender to their advantage in display ads, which appeared on websites, turning "Palin into a brand representing female empowerment."[25] One ad displayed black-and-white images from the suffrage movement, with the tagline "They demanded change," linking the McCain/Palin campaign to feminist history. An October ad featuring Palin "showed a young girl in a field, her arms spread wide with optimism: 'Inspiring a new generation of leaders,' it said."[26] Most of these internet ads appeared on women-centric sites such as iVillage and Better Homes & Gardens Online, clearly targeting the female vote with their narrative of Palin as feminist heroine.[27]

In *Adweek*, Barbara Lippert described Palin as "a classic third wave feminist:" "On the one hand, her political views (she's anti-abortion and pro-gun and an evangelical creationist) seem directly counter to the until-now traditionally liberal tenets of feminism. Yet at the same time, she's a powerful governor and mother of five, a combination that seems the very definition of what the women's movement was fighting for."[28] When Palin herself was asked directly by Katie Couric in September: "Do you consider yourself a feminist?," the governor replied: "I do. I'm a feminist who believes in equal rights and I believe that women certainly, today, have every opportunity that a man has to succeed, and to try to do it all, anyway."[29] Like Elle Woods, Palin seemed confident that she could "have it all" without becoming like one of the guys; she carried baby Trig onto countless campaign stages proudly, wearing her black boots and short skirts, without worrying that her motherhood and femininity would somehow diminish her political credibility or success. Feminism now seemed to be defined simply as women being able to make their own choices—no matter what those choices were. As Karin Agniss wrote on the conservative website Townhall.com: "Governor Sarah Palin has grown up in a world full of open doors," noting the progress for American women that occurred during her childhood and adolescence: the passage of Title IX (prohibiting discrimination against women in educational activities (including athletics), the *Roe v. Wade* decision, the Equal Pay Act, and the outlawing of employment discrimination based on sex.[30] Palin had opportunities available to her that early feminists hardly dared to dream of; but in contrast to her "feminist" contemporaries, who often "chose to reject marriage and husbands" and family, Palin was an even more "liberated" woman who embraced her femininity, married her high school sweetheart, and gave birth to five children. Now, "because of the choices she has made, she is being rejected, insulted and condemned by her feminist counterparts ... If feminism is about giving women choices, she should be cheered as an example of the success of feminism."[31] Agniss's scathing indictment of what she viewed as the hypocrisy of "feminists" not supporting Palin continued:

> National Organization for Women (NOW) PAC Chair Kim Gandy started attacking Palin within three hours of her speech in Ohio. Gandy issued a press release entitled, "Not Every Woman Supports Women's Rights," stating, "Sen. John McCain's choice of Alaska governor Sarah Palin as his running mate is a cynical effort to appeal to disappointed Hillary Clinton voters and get them to vote, ultimately, against their own self-interest." Nowhere does Gandy recognize the historical importance of this moment for women. Rather, she criticizes Palin's politics and suggests that women are not smart enough to figure out how to vote in their own self-interest. Who is sexist now?[32]

Elaine Lafferty, former editor-in-chief of the feminist magazine *Ms* and a Democrat, defended Palin as "very smart" and supporting "women's rights, deeply and passionately" after spending a short time traveling with her campaign.[33] Lafferty criticized the Democratic Party for taking women for granted, and women's groups for not buying Palin's self-declared feminism. Apparently, she scoffed, elitist feminist activists and bloggers got to decide for everyone else who was truly pro-women, and "you are not a feminist until *we* say you are."[34] She also saw a religious and class bias in the revulsion to Palin: "For the sin of being a Christian personally opposed to abortion, Palin is being pilloried by the inside-the-Beltway Democrat feminist establishment ... yes, instead of buying organic New Zealand lamb at Whole Foods, she joins other Alaskans in hunting for food. That's it. She is not a right-wing nut."[35]

Angela McRobbie theorizes this seeming contradiction of how to define Palin—as feminist role model, or post-feminist dystopian nightmare—with her definition of post-feminism as a "double entanglement" that is simultaneously a doing and undoing of feminism, a confirmation that feminism is "now common sense" but also no longer needed by modern young women.[36] Along with Rosalind Gill and Christina Scharff, she defines post-feminism not as mere backlash or antifeminism, nor as simply a historical break with second-wave feminism, evolving into a more contemporary "third wave."[37] Rather, post-feminism is a sensibility that incorporates and repudiates feminism, seeing the struggle for women's equality as both legitimate and redundant. It assumes women's equality as neoliberal workers and consumers, but undercuts their demands for equality or social change beyond an individual level. Post-feminist discourse "focuses on female achievement, encouraging women to embark on projects of individualized self-definition and privatized self-expression exemplified in the celebration of lifestyle and consumption choices."[38] As Gill explains, a post-feminist sensibility includes the

> notion that femininity is a bodily property; the shift from objectification to subjectification [in the ways that women are represented]; the emphasis on self-surveillance, monitoring and discipline; a focus upon individualism, choice and empowerment; the dominance of a 'makeover paradigm'; the articulation or entanglement of feminist and anti-feminist ideas; a resurgence of ideas of natural sexual difference; a marked sexualization of culture; and an emphasis on consumerism and the commodification of difference.[39]

The feminist/post-feminist debate surrounding Palin certainly contains many of these elements. Gill argues that femininity is no longer primarily defined by caring, nurturing, or maternal social qualities, but by possessing a sexy body. The beauty queen framing of Sarah Palin, as well as the depictions of Gracie Hart, Elle Woods, and Carrie Bradshaw and her friends in *Sex and the City*, demonstrate this. We viewers understand their femininity by their "hotness." Gill also notes that post-feminism has effectively internalized the male gaze, so that it is not men who are enforcing standards of female beauty or behavior, but women who scrutinize and self-police their bodies constantly. The irony is that women use the rhetoric of freedom and agency "to construct [themselves] as subjects closely resembling the heterosexual male fantasy that is found in pornography."[40] Neoliberal consumerism is important here, as women embrace spending their time and money on constant self-improvement rather than larger political transformation. The language of choice and individualism depoliticizes these issues, making them all "lifestyle choices" beyond judgment or reproach. As we have already demonstrated, the debate surrounding Palin's feminism is suffused with these sensibilities of individual choices, individual achievement, and reclaiming femininity, particularly in sexualized ways.

Many women disagreed with this Palinesque brand of post-feminist equality. Just as Palin had, her opponents also tried to claim the mantle of feminist history. One viral attachment floating around the web during the 2008 campaign used a picture of suffragists from 1918 protesting in front of the White House.[41] It drew on the iconography of early twentieth-century suffragists from the National Women's Party standing outside the White House gates, petitioning President Wilson to support voting rights for women, with banners asking: "Mr. President, How Long Must Women Wait for Liberty?"[42] In the viral 2008 photo, the text on the suffrage banner has been digitally replaced with "Mr. McCain, America's women have not waited two-hundred and thirty-two years for Sarah Palin." Feminist commentators and bloggers took exception to Palin on the grounds that she was pro-life, that she opposed many other "women's issues," that she was unqualified, that she played the "sexism card" hypocritically, and even because she showed poor maternal judgment.

Feminist opposition to the Palin pick was immediate. On the *Huffington Post* on August 29, Sarah Seltzer's headline declared herself "A Feminist Appalled by Palin." Seltzer was outraged by the "cynicism and condescension inherent in this choice. It's as though the McCain camp believes our irrational she-hormones will lead us, like sheep, to pull the lever for any candidate who looks like us—even if she has a strong record, as Palin does, of standing *against* women's interests" in terms of the environment, abortion, and contraception.[43] Similarly, on the day of the Palin announcement, Megan Carpentier explained on the feminist website *Jezebel* why "Choosing a Woman Might Not Be Choosing for Women."[44] She too based her disagreement with Palin on issue positions regarding healthcare, abortion, gay marriage and the Lilly Ledbetter pay equity bill, posing the rhetorical question: "is it more important to vote for a woman, or to vote for a candidate that represents the issues of importance to women? ... While getting one woman to a top position is a great symbolic victory for women, is it worth giving up other things for which we've fought really hard just to get a symbolic victory?"[45] The issue of demographic representation versus substantive representation was immediately thrown into sharp relief. Should women support one of their own, poised to "break the highest, hardest glass ceiling," simply because she was a woman and would bring women's life experience, such as being a working mom, into the White House? Or should women look beyond shared biology to their policy concerns, and choose a candidate that most closely matches their own preferences, whether Democrat or Republican, male or female?

Feminist activist Gloria Steinem chose the more orthodox feminist issue platform when she wrote a widely circulated opinion piece in the *New York Times* on September 4, 2008, entitled "Wrong Woman, Wrong Message." Like many other feminist commentators, she accused the McCain campaign of cynicism and desperation, of choosing Palin to try to bridge the electoral gender gap and pander to the right-wing base of the Republican Party. Looking at American women's responses to public opinion polls on policy issues, Steinem asserts that Palin "opposes just about every issue that women support by a majority or plurality:"

> She believes that creationism should be taught in public schools but disbelieves global warming; she opposes gun control but supports government control of women's wombs; she opposes stem cell research but approves "abstinence-only" programs, which increase unwanted births, sexually transmitted diseases and abortions; she tried to use taxpayers' millions for a state program to shoot wolves from the air but didn't spend enough money to fix a state school system with the lowest high-school graduation rate in the nation; she runs with a candidate who opposes the Fair Pay Act but supports $500 million in subsidies for a natural gas pipeline across Alaska; she supports drilling in the Arctic National Wildlife Reserve, though even McCain has opted for the lesser evil of offshore drilling.[46]

She criticizes Palin as "unqualified" and asserts that supporting her is not truly a feminist act, for "feminism has never been about getting a job for one woman. It's about making life more fair for women everywhere."[47] But as a feminist, Steinem draws the line at attacking another woman on personal grounds. She makes clear that her goal is "not to beat up on Palin" or to criticize her as a mother: "I regret that people say she can't do the job because she has children in need of care, especially if they wouldn't say the same about a father."[48] Rather, Steinem says, the real "culprit is John McCain" for choosing Palin in the first place. Eve Ensler, author of *The Vagina Monologues* and founder of the V-Day movement to end violence against women, agreed. "The Sarah Palin choice was … insidious and cynical. The people who made this choice count on the goodness and solidarity of Feminists. But everything Sarah Palin believes in and practices is antithetical to Feminism," wrote Ensler, cataloging Palin's positions on the environment, war, abortion, birth control, and sex education.[49]

Choice and reproductive rights were particular sticking points for most feminists. Palin embodied a hard-line pro-life stance, exemplified in her choice to carry a pregnancy with a special-needs child to term and her applauding of her unwed daughter's choice not to abort an unexpected teen pregnancy. While this made her extremely popular with evangelicals and other social conservatives for whom abortion politics are particularly salient, it won her disfavor from feminist groups who viewed reproductive choice as central to women exercising their economic and educational rights as well. While Palin claimed membership in a group called Feminists for Life, demonstrating how she thought a pro-life stance could be compatible with feminist and pro-women positions, most feminists found this unconvincing. Many linked her anti-abortion politics to a range of other sexual and reproductive rights issues, such as sex education, contraceptives, and women's sexual agency. In a vitriolic column posted on Salon.com, Cintra Wilson called Palin "a Christian Stepford wife in a sexy librarian costume" and "the White House bunny."[50] Here the "sexy Puritan" beauty queen, bimbo, and virgin narratives converge. Palin's candidacy represents "a Faustian bargain" for American women, according to Wilson: "To elevate your sex to power and respectability, you must first give us the keys to your chastity belt." Palin puts a pretty face on policies that want to control women's bodies, sexuality, and social roles: "Republicans seem to be saying, at least we can offer you the hope of putting women back in their place … Women, even if they are vice president, can always look pretty, worship their husbands in the fear of God and never, ever resist invasions from unwanted sperm."[51]

Because so much of Palin's self-presentation and narrative of support among social conservatives centered around her own life choices around these issues—to have a large family, to continue her pregnancy with a Down syndrome baby rather than terminating it, to stand by her unwed teenage daughter unapologetically, instead of encouraging her to have an abortion—some observers found those personal choices fair game for analysis and critique. Political journalist Beverly Davis accused Palin of "putting her ambitions ahead of her daughter's well-being" by accepting the vice presidential nomination, knowing that Bristol would be exposed to enormous media scrutiny when her pregnancy was inevitably revealed.[52] "Is Palin showing family values?" asked another blogger, wondering if Palin's "absti-nence-only" stance on sex education was hypocritical after her 17-year-old daughter got pregnant, and if accepting McCain's offer to be his running mate was a bad parenting decision at a time when Bristol and her family could have used more privacy instead.[53] Even women who wondered aloud: "Is that sexist?" opined that, pragmatically, "I would have considered [Bristol's] needs, and the needs of my Down syndrome baby, and probably begged off the VP slot." [54]A Connecticut voter echoed this sentiment in the *Los Angeles Times*: "The mom part of me says how did this woman expect to run for vice president with a 4-month-old baby with a disability and a 17-year-old about to have a baby of her own? It's not a feminist perspective … but there are times when you put your professional aspirations on hold, and this seems like it might be one of them."[55]

But most feminist critique, like Gloria Steinem's, shied away from Palin's motherhood. Just as scholars of women and politics had been urging the media for decades to stop asking women candidates "who will take care of your children if you run?," most women's groups and bloggers held the line at not attacking a woman over her maternal choices. Marie Wilson, feminist founder of the White House Project to encourage women in leadership, was typical. She criticized Palin's support for women's issues and her experience during an interview on National Public Radio, but made sure to note that she had "no concerns about how she'll take care of her family at all. Absolutely not … nor do I think we should even be talking about it."[56] Similarly, Rebecca Traister, outspoken in her disagreement with Palin, asserted that she was "perfectly capable of picking out the sexism being leveled at the Alaska governor by the press, her detractors and her own party" and bristled "every time someone doubts Palin's ability to lead and mother simultaneously."[57] The founders of the popular blog "Women Against Sarah Palin" stressed that their opposition to Palin was based on her issue positions and her lack of experience, and hoped contributors to their website would "focus on Palin's record rather than her biography."[58] Started by two art magazine editors in New York who emailed a letter to 40 friends asking for their reactions to Palin's nomination, the blog grew exponentially. Within a week they had received over 80,000 emails from women all over the country explaining why, in the words of the blog, "Ms. Palin does not represent us … or uphold our interests as American women."[59] By mid-September, over 140,000 responses had been posted; most of them concerned Palin's stance on environmental issues, education, and the economy, in addition to women's rights, as well as her lack of experience and qualifications.[60]

The debate about Sarah Palin, as an example of women's progress or a setback for women's interests, soon turned to charges by the McCain campaign that she was a victim of sexist treatment by the media.[61] Interestingly, Palin herself had weighed in on the issue of sexism during the presidential primary process. In the spring of 2008, Palin was asked about Hillary Clinton's campaign complaining of a double standard in media coverage, with sexist attitudes influencing stories and disadvantaging their candidate. Palin replied: "When I hear a statement like that coming from a woman candidate with any kind of perceived whine about that excess criticism, or maybe a sharper microscope put on her, I think, 'Man, that doesn't do us any good, women in politics, or women in general, trying to progress in this country.'"[62] Palin's statement seems to reflect a post-feminist view, in that women don't want to be seen as victims, but as already equal. Yet, in the fall, the political right had "suddenly found its inner feminist," as Anna Quindlen put it in a *Newsweek* column: "Conservatives have probably used the word 'sexist' more in the past week than they have in the past 50 years."[63] McCain strategist Steve Schmidt told reporters at the start of the GOP convention that he couldn't imagine the question of how Palin would juggle her responsibilities to her children and the vice presidency "being asked of a man. I think it's offensive, and I think a lot of women will find it offensive." Rudy Giuliani, a keynote speaker, and Cindy McCain made similar statements.[64] The McCain campaign insisted that any criticism that Palin was under-qualified and ill prepared to be a heartbeat away from the presidency—which intensified after her disastrous September interviews with Charlie Gibson and Katie Couric on national television—was, by definition, condescending and anti-woman. Feminist commentators such as Anna Quindlen responded by elucidating what they saw as hypocrisy at the Republicans' sudden concern with sexism: that social conservatives who had urged women to be stay-at-home mothers were embracing this working mother; that a party opposed to any affirmative action had picked Palin solely on the basis of her gender; that the campaign marketed her motherhood aggressively but then protested when questions were asked about her parenting; and their assertion that women are strong and smart, yet not trustworthy enough to make their own decisions about their bodies and pregnancies.[65]

Thus, the frame telling us how to read Sarah Palin—as feminist symbol or as victim of sexism—became contested. Certainly, there were moments during the election season when her gender was exploited (whether to her advantage or at her expense). One of the more striking examples, which provoked coverage of the resulting controversy at *The Washington Times* and Fox News sites, was a picture taken by wire service photographer Carlos Barria at a campaign event in Pennsylvania.[66] Taken from below and behind Palin as she stood onstage, it framed the rapt face of young male supporter directly between her legs. The young man, mesmerized expression on his face, was positioned perfectly between the V of her calves and high-heeled shoes, while the rest of Palin's body has been completely cropped out of the frame. It is hard to imagine an image that is less gender neutral and more sexualized. Palin herself implied she was a victim of "trashing" by feminists who should have shown her sisterly solidarity. At an October 2008 rally in Carson, California, she informed the crowd of a quote from Madeleine Albright found on her Starbucks cup: "There is a special place in hell for women who don't support other women."[67] Palin implied that women who didn't support her were actually the ones being sexist and anti-feminist.

However, many observers rejected this narrative of sexist victimization. Rather than feeling pity for Palin, they insisted that equal treatment and respect required, instead, holding her to the same standard of competency as any other serious (male) candidate. By that standard, even conservative women commentators found themselves dismayed by Palin's lack of knowledge, concluding "she's out of her league" and perhaps should even "bow out" of the race.[68] Was she a victim? "Palin is tough as nails. She will bite the head off a moose and move on. So, no, I don't feel sorry for her," Rebecca Traister observed, adding:

> Shaking our heads and wringing our hands in sympathy with Sarah Palin is a disservice to every woman who has ever been unfairly dismissed based on her gender, because this is an utterly *fair* dismissal, based on an utter lack of ability and readiness. It's a disservice to minority populations of every stripe whose place in the political spectrum has been unfairly spotlighted as mere tokenism; it is a disservice to women throughout this country who have gone from watching a woman who—love her or hate her—was able to show us what female leadership could look like to squirming in front of their televisions as they watch the woman sent to replace her struggle to string a complete sentence together.[69]

Some, such as CNN's Campbell Brown, threw the accusation of sexism back at the McCain campaign, wondering if they were behaving in a sexist fashion by shielding Palin from more tough media interviews and scrutiny—as if this delicate woman couldn't handle it and needed to be protected. Such "chivalrous" protection confuses a sexist double standard (such as asking female politicians how they can possibly be good mothers and hold public office, but not asking males about their parenting responsibilities and public life) with a legitimate query about qualifications (a candidate's education and experience). "Conflating the two is not combating sexism, it is exercising chivalry, and chivalry is an insult to all smart, accomplished women everywhere."[70] As Anna Quindlen put it, "all the cries of sexism suggested that, yet again, the Republicans had underestimated the ability of women to lead; when the governor finally took center stage, it was clear that she needed no protections or excuses," proving herself sharp, self-assured, and as able to "take an elbow" in the rough sport of politics as on the basketball court.[71] Quindlen noted that the goal of feminism and women's equality was for Palin to be "honored with the same tough scrutiny the guys in this race get."[72] Political cartoonist Nick Andersen summed up the irony in Republicans' charges of media sexism in a four-frame editorial cartoon on September 10. The first three frames show John McCain standing beside Palin, pointing to her and declaring: "She's Sarah Barracuda!" then "A Pit Bull With

Lipstick!" and, finally, "She Can Field Dress a Moose!" In the final frame, a reporter with a notebook appears, and McCain is throwing himself in front of Palin, arms flung wide to protect her, yelling: "No Tough Questions!"

The season-opening *SNL* skit on September 13, 2008, also contributed to the narrative debating Palin's feminism and the role of gender and sexism in political campaigns. Amy Poehler played Hillary Clinton and Tina Fey debuted her Sarah Palin impression in a sketch that had both women "crossing party lines to address the now very ugly role that sexism is playing in the campaign," as Fey put it. Poehler's Clinton added: "An issue which I am frankly surprised to hear people suddenly care about." After pointing out how both women had been described in sexual terms (in ways that depicted Clinton negatively, and Palin as appealing but in the beauty queen/bimbo narrative that undermined her credibility), the sketch turned to the historic nature of both women's achievements. "Just look at how far we've come. Hillary Clinton, who came so close to the White House, and me, Sarah Palin, who is even closer … it's truly amazing, and I think women everywhere can agree, that no matter your politics, it's time for a woman to make it to the White House!" Fey declared brightly. When Poehler's Clinton responds "No-o-o-o!! Mine! It's supposed to be mine … I didn't want a woman to be President! I wanted to be President, and I just happen to be a woman!," the audience knew to laugh at the joke mocking Hillary's ruthless ambition. But the sketch also raised serious questions about feminism: is it more feminist to support a woman in achieving high office for the first time, or to vote for one's preferred candidate without focusing first on gender? Is the media unfairly attacking women as women, or is it a sign of feminist progress to scrutinize women as closely as men candidates? Toward this point, Fey's Palin concludes the sketch by saying: "So in the next six weeks, I invite the media to be vigilant for sexist behavior." Poehler's Clinton adds: "Although it is never sexist to question female politicians' credentials. Please, ask *this* one about dinosaurs … I invite the media to grow a pair. And, if you can't, I will lend you mine."

Feminism was being debated, redefined, and deployed in a variety of ways through the Sarah Palin narrative. Was Palin a feminist? What do women want? And who speaks for them? *Newsweek's* September 22, 2008, cover story posed the question: is Sarah Palin indeed the heir to the American women's rights movement that began in Seneca Falls, New York in 1848?[73] The story is devoted to discussing the gender gap in presidential elections and Palin's effect on the electorate. It noted that women voters initially seemed to be "flocking to her:" the McCain ticket's poll numbers had climbed to 53 percent among white women, up from 44 percent in July.[74] "When Democrats question how she can do it, Republicans accuse them of sexism and cry, 'Women can do anything,' flipping feminist rhetoric about competent, unapologetic working women back in their faces," Julia Baird wrote, encapsulating a post-feminist rhetoric of individualism, equality, and rejection of victimhood. Women were "cheering her can-do attitude" and "like her most of all because she is a woman unafraid to push men around, and punch even before being provoked. She is not weak or overwhelmed. She is determined to win."[75] Like pop culture characters Gracie Hart or Elle Woods, Palin was a woman who projected a confident femininity, without "whining" or seeing sexist obstacles impossible to overcome. She embodied political "girl power," or as Baird put it in *Newsweek*, the message that "Gals can do anything!" A similar framing of Palin appeared in the *Wall Street Journal* in early September: "Maybe Sarah Palin from Wasilla is a lot closer to the way many women today see themselves than the standard feminist model" of the past 30 years, with "no victim vibes."[76] Reporter Daniel Henninger noted that among women voters he talked to, "the angry woman-as-victim drives them nuts. They hate victimology," as expressed by Hillary Clinton or traditional feminism, but admired Palin's "grit, determination and character."[77]

The frontier and feminist narratives overlapped and reinforced one another here, as the plucky Western pioneer gal fit not just a Republican trope, but also an appealing independent, strong woman frame. Women on the right embraced this "Sarah Palin feminism," enjoying the way it tied left-leaning feminists in knots. They rejected the *Roe v. Wade* litmus test and insisted that being pro-life could be pro-women.[78] They saw condescension and snobbery in critiques of Palin; white, working-class identity politics lay just below the surface of the feminist/post-feminist narrative. Barbara Amiel decried in the *Wall Street Journal*: "Caste and class have always been ammunition in the very Eastern Seaboard women's movement, and now they were (so to speak) loading for bear." Sally Quinn felt a mother of five had no business being vice president. Andrea Mitchell remarked that "only the uneducated" would vote for Mrs. Palin. "Choose a woman, but this woman?" wrote *Baltimore Sun* columnist Susan Reimer.[79] In the *National Review* online, Victor Davis Hansen condemned contemporary feminism for its "sneering stories about [Palin's] blue-collar conservatism [and] small Alaska town" and for calling women who were Christians or opposed to abortion "unsophisticated dupes," and called for a redefinition of feminism that more accurately reflected American women.[80] Another *Wall Street Journal* column exclaimed in mock-feminist horror:

> All she seems to have done was play sports, go to a no-name university and have lots of babies. She's a beauty queen! This isn't even close to your standard East Coast uber-woman. Sarah didn't go to Harvard Law and clerk for some legendary judge ... My God, she almost sounds like an Alaskan Valley Girl. This can't possibly work, can it?[81]

Perhaps, posited some, Palin was so hated by left-leaning feminists because they were jealous—of her looks, her family, and her ability to "do it all" on her own. In *Time*, Belinda Luscombe opined that Palin was too pretty and too confident, qualities sure to cause women to resent and loathe her.[82] In a blog post entitled "The Harpies Are Out to Get Sarah Palin," conservative Mary Grabar unleashed her outrage at "these feminists [who] don't care about women."[83] Grabar contrasted the "poor treatment [liberal women] get from liberal boyfriends" to her friends earning Ph.D.s while being "supported by conservative blue-collar husbands." Working-class conservatism was more authentic and better for women than elitist feminism, she seemed to argue. "The feminists are livid that Palin did it outside the movement, that—unlike Hillary Clinton—she began not out of her own ambition, but as a result of her concern for her own children, as a PTA mom," Grabar explained. Clinton and her "pro-choice sisters" were just like Lady Macbeth, the antithesis of normal femininity, who for the sake of ambition cried out: "Unsex me here, /And fill me from the crown to the toe topful /Of direst cruelty … Come to my woman breasts,/And take my milk for gall."[84] Pro-choice feminists were resentful, unsexed killers who were no longer real women because of their selfishness: "These women have blood on their hands, and they are very angry and bitter."[85] In this view, real women, with working-class husbands, families, and church membership, were poised to rise up in support of Palin and refute this type of "flawed" feminism. Indeed, while a gender gap favoring Democrats has been a staple of presidential elections since 1980, white married women are much more likely than their single, racially and ethnically diverse sisters to support Republican candidates. Perhaps Palin appealed to those women not just as a conservative, but as a powerful woman who looked like them.

Some columnists used the Palin nomination to call for a new or expanded definition of feminism. Cathy Young, in the *Boston Globe*, identified herself as a liberal but praised Palin's candidacy as a great moment for American women. "More representation for feminism across the spectrum of political beliefs is a good thing. Women, like men, should be able to disagree on gun ownership, environmental policies, taxes, even abortion while agreeing on gender equity," Young declared.[86] She also called career–family balance (not reproductive rights) "the biggest feminist issue in America today," finding inspiration in Palin's ability to juggle kids and a powerful job alongside a hands-on partner and father, and in the way that her candidacy would invalidate the right's insistence on stay-at-home-motherhood as proof of "family values."[87] Suzanne Fields called Palin "a triumph for the 'third stage' of feminism," neither a victim nor trying to prove she was manly enough: "She's comfortable balancing femininity and toughness."[88] Indeed, a fashion story on the popularity of spike-heeled shoes noted that stilettos, named after the Italian word for "dagger," were a useful tool "for the projection of an image that is both feminine and powerful. That's why … Sarah Palin donned Naughty Monkey Double Dare pumps at the Republican Convention."[89] In third-wave feminist style, heels could be seen not as crippling fashion accessories causing women to hobble and lose ease of motion, but as "the perfect shoes for negotiating the complicated landscape where authority meets beauty. Think of them as a peacock's tail—if each feather were also a poison dart."[90] Indeed, Elle Woods would definitely understand.

On October 21, 2008, Sarah Palin addressed gender equality head-on in a speech she gave at a large rally in Henderson, Nevada, just outside Las Vegas.

Surrounded on the stage by various women associated with the Democratic Platform Committee and the National Organization for Women, Palin made her case as the feminist choice in the presidential race.[91] She began by using a line from her introductory speech back in Ohio in August: "I have a question for the women in the audience. Are you willing to break the highest, hardest glass ceiling in America?" Palin lashed out at Barack Obama as a "faux feminist" who campaigned on the issue of equal pay, but failed to pay women on his own Senate staff as highly as the men (a charge refuted quickly by the Obama campaign).[92] Palin also attacked Obama for not choosing Hillary Clinton as a running mate, comparing his decision to the discrimination American women face in the workplace daily:

> Barack Obama couldn't bring himself to pick the woman who got eighteen million votes in the primary. The qualifications are there, but for some reason the promotion never comes … You've got to ask yourself, why wasn't Senator Hillary Clinton even vetted by the Obama campaign? Our opponents think they have the women's vote all locked up, which is a little presumptuous. A little presumptuous, and only our side has a woman on the ticket.[93]

Palin went on to list her feminist policy *bona fides*: flexible labor laws allowing working moms to telecommute more; a tax code that doesn't penalize working families; and advocacy for women globally, especially in ending sex trafficking and honor killings. She also talked about how she personally had benefitted from Title IX, which opened doors for women in sports and education: "Over time, that opened more than doors to just the gymnasium. It allowed us to view ourselves, and our futures, in a different way. We owed that opportunity to women, to feminists who came before us." But she expanded her view of gender equality beyond women's interest groups, noting that "a belief in equal opportunity is not just the cause of feminists. It's the creed of our country."[94]

Palin took an interesting stance, one more difficult to sell to the conservative base than an outright disavowal of left-wing, "harpy" feminists. She repeatedly called herself a feminist when it might have been easier to reject that label. She acknowledged her debt to women's activism for equal opportunity and to the women candidates who came before her (especially Democrats Geraldine Ferraro and Hillary Clinton). She asserted her belief in women's equality and spoke in support of feminist policies like Title IX. Yet, Palin's insistence that feminism could encompass an absolutist pro-life position (with abortion available only to save the life of the mother) and abstinence-only sex education, or be compatible with hawkish policies on Iraq and drilling for oil in the Arctic National Wildlife Reserve, challenged most conventional understandings of feminism. Palin seemed to think tax cuts for female small-business owners might be a more "feminist" policy than expanding reproductive rights or government-subsidized childcare.

She presented mothering not as an obstacle to holding public office, but as a possible credential for it. She opened up the conversation regarding what feminism really meant, and women all over the country added their voices to the debate.

In rejecting the stories of feminist triumph or sexist victimization, there was worry over the implications of Sarah Palin's performance for other women. The *New York Times* blogger Judith Warner was appalled by the pundits' general reaction to Palin's acceptance speech, "damning with faint praise" and betraying their low expectations for women.[95] One "marveled at Palin's ability to speak and smile at the same time," and thus "it seems we've all got to celebrate the fact that America's Hottest Governor ... could speak at all. Could there be a more thoroughgoing humiliation for America's women?" Warner's distress continued as she pondered the governor's likability and authenticity:

> Palin's not intimidating, and makes it clear that she's subordinate to a great man. That's the worst thing a woman can be in this world, isn't it? Intimidating, which appears to be synonymous with competent. It's the kiss of death, personally and politically. But shouldn't a woman who is prepared to be commander in chief be intimidating? Because of the intelligence, experience, talent and drive that got her there? If she isn't, at least on some level, off-putting, if her presence inspires national commentary on breast-pumping and babysitting rather than healthcare reform and social security, then something is seriously wrong.[96]

When Donny Deutsch opined on CNBC that Palin was "a new creation ... of the feminist ideal" because she "put a skirt on" and was sexually appealing and submissively feminine instead of intimidating, it may remind us of the double-edged sword of third-wave, individualist feminism. While there may be empowerment in reclaiming elements of femininity, and refusing to conform to a male model of life or politics, there may also be danger in remaking and redefining feminism as simply each woman having the opportunity to make her own choices, whatever they consist of: what theorist Rory Dicker terms the seduction of a "feminist free-for-all," in which politics are abandoned for an "anything goes" feminism unmoored from a political agenda.[97] The result is a feminism that fails to challenge traditional male power or hierarchy, and accepts female subordination under the guise of women's own choice. Or, as Rebecca Traister put it, "What Palin so seductively represents, not only to Donny Deutsch but to the general populace, is a form of feminine power that is utterly digestible to those who have no intellectual or political use for actual women. It's like some dystopian future ... feminism without any feminists."[98] Sarah Palin

> achieves her power by doing everything modern women believed they did not have to do; presenting herself as maternal and sexual, sucking up to men, evincing an absolute lack of native ambition, instead emphasizing her

luck as the recipient of strong male support and approval. It works because these stances do not upset antiquated gender norms … Sarah Palin's nomination is a grotesque bastardization of everything feminism has stood for … a narrative [that] could not only subvert but erase the meaning of what real progress for women means.[99]

Just two days before her Henderson speech on gender equality, Sarah Palin made her much-anticipated appearance on *SNL*. It was the largest audience for *SNL* since 1994, seen by over 14 million people.[100] On set, Palin met Alec Baldwin, who leered: "You're much hotter in person;" then Palin sat through Amy Poehler's rap satirizing the vice presidential nominee (including lyrics such as "I've got a bookish look and you're all hot for teacher" and "Shoot a mutha humpin' moose eight days of the week!") while smiling and bobbing her head. In the *New York Times*, TV critic Alessandra Stanley presciently noted that Palin was not being presented as a credible, thoughtful politician headed for the White House or a serious career, but was being "showcased as a star" with a game sense of humor, ready to "someday host her own television show" and become a celebrity.[101] Women bloggers on Slate's Double X blog also offered their opinion on Palin's *SNL* appearance, but unlike TV critic Stanley who focused on Palin's credibility and career, they delved into Palin's sexuality and the implications for larger gender politics. For example, Emily Bazelon posted on Sunday, October 19, that she felt "queasy" about Palin's appearance on *SNL* the night before, particularly because of the ogling by Alec Baldwin. Rather than seeing it as "the charming and harmless Palin equivalent of Obama Girl," Bazelon argued that "it still means something different for a male politician to be treated as a sex object than for a female one to be. Plus Obama is in no danger of being reduced to his sex appeal, whereas Palin may well be when the election is over."[102] Unlike Bazelon, several other bloggers, including Melinda Henninger, disagreed that Palin's appearance would have any bearing on the future of women in politics: "We are not that easily set back, are we?"[103] Many saw the skits as turning the tables a bit, using Baldwin's obnoxiousness as a way of mocking those who made fun of Palin so openly and vulgarly.

Blogger Maureen Sullivan noted that Palin had invited some of the leering and objectification with tactics such as winking at the debate. "When you've used your sexuality as a campaign tool as much as she has, you're fair game for that kind of mock ogling … do you really even want the protection that other feminists seem willing to afford you from being so ogled?" Sullivan wondered.[104] Palin was tough, many of the bloggers concluded; not only could she take the joke, but perhaps she had invited it. Rachael Larimore responded to all of the handwringing by raising a more "third-wave" feminist objection: "Is a candidate supposed to hide her good looks just because she's a woman?"[105] After noting that Hillary Clinton was praised and respected for her "serious" pantsuits and businesslike appearance, Larimore went on:

But I don't understand why that has to be the only choice for female politicians. Worrying over whether [Palin] can handle fake ogling and stressing that men are pointing out her hotness make it seem like she should tone it down. But why can't women be hot and be taken seriously at the same time? Isn't that kind of sexist in its own way? (I'm also thinking of all the time people oohed and ahhed over Condi Rice's kick-butt power boots.) It's like saying only ugly girls can be smart. And hence, smart girls are ugly. Heck, I'm jealous. I hope I look half that good when I'm 44 (and I probably won't have just given birth, either).[106]

Here the beauty queen and feminist narratives collided. And here was the dilemma: should Palin's sexualization be seen as exploitation, sexist, and protested by feminist women who wanted to be taken seriously? Or was her use of her sexuality freely chosen, empowering, even feminist?

To some, Palin was the new face of feminism, one that made room for more diverse women and opinions, without rigid litmus tests based on abortion or left-wing ideologies. This expanded and evolving "third-wave" feminism reclaimed femininity, saw women's sexual agency as empowering, and allowed mothers into politics while valuing their skills. Palin offered a feminism that contrasted with Hillary Clinton, one not based in Eastern elite privilege and urban condescension, or in cultivating "masculine" styles and success in the public world of law and politics. Yet others saw in Palin a post-feminist retreat, a return to the days when women's power was based more on sexual attractiveness and feminine subordination than female empowerment and equality. To all, the narratives around Palin's feminism mattered less for how they defined Palin, and more for how they shaped the debate and future for all American women. "Should we feel sorry for Sarah Palin? No. But if she fails miserably, we might be excused for feeling a bit sorry for ourselves … [because] she's yanking us back to the old assumption that women can't hack it at these heights" of power.[107] Or as Amanda Fortini put it just after the election: "Palin reinforced some of the most damaging and sexist ideas of all: that women are undisciplined in their thinking; that we are distracted by domestic concerns or frivolous pursuits like shopping; that we are not smart enough, or not serious enough, for the important jobs."[108]

7

CONCLUSION

Why did Sarah Palin touch such a nerve in American politics? Few responded to her candidacy and persona ambivalently, and she remains a prominent and controversial figure in American political and popular culture. The answer lies in the narratives with which Palin was framed as a candidate in 2008, and in how those narratives continue to resonate with the American electorate. In particular, the gendered frames surrounding Palin are grounded in provocative debates about and among women. The hockey mom frame cuts to the heart of what constitutes a good mother, and the degree to which women can be good mothers if they are also seriously committed to career ambition and performance. The beauty queen frame elicits questions of whether women can or should be "pretty" or "hot" in traditionally feminine ways in order to be taken seriously. Are we past the days when powerful women were advised to adopt more masculine traits or dress, empowering women to run for political office "as women" wearing heels and carrying babies? Have women candidates simply added another retrograde requirement to running for office—now they have to be beautiful (and maternal) as well as smart? Or are women candidates who come after Sarah Palin more likely to be dismissed as lightweights because this attractive woman was seen as pretty but not prepared, reinforcing stereotypes of women as flighty? Sarah Palin's self-framing also raised the question of whether or not conservative women can justly claim the label "feminist." Is that word being reclaimed and redefined from the Right? Finally, has Palin expanded our conceptions of women candidates, creating space for more diverse female candidates in terms of ideology? Are extreme conservative social positions best expressed by traditionally feminine and pretty faces? These are each highly contested themes, all elicited in reaction to the framing of Sarah Palin.

Our examination of news coverage, online discussions, texts from candidate campaign appearances, and other campaign materials revealed a variety of narrative frames through which Palin was defined and understood in the 2008 election. Our discussion of longstanding partisan narratives—frontier woman and political outsider—suggests that Ms. Palin was placed by herself and others easily within these familiar, time-tested frames with little resistance or objection. These narratives helped to legitimize her as a Republican vice presidential candidate, despite the unusual fact that she was the first woman to hold that role. These frames tended to evoke far less passion from voters owing to their familiar and conventional nature. On the contrary, gender frames such as ordinary hockey mom, sexy puritan beauty queen, and post-feminist role model were disputed and debated throughout the 2008 campaign and beyond.

Frames are the shared stories that citizens use to make sense of political characters and events. They allow a candidate to be understood by referencing narratives grounded in social history, past political campaigns, and popular culture. Some frames are salient to certain audiences, while simultaneously invisible or unimportant to others; multiple narrative frames for a single candidate can compete and coexist, as we have seen with Sarah Palin. The applicability of frames depends upon the other characters in the electoral context as well.

Once frames are established and understood, subsequent events can be viewed through their structuring lens. They are selectively applied and vary across individuals. As we observed earlier, the two candidates for vice president in 2008 were framed quite differently from one another. Sarah Palin was framed in part as the ditzy beauty queen, while Joe Biden was viewed as a knowledgeable, experienced policy wonk (albeit one who occasionally let his mouth get ahead of his rational brain). Each candidate made verbal gaffes during the course of the fall campaign. But Palin's misstatements were typically understood to be evidence of one thing and Biden's another. Due to the beauty queen narrative framing her candidacy, Palin's were seen to represent a lack of underlying knowledge, seriousness, or commitment. Biden's gaffes, on the other hand, were viewed as indiscretion or a lack of discipline—but never a lack of underlying intelligence or readiness to be president. Our analysis would suggest that the framing of Palin and its gendered nature has a significant impact upon the way in which new information about political events or behavior is processed and evaluated. Opponents were able to reference these negative aspects of the beauty queen frame to raise doubts about how qualified Palin was to serve at the national level.

Frames are constrained by the political environment, the candidate's own biography and behavior, and the media or audience's familiarity and resonance with the narrative schema. As communications scholar Robert Harriman has observed, effective political persuasion depends upon citizens' aesthetic reactions, and "political style is an articulation of power available in a given context."[1] As a Republican woman candidate for vice president, Sarah Palin had certain narratives available to her to use stylistically in making herself intelligible to the American electorate, while others remained unavailable or untapped by the campaign or the media. We have discussed the opportunities and limits of those frames in the preceding chapters. We would like to conclude our discussion of Palin, who remains an intriguing figure on the national political stage, by pondering how much these frames continue to define her, and how she has perhaps changed the narratives and power available to future women candidates and to American women generally.

Jennifer Lobasz demonstrates that even women in novel and non-traditional roles get interpreted by the media and the public through pre-existing gender frameworks.[2] Her work on soldiers Jessica Lynch, an American prisoner of war, and Lynndie England, involved in the infamous Abu Ghraib incidents dehumanizing Iraqi prisoners, shows that both of these atypical women were presented in media reports as conforming to familiar Victorian tropes of gender, race, and class: the woman in peril (Lynch) and the ruined woman (England). While the facts of each woman's situation in Iraq, and her own agency in responding, were fairly complex and did not fit into traditional gender roles, media reports on both women reinterpreted them into narratives that the public could easily understand. Lynch was portrayed as a demure damsel in distress, despite the fact she was a soldier in the U.S. Army. England was demonized as a monstrous woman, but the blame was placed on the fellow soldier who had impregnated and thus "ruined" her, leading her astray from morality and basic human decency. If the first American woman POW can be recapitulated to traditional gender norms, despite the extreme novelty of her situation, it stands to reason that Sarah Palin would also be constrained by gendered narratives, even as her inhabiting them stretched and changed them.

In this final chapter we discuss the evolution of these narrative frames evoked by Sarah Palin in the months and years since the 2008 campaign. We pay particular attention to events surrounding the 2010 midterm national elections and the 2012 presidential primary process. The narratives through which Palin was understood have continued to shape public perceptions, not only of her but of other female and Republican candidates. We are curious as to whether or not new political archetypes have emerged for female candidates, particularly conservative women.

The particular frames employed by and about Palin in 2008 are not unique to her candidacy. They continued into the 2010 midterm elections and into the 2012 presidential nominating process, where they are used by and applied to other candidates. Other Republican contestants are framed—and frame themselves—as frontiersmen and women, political outsiders, average moms, and beauty queens/sexy Puritans. And since 2008, intense debate has ensued over whether or not conservative women can be appropriately thought of as feminists. As we reflect on Palin's image since the 2008 race, we analyze the degree to which Sarah Palin has opened a more expansive space for women in national executive politics, evaluating the contours of the environment and possibilities for women in future elections.

Hillary Clinton, Sarah Palin, and Sexism in Electoral Politics

In the aftermath of the 2008 election, the status of women in politics garnered study and debate. Observers wondered if 2008 represented a sign of imminent breakthrough for women, a non-event, or even a setback on the path toward gender equality in the political arena. In *Notes from the Cracked Ceiling*, journalist Anne Kornblut pessimistically summed up the 2008 race as a lesson in persistent sexism, "a severe letdown, with damaging consequences. It revived old stereo-types, divided the women's movement, drove apart mothers and daughters, and set back the cause of equality in the political sphere by decades."[3] Rebecca Traister's *Big Girls Don't Cry* bemoaned Hillary's loss, sexist pundits and voters, and Palin's poorly reviewed performance. But Traister was thrilled to note that the somewhat ignored notion of feminism "was back, embraced in a manner that broadened its reach, relaxed the rules about how it might be deployed, extended it so far outward that, yes, it became imperiled again. But its return also meant that someday feminism's legacy would bear fruit with regard to the presidency, even if it's not as sweet as many of us might have hoped."[4]

The candidacies of Hillary Clinton and Sarah Palin would be forever joined owing to their coincidental timing. However, a significantly greater amount of attention was paid to the treatment Hillary Clinton received over the course of her primary run and the degree to which she was the victim of sexism than to Sarah Palin's experience. Much of the ensuing scholarly discussion of women candidates and their treatment in 2008 focused on the perceived sexist treatment Clinton received during the Democratic nomination contest, although a few studies juxtaposed her candidacy with Sarah Palin's. Few analysts overtly addressed how one should factor in a candidate's own choices and behavior into evaluations of media treatment. The consideration of Hillary Clinton's candidacy was exten-sive enough that it led one observer of political communication to describe the efforts as "Hillary Studies".[5] In her comprehensive review of four works focused primarily on Hillary Clinton's presidential candidacy, Janis Edwards offered the view that:

> Hillary occupies the center of attention to the subject of women and politics, not just because she is a polarizing and controversial figure, not just because of her relationship to a similarly larger-than-life spouse (and ex-president), but also because she embodies the issues that define the intersection of gender studies and contemporary political communication scholarship.[6]

Sarah Palin's 2008 candidacy received less attention from scholars despite the intense media and popular interest in her behavior.[7] Some aspects of her run for vice president evoked familiar challenges faced by female candidates. But Palin also defied many of the assumptions about prominent women in public life.

Most significantly, she did not fit the mold of liberal feminism that has characterized such second-wave feminist political icons as Geraldine Ferraro, Pat Schroeder,
and Hillary Clinton.[8] Sarah Palin's toughness was grounded in her private, individualistic pursuits and was implicit in these choices rather than explicitly argued.
As a result, she did not seem to be as captured by the double bind experienced by
Clinton that resulted in a common perception of her as shrill and unpleasant.[9]

Some case studies and journalistic accounts centered on self-presentation and
fashion, directly contrasting Palin and Clinton. Hillary Clinton was presented as
an iconic exemplar of candidates dressing "like men:" outwardly unconcerned
with femininity, focused on appearing serious and prepared, and almost de-
sexualized. Ruth LaFerla, after describing Ms. Clinton's rainbow collection
of boxy utilitarian pantsuits for the *New York Times*, concluded that women politicians had stayed close to the Clinton example in the 2010 election cycle:

> On their own steam—or perhaps at the suggestion of a battery of campaign
> advisers … [they] are retreating, as they have for decades, to the relative
> safety of an anodyne uniform. Understated to a fault, its chief components
> are a formless suit, flat or low-heeled shoes and a noncommittal hairstyle.
> It's a brusquely masculine image tempered occasionally by a strand of pearls
> and dainty, never dangly, earrings.[10]

Sarah Palin was described as firmly on the other end of the spectrum, politically
and sartorially. In her assessment of Palin's "bright, curve-enhancing garments
and loose, shoulder-grazing hair," LaFerla suggested that "Ms. Palin—she of the
designer jackets, rump-hugging skirts and knee-high boots—would seem to have
been a game changer, loosening up a restrictive, if unwritten, campaign dress
code with one that expresses a more conventionally feminine look."[11] But she
concluded that not many actually followed Palin's example of more edgy or sexy
style.

After 2008, analyses seemed to suggest that one impact of Palin's candidacy was
to open up more space for women candidates' self-expression in fashion. Ann
McGinley provided the view that Palin's choices were, in a sense, strategic performances of gender that she actively managed. "Palin's success resulted largely from
her failure to challenge gender norms while strategically emphasizing femininity
or masculinity as needed."[12] However, by 2010 one had to wonder if there really
was more room for a variety of acceptable options for women's self-presentation,
or if instead a different set of singular expectations had emerged. Were women
candidates now expected to look like Sarah Palin—to be "hot" in addition to
all the other qualifications for political office? Rather than simply putting to
rest false choices for women candidates—attractive or intelligent, pretty or
tough—Palin's experience indicates women may instead now face expanded and
demanding expectations: attractive *and* intelligent, pretty *and* tough. The attempt
to balance the set of partisan and gender frames encountered in 2008 may have

brought women full circle, to the point where the door has been opened wider for commentators and pundits to sexualize women candidates. It may seem as if they are complimenting their femininity, but it may also serve as a means of diminishing their legitimacy as potential leaders.

The controversy surrounding the November 23, 2009, cover of *Newsweek* encompasses many of the tensions surrounding issues of femininity and serious-ness implicit in the narrative frames we have discussed. The cover featured a photograph of Sarah Palin dressed in running gear—short shorts, bare legs, and running shoes. *Newsweek* was roundly criticized for appropriating the photo from a sister fitness magazine that had commissioned the photographs as part of a story about Palin's participation in marathons. Critics suggested that by decontextual-izing the photo, *Newsweek* presented Palin in a way that diminished her stature. The accompanying headline exacerbated the situation by posing the question: "How Do You Solve a Problem like Sarah? She's Bad News for the GOP—And for Everybody Else, Too." The coupling of the cover line with the sexy photo implied that Palin's appearance had its own kind of political power: it enchanted those inclined to agree with her politics—and frustrated or confused those who are not. Her looks have become not only part of her public persona but also a commodity unto themselves.[13]

The 2008 frames continue to provide insight into the challenges faced by Palin and other women candidates. Would people have reacted to a photograph of a prominent male politician in the same way? Would a cover of that kind have ever been created in the first place? The gendered double standards for politicians' images reflect discrepancies in the culture at large. If *male politician in shorts = athleticism; female politician in shorts = sexy* then it may be only one small step removed from *male politician as president = natural; female politician as president = unnatural*. The implications of how those images get read have a great deal to do with legitimizing the distribution of power and women's ways of accessing it.[14]

While differences in appearance and dress seemed to dominate comparisons between Sarah Palin and Hillary Clinton, these are not the only points of distinc-tion drawn by scholars. In their analysis of Hillary Clinton's run for the White House, Regina Lawrence and Melody Rose contrasted the two women's approach to the 2008 contest. In their view, Clinton focused on a rhetoric of equality, while Palin's rhetoric focused on difference. Palin generally presented herself in more traditionally feminine ways, appealing to motherhood to justify her power. She applied faith-based metaphors to justify her activism, suggesting she was "chosen" and "called" to her candidacy by John McCain and avoiding the ambition problem faced by many women candidates (including Clinton). Palin effectively combined masculine and feminine images—cooking, wearing high heels, and being a mom to five while also hunting and shouldering a gun. She is not just another woman who got close to the White House: "Palin brought with her an almost utterly different 'version of gender' that signals a contempo-rary struggle for the 'proper' articulation of female power."[15]

Amanda Fortini worried that the two most successful women candidates in the history of the republic might not have been a step forward for women at all. In her comparison of Clinton and Palin, she concluded that the discourse accompanying the 2008 campaign did little to open new paths, rather, it reinforced two particularly problematic stereotypes of women—the bitch and the ditz. "Clinton took the first label, even though she tried valiantly, some would say misguidedly, to run a campaign that ignored gender until the very end."[16] Conversely, at the moment she entered the national stage, Palin "seemed to have achieved what so many of us were struggling for: an enviable balance between career and family."[17] Over time, her interview performances and apparent lack of significant foreign policy knowledge led to a recasting of Palin "as the charmer, the glider, the dim beauty queen, the kind of woman who floats along on a little luck and the favor of men." Fortini opined that while Clinton "was a grind, scold, harpy, shrew, priss, teacher's pet, killjoy," Sarah Palin got her opportunity because of her looks and social skills. Neither is a particularly positive or empowering view of women candidates for office.

While two models for how to be a successful woman in politics is certainly preferable to a singular notion, we are left to wonder if this dualistic, oppositional approach to conceptualizing women as political candidates is really sufficient or appropriate? This dualism implies an underlying truth that women can be grouped into just two categories. Further, it suggests that women within each model might be viewed as fungible: conservative women look "all alike" or liberal women are all the same. This type of thinking can lead observers and participants to question (just as we saw in 2012) whether or not there is room for more than one woman in a single race. Pundits seemed confounded by the thought that Michele Bachmann might run for president if Sarah Palin also declared her candidacy, as if the two women were identical, though they have different political résumés and governing experience, not to mention different relationships to feminism. Male candidates are allowed to exist within a multidimensional space, constituting a variety of options for voters. Why not a spectrum of options for women as well?

2009 Resignation from Office

After the furor of the 2008 race died down, interest turned to where Palin would go next in her political career. Her popularity as a fundraiser, speaker, and commentator in the lower 48 states remained high. On July 3, 2009, in a hastily organized address to journalists and supporters, Sarah Palin announced her impending resignation as Alaska governor. Her choice to not only forego a run for re-election but to also leave her position midway through her term came as a surprise to most political observers. Palin presented her resignation squarely from the perspective of the outsider/maverick frame employed throughout the 2008 campaign. She spoke from her own suburban backyard surrounded by casually dressed friends and neighbors. Addressing the crowd in her typical folksy style, Palin suggested at multiple points in her remarks that her decision to resign centered on an assessment of her ability (or frustrating lack thereof) to redefine the rules of politics going forward.[18] At one point in her address Palin implored: "All I can ask is that you trust me with this decision and know that it is no more politics as usual." She later elaborated along the same lines:

> My choice is to take a stand and effect change—not hit our heads against the wall and watch valuable state time and money, millions of your dollars, go down the drain in this new environment. Rather, we know we can effect positive change outside government at this moment in time.[19]

Officials and commentators across the political spectrum weighed in on her decision. Most found Palin's choice problematic and her rationale difficult to accept at face value.[20] Even *People* magazine covered her choice to step down. Her actions provided an opportunity to revisit negative aspects of many of the gender frames we have discussed in the preceding chapters—the flightiness of the beauty queen narrative, questions about women's ability to balance career ambitions with family commitments from the hockey mom frame, and evaluations of how her choice would affect perceptions of women leaders from the post-feminist narrative. Generally, Palin's choice was viewed as one that no serious political player would make. Republican strategist Ron Bonjean summed up his view that "Republicans are getting tired of the constant drama that surrounds her family ... To win over mainstream Republicans and independents, Palin will need to start talking about important ideas and solutions instead of creating or reacting to tabloid issues."[21]

Palin argued in her own defense with a statement on her Facebook page, presented again from the perspective of the outsider/maverick reformer frame with its accompanying sense that Washington is somehow out of touch with average Americans' motivations and state of mind:

> How sad that Washington and the media will never understand; it's about country ... And though it's honorable for countless others to leave their positions for a higher calling and without finishing a term, of course we know by now, for some reason a different standard applies for the decisions I make. But every American understands what it takes to make a decision because it's right for all, including your family.[22]

Many Alaskans were left confused and unimpressed by her rationale. Their objections seemed grounded in the frontier woman frame that had introduced Palin as a tough character long on perseverance and self-sufficiency: "Astounding. Risky. Quitter. And that's what fellow conservatives had to say Sunday about

Alaska Governor Sarah Palin and her decision to step down with 18 months left in her term."[23] A blog post about Palin continued along similar lines:

> One cause of the 49th state's newly icy relationship with our ex-governor that cannot be overestimated is simply this—she quit. Quitters don't make it far in the frontier, and Alaskans lose respect quickly for those who flee when the going gets tough. Surviving discomfort and hardship and risk is a badge of honor here. It's practically the price of admission. We are the home of the bootstraps by which we tell everyone to pull themselves up. Alaskans don't like a whiner, and we don't like a quitter. Case closed.'[24]

Palin's decision to resign served to highlight the growing divide between the interests, skills, and competencies suited to electoral politics and those needed to govern effectively. She flourished in campaign settings, but seemed to lack interest and engagement with the day-to-day details and challenges of governing. In 1988, political scientist Michael Nelson articulated competencies that might be evaluated in selecting vice presidential nominees—governance criteria and election criteria. His analysis suggested that election criteria, particularly a candidate's ability to unite a partisan base, could dominate the vice presidential selection process.[25]

Palin's selection in 2008, while a game changer because she was relatively unknown, inexperienced at the national level, and a woman, was firmly focused on the traditional election competencies and criteria that dominate vice presidential selections in years of significant partisan conflict. Her choice to leave office early in 2009 only emphasized the growing divide between the capacity to get elected and the ability to attentively and effectively govern from that position. The power of the outsider frame within the electoral context is unquestionable. However, it offers little guidance regarding governance issues. One must wonder how outsiders are expected to effectively build coalitions or populate bureaucratic agencies when they come to Washington, DC, without historical and experiential alliances. The American propensity to curb elitism plays into this continuing divide. Do outsiders possess the knowledge and experience (and bank account of favors) to effectively face the challenges of governance?

2010 Susan B. Anthony List Speech: Redefining Feminism

Sarah Palin's May 14, 2010, keynote remarks to the Susan B. Anthony List's Celebration of Life breakfast ignited a firestorm of commentary, controversy, and debate as she reclaimed the label feminist yet again.[26] The speech integrated and reiterated many of the frames from the 2008 campaign that we have discussed. It introduced the notion of Mama Grizzlies as a political movement: passionately protective mothers angered that politicians were putting the nation in peril by stealing from future generations to pay today's extravagant bills. According to Palin, these motivated, strong, and self-sufficient moms were ready to band together and take control of the situation in order to spearhead the fundamental changes necessary to right the current course of the country: "You don't want to mess with moms who are rising up ... If you thought pit bulls were tough, you don't want to mess with mama grizzlies."[27] The image of Mama Grizzlies became one of the defining narrative frames of the 2010 election cycle, rooted in the hockey mom of 2008 that had grown more motivated and angry.

Some observers focused on the pro-life theme of Palin's speech, and in particular her revelation that while pregnant with her youngest child, she had momentarily considered abortion.[28] But columnists, bloggers, and activists soon focused on the efforts that Palin made to place herself at the front of a feminist movement led by "gun-toting, pro-life moms."[29] Palin had used the opportunity presented by the Susan B. Anthony forum to lay explicit claim to the mantle of feminism for conservative pro-life women like her. Referring to her vision as "frontier feminism," Palin suggested that:

> It's an emerging conservative feminist identity. Far too long, when people heard the word 'feminist,' they thought of the faculty lounge at some East Coast women's college, right? And no offense to them, they have their opinions and their voice, and God bless them; they're just great.
>
> But that's not the only voice of women in America. I'd like to remind people of another feminist tradition, kind of a Western feminism. It's influenced by the pioneering spirit of our foremothers, who went in wagon trains across the wilderness, and they settled in homesteads. And these were tough, independent pioneering mothers, whose work was as valuable as any man's on the frontier ... They went where no woman had gone before ... As an Alaskan woman, I'm proud to consider myself a frontier feminist like those early pioneering women of the West.[30]

Palin linked her feminism to motherhood, seeing it as empowering rather than as a limitation or obstacle to women's other achievements. Truly feminist women, Palin suggested, "can give their child life, in addition to pursuing career and education and avocations. Society wants to tell these young women otherwise."[31]

In one 30-minute address, Palin pulled together the down-home folksy language and geographic appeals from the 2008 outsider frame, the gun-toting toughness and pioneer independence of the frontier frame, the protective mother from the hockey mom frame, and the pro-life culture warrior of the outsider frame, and leveraged them all to reframe and plant her flag firmly on feminist territory. The resulting firestorm about her remarks centered on the gender frames. As in 2008, there was little discussion of whether or not she was justified in claiming the mantle as the representative average American—an "outsider" to all the politics as usual in Washington. No one questioned seriously whether or not the frontier frame was an apt narrative as applied to her persona and political credentials. However, columnists were not the least bit shy in questioning how

Ms. Palin could ever be considered a feminist. In an opinion piece entitled "The Fake Feminism of Sarah Palin," Jessica Valenti asserted:

> Just as consumer culture tries to sell "Girls Gone Wild"-style sexism as "empowerment," conservatives are trying to sell anti-women policies shrouded in pro-women rhetoric ... By tying their "feminism" to the suffragists, whose goal was realized nearly 100 years ago, they're not-so-subtly saying that women in America have achieved equality. In fact, they don't believe that systemic sexism exists.[32]

Others responded with the familiar refrain that the left was reacting to Governor Palin's declarations in a hypocritical and elitist fashion, while misunderstanding real women and their views. In a column for *National Review* online, Kathryn Jean Lopez noted that "When Sarah Palin speaks, liberal feminists go wild. The woman is like a stilettoed catalyst for backlash from the professional political sisterhood."[33] Conservative blogger Lori Ziganto argued in Palin's defense that:

> self-avowed modern day feminists are anything but feminist. In fact, they are diametrically opposed to feminism, by its very definition, because their entire agenda is actually harmful to women ... and I'm taking the term feminist back.
>
> True feminists are women like Sarah Palin and Nikki Haley. *They* are the new faces of feminism. That has a great built-in bonus, too—they are far easier on the eyes and exhibit none of that irksome hysterical screeching ... We are tired of being sneered at as gender traitors for not toeing the faux feminist line and by daring to be pro-life. We are tired of the attempts to diminish Motherhood. We are tired of women being painted as perpetual victims by the left, in need of Big Daddy Government to save us.[34]

Jessica Valenti complained that Palin and her supporters were hijacking the feminist label for strategic purposes. While this constituted an effective approach, in her view they were highly inaccurate in their assertions, painting feminists as "condescending hypocrites who simply don't believe in young women" enough to think they are capable of having both a career that requires education and commitment, and bearing an unplanned child.[35] True feminism, Palin had argued, was actually more affirming of women, believing women are "strong enough and smart enough" to handle finishing school and giving a child life. Stephanie Schriock, president of EMILY's List, the political action committee (PAC) committed to electing more pro-choice Democratic women and precursor to the Susan B. Anthony List, weighed in with her view that "Sarah Palin talks a good game about 'grizzly bear moms' taking the country back." Schriock added that "Palin doesn't seem to trust American women to make their own decisions—though she speaks movingly about her own."[36]

Feminist rhetoric has been co-opted in the past to support conservative policies and agendas. For example, in six speeches between November 17, 2001, and May 21, 2002, about the rights of women and children in Afghanistan, First Lady Laura Bush used the rhetoric of feminism to justify the Bush administration's war on terror. Bush used liberal feminist language idealizing women's rights to health, education, and independence, along with maternal language demonstrating a more traditional understanding of womanhood, to undergird a conservative political vision.[37] Similarly, some scholars see the pro-life movement shifting its rhetoric toward a more "pro-woman" frame. While opposition to abortion has often been couched in language regarding immorality or the rights of the fetus, this rhetorical shift uses the language of women's rights to argue that abortion is bad for women, rather than a necessary right that women need. Rather than pitting the rights of the fetus against the rights of the woman carrying it, this new language frames abortion as something that victimizes women and gives them less "choice" rather than more. Thus, a basic tenet of feminism—reproductive rights and, specifically, abortion—is turned into an antifeminist position, while the pro-life position that has been seen as antifeminist becomes the more genuinely feminist one in this reframing.[38]

Meghan Daum, columnist for the *Los Angeles Times* and self-identified feminist, provoked the most debate when she defended Palin's right to call herself a feminist as well. Despite the fact that she disagreed with Sarah Palin's policy positions on reproductive rights, Daum suggested it would be hypocritical not to allow Palin to claim the term. Daum pointed the finger of blame back at liberal women themselves for providing an opportunity for Palin to seize upon in the first place:

> think hard about who or what is to blame for increasingly narrow definitions of feminism, definitions that often have more to do with armpits and their discontents than with policy, pay rates and other matters of substance. Part of the fault lies with those who believe in gender equality but avoid the word, souring its reputation and undermining principles they actually hold quite dear. In other words, too many people are walking the walk without talking the talk.
>
> Is there a place in politics for "conservative feminists?" According to my definition of feminism, it would be hypocritical to say no. More hypocritical, though, is to not drop that F-bomb at every reasonable opportunity. If a grizzly bear can do it, anyone can.[39]

A month after Palin's speech, *New York Times* columnist Russ Douthat marveled at all the hand wringing across the political spectrum over who did and who did not qualify as a feminist, commenting that:

> The question of whether conservative women get to be feminists is an interesting and important one. But it has obscured a deeper truth: Whether or not Palin or Fiorina or Haley can legitimately claim the label feminist, their rise is a testament to the overall triumph of the women's movement.[40]

As part of the aftermath of the Anthony List speech, *Newsweek* ran a cover story entitled "Saint Sarah" on June 11, 2010. Lisa Miller described Palin's popularity with conservative, pro-life women and posited that Palin was turning the religious right into a women's movement, as she "gathers up the Christian women that traditional feminism left behind." While these women had not been attracted to the feminist label or seen themselves reflected in the candidacy of Hillary Clinton, they could relate to Palin's image of strength and empowerment on feminine terms. "There is very much an ideal Christian woman model" in these circles, noted religion Professor R. Marie Griffith: "It's an image that blends this kind of submissive, pretty, aw-shucks demeanor with a fiery power, a spiritual warfare."[41] To the echoes of the biblical Esther story on the 2008 campaign trail is added the "Proverbs 31 woman," who is described as a successful businesswoman, wife, and mother who wears beautiful clothes, rises before dawn, and cares for the needy. "No exhausted careerist is she: the Proverbs 31 woman laughs easily; her children are happy. Christian women have long puzzled in their Bible study groups over how she does it, and in Palin they finally have an example—not just for themselves, but for their daughters," wrote Miller.[42] Palin's cooptation of feminist language was also reaching a different, untapped audience of women who saw themselves as capable and energetic, but unwilling to give up their own notions of femininity in exchange for power. Here the post-feminist narrative not only re-emerges, but overlaps with a Republican religious base.

2010 Midterm Election: "Mama Grizzlies"

Palin embraced a dynamic role in the 2010 elections, endorsing candidates in numerous gubernatorial and congressional races, aggressively raising funds for Republicans and making appearances on behalf of her chosen contenders. Her endorsements garnered a tremendous amount of attention, as pundits and media attempted to analyze her impact and power in the party. *The Washington Post* recognized her visibility and influence by posting a widely linked tool tracing the success of her endorsements throughout the election season.[43] In total, Palin endorsed 64 candidates in national races. Ten of these individuals lost in their primary contests, 33 won their general election contest, and 21 lost in the general election stage.[44]

The salience and success of frames in any particular election relies on the political environment and electoral context. In 2010, the state of the U.S. economy had driven the electorate to a point of deep doubt and frustration with the continuing economic downturn and mortgage crisis. A majority of Americans seemed angry and disillusioned about the national government's inability to work together to offer meaningful solutions to these serious challenges, and the anti-taxation Tea Party movement emerged from the conservative grassroots. In hopes of electing sympathetic representatives to Congress, Tea Party activists focused their efforts on defeating moderate Republican incumbents and candidates at the primary election stage. Sarah Palin was a popular political figure among Tea Partiers, endorsing several Tea Party candidates and expressing their populist rage in a feminine voice. This gave rise to a new frame, as Palin began describing herself as a "Mama Grizzly," angry about trends in American politics and on the attack to protect her cubs and her values. In June 2010, just after the Susan B. Anthony List speech, Palin's political action committee, SarahPAC, promoted the Mama Grizzly frame in an internet campaign commercial with the same title. In it, she compared the rise of conservative women opposed to the Obama administration's policies to Alaska's "Mama Grizzly bears, who rise up on their hind legs when someone is coming to attack their cubs … you thought pit bulls were tough? Well, you don't want to mess with the Mama Grizzlies!" and declared that women were "rising up, saying no, this isn't right for our kids and our grandkids."[45] Palin also devoted an entire chapter in her book *America by Heart*, released in November 2010, to "The Rise of the Mama Grizzlies."[46]

The Mama Grizzly frame demonstrated continuity with many of the narratives and appeals used by Palin in 2008. It evoked the fierce spirit of the frontier woman (and the imminent dangers that must be fought in the wilderness). It took the hockey mom one step further: from strong and aggressive to downright angry, provoked to fight back. The Mama Grizzly was on the attack, hostile to Washington insiders, Democratic incumbents, Republicans-in-name-only, and the liberal "lamestream" media. She was the ultimate citizen outsider (from all the way out in the woods), hostile to all that was wrong with experts and entrenched political elites. And the Mama Grizzly was not alone. Both the media and Palin herself began to refer to a cadre of "commonsense conservative women" by the same label—such as Delaware Senatorial candidate Christine O'Donnell, South Carolina gubernatorial candidate Nikki Haley, Nevada Senatorial candidate Sharon Angle, and Minnesota Congresswoman Michele Bachmann.

The narrative (and primary election successes) of Mama Grizzlies opened up space for a wider ideological range of female candidates, and extends beyond the usual advice to women on how to win office. Female office-seekers have conventionally been told that remaining calm and coolly competent is the path to success (defying those feminine stereotypes of emotion and weakness). But the Mama Grizzly frame made space for women to express anger—albeit not the shrill hysteria (or the righteous indignation about sexism) voters might fear. Mama Grizzlies roared in conservative outrage. They claimed new political space for women's anger, aggression, and even violence—legitimized by protecting what they held dearest. But they were not fighting to protect "cubs" traditionally by supporting child-centered public policies in areas such as healthcare, education, day care, or social supports to prevent poverty. Instead, they were attempting to reclaim issues traditionally thought of as "masculine"—reducing the size of government, the economy, free markets, lower taxes—as areas where women were needed to protect the futures of their children. They were roused as fierce Mama Grizzlies to protect American freedom and the future, as only protective mothers can.

Importantly, this recasting of issues and ideology was still couched in terms of motherhood and traditional femininity. These were not the caricatures of "angry feminists," rejecting men and family. Their attractive, stylish, feminine personas were crucial to their success in using harsh populist rhetoric, and not in contradiction to it. As blogger Peggy Drexler noted:

> there is something going on with these Republican women that goes beyond good looks. It's deft packaging. In the same way a hardened commie-fighter like Richard Nixon was the one to open China, these women are a fascinating vessel for conservative thought. Take perfect teeth, glossy hair, sparkling eyes, flawless make up and clicking heels. Now combine that with values much more likely associated with a sensibly-shoed audience gathered on the state-house lawn in their Uncle Sam hats and Tea-Party T-shirts. Anti stem cells, anti abortion, anti gay marriage, anti big-city smart asses suddenly have star power. It's a juxtaposition that flummoxes opponents—like Barbra Streisand supporting assault-rifles.[47]

These pretty conservatives re-invoked and invigorated the paradox of the sexy Puritan from 2008. The cover of *Newsweek*'s October 4, 2010, edition featured the striking juxtaposition of images of four Republican women: Sarah Palin, Nikki Haley, Christine O'Donnell, and Michelle Bachmann.[48] Under the headline: "The Bear Truth: Will the Mama Grizzlies Really Protect America's Kids?" the four appeared in equal quadrants of the cover, in photos that maximized the similarity across the four women. They looked like identical quadruplets, or perhaps mirror images of the same woman. All were brunettes, wearing power red suits and smiling brightly, showing gleaming white teeth. Clearly attractive and poised, this cohort of conservative candidates did not fit neatly into pre-existing political narratives. If they were sexy Puritan beauty queens, weren't they supposed to be dismissed as silly? Yet, here they were, winning primaries and poised to do well in the general elections. Perhaps, the cover suggested visually, they were simply Sarah Palin clones? This imagery raises the question of whether individual women identified as part of Palin's "Mama Grizzlies" movement were being conceptualized as merely interchangeable. Would voters be as willing to accept the suggestion that men who shared political views with each other would also be inspired to dress alike, with similar hairstyles and eyeglasses? Voters and the media seemed to be grappling with how to tell or understand the story of a new type of female political candidate on the national stage.

Giffords Shooting

The issue of anger became even more salient when Democratic Representative Gabrielle Giffords and 18 other people were shot in January 2011 at a scheduled public meeting outside a Tucson, Arizona, grocery market. In the heated fall election season preceding the tragedy, Sarah Palin had posted to Facebook a map placing cross hairs over the home districts of candidates whom her political action committee (SarahPAC) had targeted for defeat in the midterm election. When the map had originally been posted online, Giffords herself had criticized the imagery on MSNBC: "The way they've got it depicted it has the crosshairs of gun sight over our district … they've got to realize there are consequences to that action."[49] Following the shooting, uproar ensued over the map and its accompanying crosshairs. Facebook executive Randi Zuckerberg noted that many Facebook users were discussing whether or not Governor Palin was in part to blame for the tragedy, indicating that this was the "#1 question on the social network behemoth following the Tucson shooting."[50]

There was some discussion and debate regarding whether or not the images Palin employed really represented crosshairs or not. Palin herself had, at times, referred to the symbols as bull's-eyes rather than targets.[51] Journalist John Berman offered his assessment that the symbols carried with them no ill intent, arguing that "anyone who has seen 'Sarah Palin's Alaska' [has] … seen that Palin has a deep connection and love for hunting … Language surrounding gun-use and hunting is something she uses often, and often with no political overtones."[52]

Palin's detractors disagreed. Representative Emanuel Cleaver, Democrat from Missouri, offered his view that "We are in a dark place in this country right now; the atmospheric condition is toxic … much of it originates here in Washington, DC, and we export it around the country."[53] Paul Krugman asserted that the ramped-up rhetoric helped to create what he referred to as a "climate of hate" in which this occurred.[54] It did not help the situation that along with the cross hairs visual, Palin had used the slogan "Don't retreat, RELOAD," both in speeches and in social media venues throughout the fall.[55]

The controversy provided Palin's opponents an opportunity to revisit the wisdom of emotional justifications within the frontier woman frame that Palin had embraced so strongly during her time in the political spotlight. Much like the successful counter-strategy Lyndon Johnson employed during the 1964 presidential race against cowboy conservative Barry Goldwater, Palin's detractors tried to turn the building blocks of the frontier frame against Ms. Palin. Instead of conceptualizing the frame as one filled with noble, hard-working, trailblazing pioneers or with white hat-wearing cowboys, Palin's opponents now argued she advocated a hazardous approach to solving disagreements. In their alternate narrative, Sarah Palin was the dangerous gunslinger—slow to analyze situations before reacting, quick to shoot, and often driven by anger, passion, and perceived slights or injustices. This alternative application of the frame was designed to raise questions about her prudence and professionalism.[56]

"Celebritician"

Palin seemed to chafe within the confines of traditional media and political frameworks. While highly adept with audiences and direct voter contacts, beginning in late 2008 McCain campaign staffers commented frequently and widely about her unwillingness or inability to stay on message or to approach campaign discourse in a disciplined fashion. They suggested that at some point midway through the fall campaign, Palin made a decision to "go rogue" and choose her own message and strategy. Her perspective appears to be that traditional journalistic outlets question her too much on terms she neither appreciates nor excels at addressing. These venues expect her to play by their rules. Conversely, social media outlets, entertainment venues, and reality television programs allow her significantly more control over the manner in which her own image is presented. These "new media" provide far less mediation and management of the messenger. The message goes out essentially unchallenged and uninterrupted.

In the months and years following the 2008 elections, Sarah Palin and her family became mainstays of the "celebrity" culture, participating in a dizzying array of venues not typically embraced by political families. The Palins participated in the cable TV reality series *Sarah Palin's Alaska*. Bristol Palin became a contestant on *Dancing with the Stars*, bringing with her higher ratings for evenings when Sarah Palin attended in support of her daughter. Celebrity magazines chronicled the on-and-off relationship between Bristol Palin and Levi Johnston, announcing their breakup, custody fights, reconciliation, and final separation. Bristol and Levi gave interviews and appeared at red carpet events, discussing her mother's reaction to their temporarily renewed plans to build a life together. Bristol's plastic surgery was covered and evaluated in the celebrity press. Levi Johnston posed for Playgirl and appeared on Kathy Griffin's reality show *My Life on the D List*, pretending to be Griffin's date to garner publicity. In 2012, Palin's daughter starred in a reality series on TLC entitled *Bristol Palin: Life's a Tripp*. What are we to make of these developments?

The Palins' embrace of the celebrity culture provided opportunities to revisit, reinforce, and even rework the frames from 2008. The cable television reality series *Sarah Palin's Alaska* is a case in point. The show built explicitly on the frontier frame. The show's network website teased the show: "'Sarah Palin's Alaska' takes viewers into the nation's 'final frontier' through the eyes of one of its most famous citizens." Episodes from the series showed run-ins with grizzly bears on a family fishing trip, gold panning expeditions, camping and hunting in the remote wilderness, and packing up extended family members for a road trip in a rented RV. The sense of the frontier pervaded the series, as did the effort to make the Palins appear to be living the life of the average American family. As Palin's voice-over declared in the opening credits: "I'd rather be out here, being free, than in some stuffy old political office."

The culture wars discussed as one aspect of the outsider frame continued as well. Much like Tim Tebow months later, Palin served as a signpost for conservatives, particularly religious conservatives, unaccustomed to seeing their icons in popular culture. Conservative supporters used these popular celebrity figures as vehicles through which to demonstrate their support for certain viewpoints and policy choices. Votes poured in for Bristol Palin with each week's appearance on *Dancing with the Stars.* Discussion boards filled with posts about the degree to which call-in votes for her on the television show represent potential political support for her mother or for Christian ideals more generally. But we are left to wonder about the consequences of treating Sarah Palin (and politicians more generally) as if they are simply celebrities. Again, the opportunity to focus on negative aspects of the gender frames appears all too easy to embrace.

2012 Presidential Horserace

After an extended flirtation with the idea of running for president, Palin eventually opted to sit out the 2012 Republican nominating process. However, during the period she considered her path, the framing process continued unabated. Even after she announced her decision to remain on the sidelines, frames that had been employed by and about Palin were being applied to other candidates in the race. Michelle Bachmann embraced the mothering frame; Rick Santorum portrayed himself as an outsider and champion of traditional religious values; Herman Cain was a Washington outsider having never held elective office before his run for the presidency; and Rick Perry claimed the frontiersman-cowboy conservative mantle. As expected, the partisan (Republican) frames were all clearly apparent, largely uncontested, and consistently defined. The gender frames were dependably more complicated.

Commentators seemed compelled to view Bachmann's candidacy in dualistic relationship to Palin's. Some offered objective comparison and contrast stories. *Newsweek* contributor Lisa Miller, for example, suggested that:

> Like Palin, Bachmann lives out her pro-life views convincingly. Over the years she has cared for twenty-three foster children—in addition to five of her own ... As a state legislator, Bachmann pushed for anti-abortion initiatives, such as the 2005 Positive Alternatives Act, which has provided some $2.4 million in state Department of Health grants to programs that encourage and assist women in carrying their pregnancies to term and caring for their babies.[57]

The Washington Post blogger Chris Cilizza posted his assessment that Michelle Bachmann was "no Sarah Palin."[58] Other writers could not resist the opportunity to tap into female stereotypes. In a June 2011 *Telegraph* piece, Toby Harnden offers his prediction that "Sarah Palin and Michelle Bachmann head for 2012 'cat fight.'"[59] The discussion seemed to realize our concern that these conservative women were seen as interchangeable and given that reality, there was room for only one of them in the nomination battle. But given that there were a multitude of men in the race, one had to wonder why no one was asking the same about them? Their images were not at all tied to their gender but instead to their individual personas. Why is the analysis of Bachmann and Palin presented first and foremost through that gendered lens? These are particularly important questions when one considers that there are significant differences in background and belief between Palin and Bachmann. While Palin may be ready to define the Christian right as a women's movement and to take ownership of the feminist label for pro-life women, Bachmann is a far more typical fundamentalist who would be unlikely to ever move in such an unconventional direction.

The framing of Sarah Palin provides significant insight into the ever-present struggles women face as the result of unresolved and conflicting attitudes about their appropriate role and conduct in the electoral arena. Sarah Palin certainly blazed a new trail; but it remains to be seen whether or not she has opened up room for other women in addition to her. Her candidacy suggests that a higher level of scrutiny ought to be given to generic advice about how women should present themselves as candidates. Cookie-cutter advice about how to speak, what issues to avoid, which clothes and jewelry to wear, or what haircut to get may be unnecessarily limiting for women. If nothing else, the reception to the narrative frames employed by Palin suggests the power of authenticity and self-confidence. Writing for *Slate.com*, Libby Copeland argued that:

> Even when her logic is frustrating, even when she contradicts herself, Palin's unselfconscious brashness is a good thing for women because it is so needed and so exceptional. There are simply not enough women willing to tout their own greatness, to correct hosts who underestimate their popularity, to predict that, yes indeed, they could be elected president. This is in great part because women expect to be punished for anything that smacks of self-promotion.[60]

Our analysis reinforces the fact that gender frames are still being contested: they are nowhere near as resolved as the partisan frames that Palin also employed. Palin's history certainly suggests that women may be finding new ways to expand the opportunities available to all women in the political arena by intersecting and balancing various narrative frames as part of their political personas. The overlap and juxtaposition of partisan and gender frames belies the continued relevance of the geographic, class, and racial appeals to the Republican electorate. Her experience also sheds light on the degree to which candidates must seize all available strategic resources they can through the framing process and be prepared to respond when opponents attempt to reframe them in response. The frames through which we understood Sarah Palin in the 2008 election and beyond illuminate the importance of political narratives, the opportunities and constraints still faced by women candidates, and the gendered questions with which American women and men continue to grapple.

NOTES

Chapter 1

1 Karrin Vasby Anderson and Kristina Horn Sheeler, *Governing Codes: Gender, Metaphor, and Political Identity* (Lanham, MD: Lexington Books, 2005), 3.
2 Shanto Iyengar and Donald Kinder, *News That Matters: Television and American Opinion* (Chicago, IL: University of Chicago Press, 1987).
3 Brian F. Schaffner and Mary Layton Atkinson, "Taxing Death or Estates? When Frames Influence Citizens' Issue Beliefs," in *Winning with Words: The Origins & Impact of Political Framing*, eds. Brian F. Schaffner and Patrick J. Sellers (New York: Routledge, 2010), 121–135.
4 Shanto Iyengar, *Is Anyone Responsible? How Television Frames Political Issues* (Chicago, IL: University of Chicago Press, 1991), discussed in Vincent Price and David Tewksbury, "News Values and Public Opinion: A Theoretical Account of Media Priming and Framing," eds., George A. Barnett and Franklin J. Boster, vol. 13 of *Progress in Communication Sciences: Advances in Persuasion* (Greenwich, CT: Ablex Publishing, 1997), 182–183.
5 Frank R. Baumgartner, Suzanna Linn, and Amber E. Boydstun, "The Decline of the Death Penalty: How Media Framing Changed Capital Punishment in America," in *Winning with Words: The Origins & Impact of Political Framing*, eds. Brian F. Schaffner and Patrick J. Sellers (New York: Routledge, 2010), 159–184.
6 Nicholas J. G. Winter, *Dangerous Frames: How Ideas About Race & Gender Shape Public Opinion* (Chicago, IL: University of Chicago Press, 2008), 146.
7 George Lakoff, *The Political Mind: Why You Can't Understand 21st Century American Politics with an 18th Century Brain* (New York: Viking Publishers, 2008), 24.
8 Ibid., 27.
9 Ibid., 35.
10 Drew Westen, *The Political Brain: The Role of Emotion in Deciding the Fate of the Nation* (New York: Public Affairs, 2007), 3.
11 Ibid., 12.
12 Beth Waggenspack, "Deceptive Narratives in the 2008 Presidential Campaign," in *Studies of Identity in the 2008 Presidential Campaign*, ed. Robert E. Denton, Jr. (Lanham, MD: Lexington Books, 2010), 161.

13 Westen, *The Political Brain*, 264.
14 Dennis Chong and James N. Druckman, "Identifying Frames in Political News," in *Sourcebook for Political Communication Research: Methods, Measures, and Analytical Techniques,* eds. Erik P. Bucy and R. Lance Holbert (New York: Routledge, 2010), 238–267.
15 James N. Druckman, "Competing Frames in a Political Campaign," in *Winning with Words: The Origins & Impact of Political Framing,* eds. Brian F. Schaffner and Patrick J. Sellers (New York: Routledge, 2010), 101–120.
16 Ibid., 103; Vincent Price and David Tewskbury, "News Values and Public Opinion: A Theoretical Account of Media Priming and Framing," in *Progress in Communication Sciences: Advances in Persuasion,* vol. 13, eds. George A. Barnett and Franklin J. Boster (Greenwich, CT: Ablex Publishing Corporation, 1997), 173–212.
17 See Druckman 2010, 103 for this and similar examples.
18 Ibid., 114.
19 Kimberle Crenshaw, "Whose Story Is It, Anyway? Feminist and Anti–Racist Appropriations of Anita Hill," in *Race-ing Justice, En-Gendering Power: Essays on Anita Hill, Clarence Thomas, and the Construction of Social Reality,* ed. Toni Morrison (New York: Pantheon, 1992), 402–420.
20 Winter, *Dangerous Frames*, 46.
21 Ibid., 23.
22 Brian F. Schaffner and Patrick J. Sellers, eds., *Winning with Words: The Origins & Impact of Political Framing* (New York: Routledge, 2010), 3–4.
23 Winter, *Dangerous Frames*, 171.
24 Jeffrey P. Jones, *Entertaining Politics: Satiric Television and Political Engagement*, 2nd edition (Lanham, MD: Rowman & Littlefield, 2010).
25 Liesbet van Zoonen, *Entertaining the Citizen: When Politics and Popular Culture Converge* (Lanham, MD: Rowman & Littlefield, 2005), 3.
26 Ibid., 145.
27 Ibid.
28 Jones, *Entertaining Politics*, 23–24.
29 Ibid., 211.
30 For examples of how audience members make use of television narratives, see Michael X. Delli Carpini and Bruce A. Williams, "Constructing Public Opinion: The Uses of Fictional and Nonfictional Television in Conversations about the Environment," in *The Psychology of Political Communication,* ed. Ann N. Crigler (Ann Arbor: University of Michigan Press, 1996); and Andrea L. Press and Elizabeth R. Cole, *Speaking of Abortion: Television and Authority in the Lives of Women* (Chicago, IL: University of Chicago Press, 1999).
31 Jones, *Entertaining Politics*, 17.
32 Stephen J. Wayne, *The Road to the White House 2004: The Politics of Presidential Elections* (Belmont, CA: Wadsworth/Thomson Learning, 2004), 65–66.
33 Ibid., 93.
34 Paul R. Abramson, John H. Aldrich, and David W. Rohde, *Change and Continuity in the 2008 Elections* (Washington, DC: CQ Press, 2010), 116–141.
35 Ibid., 10–13.
36 For fuller reviews of 2008 election context and influences see, for example, Kathleen Hall Jamieson, ed., *Electing the President 2008* (Philadelphia: University of Pennsylvania Press, 2009); Janet Box Steffensmeier and Steven E. Schier, eds., *The American Elections of 2008* (Lanham, MD: Rowman and Littlefield, 2009); Paul R. Abramson, John H. Aldrich, and David W. Rohde, *Change and Continuity in the 2008 Elections* (Washington, DC: CQ Press, 2010); Stephen J. Wayne, *The Road to the White House 2008*, 8th edition (Belmont, CA: Wadsworth/Thomson Learning, 2008).

37 Virginia Sapiro, "If U.S. Senator Baker Were a Woman: An Experimental Study of Candidate Images," *Political Psychology* 2 (1982): 61–83; Monika McDermott, "Voting Cues in Low Information Elections: Candidate Gender as a Social Information Variable in Contemporary United States Elections," *American Journal of Political Science* 41 (1997): 270–283; Kathleen Dolan, "The Impact of Candidate Sex on Evaluations of Candidates for the U.S. House of Representatives," *Social Science Quarterly* 85 (2004): 206–217; Kira Sanbonmatsu and Kathleen Dolan, "Do Gender Stereotypes Transcend Party?" *Political Research Quarterly* 62 (2009): 485–494.

38 Classic studies of gender trait stereotyping are: Sandra Bem, "The Measurement of Psychological Androgyny," *Journal of Clinical and Consulting Psychology* 42 (1974): 155–162; Inge Broverman et al. "Sex-Role Stereotypes: A Current Appraisal," *Journal of Social Issues* 28 (1972): 59–78. These are replicated and reconfirmed by Deborah Prentice and Erica Carranza, "What Women and Men Should Be, Shouldn't Be, Are Allowed to Be, and Don't Have to Be: The Contents of Prescriptive Gender Stereotypes," *Psychology of Women Quarterly* 26 (2002): 269–281; and Susan Rachael Seem and M. Diane Clark, "Healthy Women, Healthy Men, and Healthy Adults: An Evaluation of Gender Role Stereotypes in the Twenty-first Century," *Sex Roles* 55 (2006): 247–258.

39 Prentice and Carranza, "What Women"; Seem and Clark, "Healthy Women".

40 Seem and Clark, "Healthy Women".

41 Ibid.

42 Prentice and Carranza, "What Women," 275.

43 Seem and Clark, "Healthy Women," 255.

44 Prentice and Carranza, "What Women," 275.

45 Kim Fridkin and Patrick Kenney, "The Role of Gender Stereotypes in U.S. Senate Campaigns," *Politics & Gender* 5 (2009): 301–324; Barbara Burrell, *A Woman's Place is in the House: Campaigning for Congress in the Feminist Era* (Ann Arbor: The University of Michigan Press, 1994); Leonie Huddy and Nayda Terkildsen, "Gender Stereotypes and the Perception of Male and Female Candidates," *American Journal of Political Science* 37 (1993): 99–147; Barbara Lee Family Foundation, *Positioning Women to Win* (Brookline, MA: Barbara Lee Family Foundation, 2007).

46 Shirley Rosenwasser and Norma Dean, "Gender Role and Political Office," *Psychology of Women Quarterly* 13 (1989): 77–85; Jennifer Lawless, "Women, War and Winning Elections: Gender Stereotyping in the Post-September 11 Era," *Political Research Quarterly* 57 (2004): 479–490.

47 Lawless, "Women, War;" Jessi L. Smith, David Paul, and Rachel Paul, "No Place for a Woman: Evidence for Gender Bias in Evaluations of Presidential Candidates," *Basic and Applied Social Psychology* 29 (2007): 225–233; Shirley M. Rosenwasser and Jana Seale, "Attitudes toward a Hypothetical Male or Female Presidential Candidate: A Research Note," *Political Psychology* 9 (1988): 591–598.

48 See description of the New Hampshire conversation and its aftermath in Anne E. Kornblut, *Notes from the Cracked Ceiling: Hillary Clinton, Sarah Palin, and What it Will Take for a Woman to Win* (New York: Crown Publishing, 2009), 58–62; Rebecca Traister, *Big Girls Don't Cry* (New York: Free Press, 2010), 93–106.

49 Barbara Burrell, *Public Opinion, the First Ladyship and Hillary Rodham Clinton* (New York: Routledge, 2001).

50 Judith Warner, "Emotion without Thought in New Hampshire," *New York Times* Opinionator Blog (January 10, 2008), http://opinionator.blogs.nytimes.com/2008/01/10/emotion-without-thought-in-new-hampshire/.

51 Traister, *Big Girls*, 102; Maureen Dowd, "Can Hillary Cry Her Way Back to the White House?" *New York Times* (January 9, 2008), http://www.nytimes.com/2008/01/09/opinion/08dowd.html?pagewanted=all.

52 Traister, *Big Girls*.

53 Huddy and Terkildsen, *Gender Stereotypes*; Paul S. Herrnson, Celeste Lay, and Atiya Stokes, "Women Running 'As Women': Candidate Gender, Campaign Issues, and Voter Targeting Strategies," *Journal of Politics* 65 (2003): 244–255; Fridkin and Kenney, "The Role of Gender."

54 Sue Thomas, *How Women Legislate* (New York: Oxford University Press, 1994); Michele Swers, *The Difference Women Make: The Policy Impact of Women in Congress* (Chicago, IL: University of Chicago Press, 2002).

55 Mark S. Leeper, "The Impact of Prejudice on Female Candidates: An Experimental Look at Voter Inference," *American Politics Quarterly* 19 (1991): 248–261; Carol M. Mueller, "Nurturance and Mastery: Competing Qualifications for Women's Access to High Public Office?" in *Women and Politics: Activism, Attitudes, and Office-Holding*, eds. Gwen Moore and Glenna D. Spitze (Greenwich, CT: JAI Press, 1986); Rosenwasser and Seale, "Attitudes Towards;" Burrell, *Public Opinion*; McDermott, "Voting Cues in Low."

56 Lawless, "Women, War."

57 Barbara Lee Family Foundation, *Cracking the Code: Political Intelligence for Women Running for Governor* (Brookline, MA: Barbara Lee Family Foundation, 2004).

58. Kim Fridkin Kahn, *The Political Consequences of Being a Woman: How Stereotypes Influence the Conduct and Consequences of Political Campaigns* (New York: Columbia University Press, 1996).

59 Lesa Major Hartley and Renita Coleman, "The Intersection of Race and Gender in Election Coverage: What Happens When the Candidates Don't Fit the Stereotypes?" *The Howard Journal of Communications* 19 (2008): 315–333.

60 Kathleen Dolan, "Do Women Candidates Play to Gender Stereotypes? Do Men Candidates Play to Women? Candidate Sex and Issues Priorities on Campaign Websites," *Political Research Quarterly* 58 (2005): 31–44.

61 Ibid., 41.

62 Danny Hayes, "When Gender and Party Collide: Stereotyping in Candidate Trait Attribution," *Politics & Gender* 7 (2011): 133–165.

63 Ibid., 147–149.

64 Ibid.

65 Sanbonmatsu and Dolan, "Do Gender Stereotypes Transcend Party?".

66. Ibid.

67 Ibid.; David C. King and Richard E. Matland, "Sex and the Grand Old Party: An Experimental Investigation of the Effect of Candidate Sex on Support for a Republican Candidate," *American Politics Research* 31 (2003): 595–612.

68 Lynda Lee Kaid, Sandra L. Myers, Val Pipps, and Jan Hunter, "Sex Role Perceptions and Televised Political Advertising: Comparing Male and Female Candidates," *Women & Politics* 4, no. 4 (1984): 41–53.

69 Eleanor Clift and Tom Brazaitis, *Madame President: Women Blazing the Leadership Trail* (New York: Routledge, 2003), 99–102.

70 Barbara Lee Family Foundation, *Cracking the Code*.

71 Ibid.

72 Hayes, "When Gender," 155–159.

73 Ibid., 158–159.

74 Kahn, *The Political Consequences*.

75 Ibid.

76 Erika Falk, *Women for President: Media Bias in Eight Campaigns* (Urbana: University of Illinois Press, 2008).

77 Diane J. Heith, "The Lipstick Watch: Media Coverage, Gender, and Presidential Campaigns," in *Anticipating Madam President*, eds. Robert P. Watson and Ann Gordon (Boulder, CO: Lynne Rienner, 2003), 123–130; Falk, *Women for President*; Linda

Witt, Karen M. Paget, and Glenna Matthews, *Running as a Woman: Gender and Power in American Politics* (New York: Free Press, 1994).

78 Clift and Brazaitis, *Madame President*.

79 Susan J. Carroll and Kelly Dittmar, "The 2008 Candidacies of Hillary Clinton and Sarah Palin: Cracking the Highest, Hardest Glass Ceiling," in *Gender and Elections: Shaping the Future of American Politics*, eds. Susan J. Carroll and Richard L. Fox (New York: Cambridge University Press, 2010), 46.

80 Clift and Brazaitis, *Madame President*.

81 Falk, *Women for President*.

82 Ibid., 72; Clift and Brazaitis, *Madame President*, 99–102.

83 Falk, *Women for President*, 125–126.

84 Frank Newport, "Americans Today Much More Accepting of a Woman, Black, Catholic, or Jew as President," *Gallup News Service*, March 29, 1999.

85 Newport, "Americans Today."

86 David Paul and Jessi L. Smith, "Subtle Sexism: Examining Vote Preferences When Women Run Against Men for the Presidency," *Journal of Women, Politics & Policy* 29, no. 4 (2008), 452.

87 Ibid.

88. Ibid.

89 Ibid., 459–461.

90 Ibid., 467.

91 Jennifer Harper, "'Gender Bias' Did in Clinton?" *Washington Times* (June 6, 2008).

92 Michelle Goldberg, "3 a.m. for Feminism," *New Republic* (June 6, 2008).

93 Jodi Kantor, "Gender Issue Lives On as Clinton's Bid Wanes," *New York Times* (May 19, 2008).

94 Ibid.

95 Ibid.

96 Copeland, Libby. "Shooting from the hip, with a smile to boot." *The Washington Post*, October 1, 2008, http://www.washingtonpost.com/wpsrv/artsandliving/style/features/2008/rhetoric/gallery.html (accessed March 9, 2012).

Chapter 2

1 Jen Murphy, "Gov. Sarah Palin: Midnight Runs and Caribou Dinners," *Wall Street Journal* (September 22, 2008), under "Politics, Election 2008" http://online.wsj.com/article/SB122002155637283431.html?KEYWORDS=%22midnight+runs+and+caribou+dinners%22 (accessed March 9, 2012).

2 Julia Baird, "From Seneca Falls to … Sarah Palin?" *Newsweek*, September 12, 2008, under "U.S. Politics" http://www.thedailybeast.com/newsweek/2008/09/12/from-seneca-falls-to-sarah-palin.html (accessed March 9, 2012).

3 Libby Copeland, "Shooting from the Hip, With a Smile to Boot," *The Washington Post*, October 1, 2008, under "Arts and Living," http://www.washingtonpost.com/wpsrv/artsandliving/style/features/2008/rhetoric/gallery.html (accessed March 9, 2012).

4 Fred Barnes, "The Most Popular Governor: Alaska's Sarah Palin is the GOP's Newest Star," *Weekly Standard*, July 16, 2007, http://www.weeklystandard.com/Content/Public/Articles/000/000/013/851orcjq.asp (accessed March 17, 2009).

5 Ibid.

6 Kathleen Parker, "Palin Problem: She's out of Her League," *National Review*, September 26, 2008, http://www.nationalreview.com/articles/225784/palin-problem/kathleen-parker (accessed September 29, 2008).

7 William Yardley, "Sarah Heath Palin, an Outsider with Charms," *New York Times* (August 29, 2008).

8 "Anna Wintour Takes Hillary Clinton to Task," first posted to *Huffington Post* from Women's Wear Daily (WWD) (March 28, 2008), under "2008, Anna Wintour," http://www.huffingtonpost.com/2008/01/18/anna-wintour-takes-hillar_n_82132. html (accessed April 1, 2012).

9 Evan Cornog, *The Power and the Story: How the Crafted Presidential Narrative Has Determined Political Success from George Washington to George W. Bush* (New York: Penguin, 2004), 50.

10 Frederick Jackson Turner, "The Significance of the Frontier in American History," in *Frederick Jackson Turner: Wisconsin's Historian of the Frontier*, ed. Martin Ridge (Madison: State Historical Society of Wisconsin, 1986), 1–19.

11 Turner, 1–19.

12 Ibid., 18.

13 Ibid.

14 Cornog, *The Power and the Story*, 19.

15 Karrin Vasby Anderson, "Framing Gender: Pioneers, Beauty Queens, and Unruly Women," *Communication Currents*, special edition publication of the National Communication Association (October 2008), under "Communication Currents" http://www.natcom.org/CommCurrentsArticle.aspx?id=1083 (accessed March 18, 2012).

16 Laura Browder, "Guest Blogger Laura Browder: Sarah Palin: A 'Pioneer Mother' in Hockey Mom's Clothes?" *The University of North Carolina Press* blog (October 15, 2008), under "Laura Browder" http://uncpressblog.com/2008/10/15/guest-blogger-laura-browder-sarah-palin/(accessed April 3, 2012).

17 Ibid.

18 Sarah Palin, "Vice-Presidential Nomination Acceptance Speech" (speech, Republican National Convention, Saint Paul, Minnesota, September 3, 2008).

19 Gerald Seib, "Palin Pitches Sam's Club Tent," *Wall Street Journal* (September 3, 2008), under "Politics, Election 2008" http://online.wsj.com/article/SB122039959157792985. html?KEYWORDS=gerald+seib (accessed March 12, 2012).

20 Ibid.

21 David Farber, *The Rise and Fall of Modern Conservatism: A Short History* (Princeton, NJ: Princeton University Press, 2010).

22 Barry Goldwater, quoted in Bart Barnes, "Barry Goldwater, GOP Hero Dies," *The Washington Post* (May 30, 1998), "under Politics, 1998, Goldwater" http://www.washingtonpost.com/wp-srv/politics/daily/may98/goldwater30.htm (accessed April 1, 2012).

23 Barry Goldwater, "Presidential Nomination Acceptance Speech" (speech, 28th Republican National Convention, San Francisco, California, July 15, 1964).

24 Farber, *The Rise and Fall*, 5.

25 Ibid.

26 Ibid.

27 Michael E. Welsh, quoted by Richard W. Slatta, *The Cowboy Encyclopedia* (New York: W. W. Norton, 1994), 306.

28 See as examples: Harrold Hough, "John Kerry, Hunter?" *Enter Stage Right Online* (May 24, 2004), under "Archive, Articles, John Kerry" http://www.enterstageright. com/archive/articles/0504/0504kerryhunter.htm (accessed March 31, 2012); Michelle Malkin, "You Can't Fool a Sportsman," *Michelle Malkin.com* (October 21, 2004), http://michellemalkin.com/2004/10/21/you-cant-fool-a-sportsman/(accessed April 1, 2012); and "Cheney Pokes Fun at Kerry Hunting Trip," *Fox News* (October 22, 2004), under "2004, Cheney" http://www.foxnews.com/story/0,2933,136242,00. html (accessed April 1, 2012).

29 Copeland *"Shooting from the Hip,"* emphasis added.

30 Palin★tol★ogy, Cover of *Newsweek* (September 15, 2008).

31 Browder, "Sarah Palin: 'A Pioneer Mother.' "

32 Bernadette Barker-Plummer, "Reading Sarah Palin," *FlowTV* 8.10 (October 18, 2008), under "2008, October, Reading Sarah Palin" http://flowtv.org/2008/10/reading-sarah-palin-bernadette-barker-plummer-university-of-san-francisco/(accessed December 3, 2008).
33 Peggy Noonan, "A Servant's Heart," *Wall Street Journal* (September 6, 2008), under "Politics, Peggy Noonan" http://online.wsj.com/article/SB122059352189503479.html?KEYWORDS=Peggy+Noonan (accessed April 1, 2012).
34 Ibid.
35 Sara Hayden, "Negotiating Femininity and Power in the Early Twentieth Century West: Domestic Ideology and Feminine Style in Jeanette Rankin's Suffrage Rhetoric," *Communication Studies* 50, no. 2 (1999), 83–102.
36 Daniel Henninger, "What's So Special about Sarah?" *Wall Street Journal* (September 4, 2008), under "Politics, Daniel Henninger" http://online.wsj.com/article/SB122048635407597177.html?KEYWORDS=Daniel+Henninger (accessed April 1, 2012).
37 Ibid.
38 John Heileman, "The Sixty-Day War," *New York Magazine* (September 15, 2008), under "News, Politics" http://nymag.com/news/politics/49961/(accessed April 1, 2012).

Chapter 3

1 American National Election Study (ANES), *The ANES Guide to Public Opinion and Electoral Behavior* (2008), http://www.electionstudies.org/nesguide/toptable/tab5a_5.htm (accessed March 3, 2012).
2 Ibid.
3 Frank Capra, dir., *Mr. Smith Goes to Washington*, DVD (Culver City, CA: Columbia Pictures Corporation, 1939).
4 Ivan Reitman, dir., *Dave*, DVD (Burbank, CA: Warner Bros. Pictures, 1993).
5 John McCain, "McCain Announces Sarah Palin as His VP" (speech given at a rally in Dayton, OH, August 29, 2008), full transcript of speech at http://www.npr.org/templates/story/story.php?storyId=94116743 (accessed April 5, 2012).
6 Nicole Wallace, as quoted in Kathleen Hall Jamieson, ed., *Electing the President, 2008: The Insiders' View* (Philadelphia: University of Pennsylvania Press, 2009).
7 McCain, "McCain Announces."
8 Sarah Palin, "Vice-Presidential Nomination Acceptance Speech" (speech given at the Republican National Convention, in Saint Paul, MN, September 3, 2008).
9 Daniel Henninger, "What's so Special about Sarah?" *Wall Street Journal* (September 4, 3008), http://online.wsj.com/article/SB122048635407597177.html?KEYWORDS=Daniel+Henninger (accessed April 1, 2012).
10 *Saturday Night Live*, NBC, Palin skit (October 4, 2008).
11 "American Experience Episode: Reagan," PBS, under "Features, Reagan" http://www.pbs.org/wgbh/americanexperience/features/general-article/reagan-quotes/(accessed April 4, 2012).
12 Yuval Levin, "The Meaning of Sarah Palin," *Commentary Magazine* (February 2009): 19.
13 Libby Copeland, "Shooting From the Hip, With a Smile to Boot," *The Washington Post* (October 1, 2008), http://www.washingtonpost.com/wpsrv/artsandliving/style/features/2008/rhetoric/gallery.html (accessed March 9, 2012).
14 Levin, "The Meaning of Sarah Palin," 17.
15 Ibid.
16 Ann E. Kornblut, *Notes from the Cracked Ceiling: Hillary Clinton, Sarah Palin, and What It Will Take for a Woman to Win* (New York: Crown Publishing, 2009), 134.

17 Thomas E. Cronin and Michael A. Genovese, *The Paradoxes of the American Presidency*, 3rd edition (New York: Oxford University Press, 2010).
18 Elisabeth Bumiller and Michael Cooper, "Advisers Say Conservative Ire Pushed McCain Away From Picking Lieberman," *New York Times* (August 31, 2008).
19 Ibid.
20 Matthew Continetti, "Two-Front Republicans," *New York Times* (August 30, 2008).
21 Levin, "The Meaning of Sarah Palin," 19.
22 Palin, "Nomination Acceptance Speech."
23 Kim Severson, "The Spotlight Arrives, to Some Unease, in a State that Savors Its Isolation," *New York Times* (August 31, 2008).
24 Ibid.
25 Palin, "Nomination Acceptance Speech."
26 David Brooks, "What the Palin Pick Says," *New York Times* (September 2, 2008).
27 Kate Kenski, Bruce W. Hardy, and Kathleen Hall Jamieson, *The Obama Victory: How Media, Money, and Message Shaped the 2008 Election* (for Kindle) (New York: Oxford University Press, 2010), 202–203.
28 *Saturday Night Live.*
29 John Heileman and Mark Halperin, *Game Change: Obama and the Clintons, McCain and Palin, and the Race of a Lifetime* (New York: Harper Collins, 2010), 411.
30 Levin, "The Meaning of Sarah Palin," 17.
31 Ibid.
32 "Palin as Proud Redneck," Time/CNN's *The Page* (October 23, 2008) http://thepage.time.com/2008/10/23/palin-as-proud-redneck/(accessed April 5, 2012).
33 John Heileman, "The Sixty-Day War," *New York Magazine* (September 15, 2008), http://www.nymag.com/news/politics/49961 (accessed April 1, 2012).
34 Levin, "The Meaning of Sarah Palin," 18.
35 Ibid.
36 Mark Noll, *American Evangelical Christianity: An Introduction* (Malden, MA: Blackwell Publishers, 2001), 22.
37 Ibid.
38 Ibid.
39 Bruce Nesmith, *The New Republican Coalition: The Reagan Campaigns and White Evangelicals* (New York: Peter Lang, 1994).
40 Ibid., 23–24.
41 Daniel K. Williams, *God's Own Party: The Making of the Christian Right* (New York: Oxford University Press, 2010), 3.
42 Ibid., 5; Nancy T. Ammerman, "American Evangelicals in American Culture: Continuity and Change," in *Evangelicals and Democracy in America, volume I*, eds. Steven Brint and Jean Reith Schroedel (New York: Russell Sage Foundation, 2009), 62.
43 Ammerman, "American Evangelicals," 62.
44 Nesmith, *New Republican Coalition,* 110–111.
45 Williams, *God's Own Party,* 6–7.
46 Corwin Smidt, Kevin R. den Dulk, Bryan T. Froehle, James M. Penning, Stephen V. Monsma, and Douglas L. Koopman, *The Disappearing God Gap: Religion in the 2008 Presidential Election* (New York: Oxford University Press, 2010), 202.
47 Ibid., 200.
48 Ibid., 196.
49 Ibid.
50 Ibid.
51 Palin, "Nomination Acceptance Speech" (italics added).
52 Rick Warren, *The Purpose-Driven Life* (Grand Rapids, MI: Zondervan, 2002).
53 Charles Swindoll, *Improving Your Serve* (Nashville, TN: Thomas Nelson, 1981).

54 George W. Bush (State of the Union Speech delivered to Congress, Washington, DC, January 28, 2003), http://www.americanrhetoric.com/speeches/stateoftheunion2003. html (accessed April 5, 2012).
55 Michael Cooper and Elisabeth Bumiller, "Alaskan is McCain's Choice; First Woman on the G.O.P. Ticket," *New York Times* (August 30, 2008).
56 Adrienne Gaines, "Evangelical Voters Energized by McCain VP Pick," *Charisma* (September 2, 2008).
57 Ibid.
58 Sarah Pulliam Bailey, "McCain Picks Alaska Gov. Sarah Palin for VP," *Christianity Today* Politics Blog (August 29, 2008); Steven Ertelt, "More Pro-life Reaction to John McCain Picking Abortion Opponent Sarah Palin," *LifeNews.com* (August 29, 2008); J. Lee Grady, "Sarah Palin and the Deborah Anointing," *Fire in My Bones* blog (September 10, 2008).
59 Grady, "Sarah Palin and the Deborah Anointing."
60 Quoted in Sarah Posner, "Where She Was Saved," *Slate* (September 11, 2008), http://www.salon.com/2008/09/11/assemblies_of_god/ (accessed March 24, 2012).
61 Randi Kaye, "Pastor: GOP may be downplaying Palin's religious beliefs," *CNN Politics Online* (September 8, 2008), http://articles.cnn.com/2008-09-08/politics/palin. pastor_1_meghan-stapleton-wasilla-bible-church-sarah-palin?_s=PM:POLITICS (accessed March 25, 2012); Amy Sullivan, "Does Sarah Palin Have a Pentecostal Problem?" *Time* (October 9, 2008), http://www.time.com/time/politics/article/ 0,8599,1848420,00.html (accessed March 25, 2012).
62 Sullivan, "Does Sarah Palin Have a Pentecostal Problem?"
63 Ibid.
64 Dan Gilgoff, "God-o-Meter Q&A with Sarah Palin's Biographer" (interview with Kaylene Johnson), *Christianity Today* Politics blog (September 3, 2008).
65 Jeffrey Barholet and Karen Breslau, "An Apostle of Alaska," *Newsweek* (September 15, 2008).
66 Kirk Johnson and Kim Severson, "Bible is Palin's Professional Guide, Friends and Pastors Say," *New York Times* (September 7, 2008).
67 Kaylene Johnson, "America, Meet Sarah Palin," *CNN Politics.com* (September 3, 2008), http://www.cnn.com/2008/POLITICS/09/02/kaylene.johnson.palin/?iref= hpmostpop (accessed April 5, 2012).
68 Joe Hilley, *Sarah Palin: A New Kind of Leader* (with foreword by Charles Colson) (Grand Rapids, MI: Zondervan, October 2008).

Chapter 4

1 Jane Lawler Dye, "Fertility of American Women: 2008," U.S. Census Bureau (November 2010), http://www.census.gov/prod/2010pubs/p20-563.pdf.
2 Nathan Thornburgh, "The Education of Sarah Palin," *Time* (September 15, 2008): 24–30.
3 Ibid.
4 Lois Romano, "Gov. Mom; The Land of the Midnight Sun's Claim to Fame: Being Led by a 24-Hour Mother," *The Washington Post* (September 2, 2008).
5 Ibid.
6 Sarah Palin (speech given at the Republican National Convention, Dayton, OH, September 3, 2008).
7 Sarah Palin (speech given at the Republican National Convention, St. Paul, MN, September 3, 2008).
8 Linda Kerber, *Women of the Republic* (Chapel Hill: University of North Carolina Press, 1980).

9 Suzanne Lebsock, "Women and American Politics, 1880–1920," in *Women, Politics and Change*, eds. Louise A. Tilly and Patricia Gurin (New York: Russell Sage, 1992).
10 Edith P. Mayo, "Motherhood, Social Service, and Political Reform: Political Culture and Imagery of American Woman Suffrage," *National Women's History Museum*, http://www.nwhm.org/online-exhibits/votesforwomen/tour_02-02j.html.
11 Jane Addams, "Why Women Should Vote," *Modern History Sourcebook* (1915) http://www.fordham.edu/halsall/mod/1915janeadams-vote.html.
12 Mayo, "Motherhood."
13 Linda Gordon, "Putting Children First: Women, Maternalism and Welfare in the Early Twentieth Century," in *U.S. History as Women's History: New Feminist Essays*, eds. Linda K. Kerber, Alice Kessler-Harris, and Kathryn Kish Sklar (Chapel Hill: University of North Carolina Press, 1995).
14 Celia Morris, *Storming the Statehouse: Running for Governor with Ann Richards and Dianne Feinstein* (New York: Macmillan, 1992).
15 Clara Bingham, "The Women on the Hill," *Vogue* (August 1993): 266.
16 Ibid., 267.
17 Barbara Boxer and Nicole Boxer, *Strangers in the Senate: Politics and the New Revolution of Women in America* (Washington, DC: National Press Books, 1994), 70.
18 Nancy Pelosi, interview by Jim Lehrer, *News Hour with Jim Lehrer* (March 30, 2006). Interestingly, Pelosi's self-depiction here is a fierce maternalism, perhaps what she felt was most appropriate in the years just after the September 11, 2001 terrorist attacks. But with the line comparing herself to a lioness or mother bear, perhaps Pelosi deserves some credit for introducing the "Mama Grizzly" image into the American political lexicon. Ironically, her ideological antithesis, Sarah Palin, would be credited with the inventing the term in the 2010 elections.
19 Linda Witt, Karen M. Paget, and Glenna Matthews, *Running as a Woman: Gender and Power in American Politics* (New York: Free Press, 1994).
20 Nancy Felipe Russo, "The Motherhood Mandate," *Journal of Social Issues* 32, no. 3 (1976): 143–153.
21 Jane Maree Maher and Lise Saugeres, "To Be or Not to Be? Women Negotiating Cultural Representations of Mothering," *Journal of Sociology* 43, no. 1 (2007): 6.
22 Ibid.
23 "The Gender Gap: Voting Choices in Presidential Elections," Center for The American Woman and Politics (CAWP), Eagleton Institute for Politics, Rutgers University (2008) http://www.cawp.rutgers.edu/fast_facts/voters/documents/GGPresVote.pdf; Susan J. Carroll, "Voting Choices: The Politics of the Gender Gap," quoted in *Gender and Elections: Shaping the Future of American Politics*, 2nd edition, eds. Susan J. Carroll and Richard L. Fox (New York: Cambridge University Press, 2010), 125–128.
24 Carroll, "Voting Choices," 132.
25 Susan J. Carroll, "Security Moms and Presidential Politics," in *Voting the Gender Gap*, ed. Lois Duke Whitaker (Urbana: University of Illinois Press, 2008), 75–90.
26 Susan Page, "Married? Single? Status Affects How Women Vote," *USA Today* (August 25, 2004), http://www.usatoday.com/news/politicselections/nation/polls/2004-08-25-female-vote_x.htm.
27 Ibid.; Margie Omero, "The Marriage and Gender Gaps," *Huffington Post* (August 1, 2008), http://www.huffingtonpost.com/margie-omero/marriage_gender_gaps1_b_729194.html.
28 Page, "Married?"
29 Kathleen Hall Jamieson, *Beyond the Double Bind* (New York: Oxford University Press, 1995).
30 Vanessa Gerzai, "Where to Now? Women's Leadership Needs New Direction," *The Washington Post* (March 15, 2009), http://www.washingtonpost.com/wp-dyn/content/article/2009/03/06/AR2009030601712.html.

31 Witt, *Running as a Woman.*

32 Georgia Duerst-Lahti, "Presidential Elections: Gendered Space and the Case of 2008," in *Gender and Elections: Shaping the Future of American Politics*, 2nd edition, eds. Susan J. Carroll and Richard L. Fox (New York: Cambridge University Press, 2010), 11–37; Linda Beail and Rhonda S. Kinney, "Gender and the Study of the Presidency" (paper presented at the annual meeting of the American Political Science Association, San Francisco, CA, September 1996).

33 Wendy Atkins-Sayre, "Governor Mom: Jane Swift and the Body Politic," in *Gender and Political Communication in America: Rhetoric, Representation, and Display*, ed. Janis L. Edwards (Lanham, MD: Lexington Books, 2009), 129–148.

34 Jaime Loke, Dustin Harp, and Ingrid Bachmann, "Mothering and Governing," *Journalism Studies* 28 (2010).

35 Ibid.

36 Atkins-Sayre, "Governor Mom," 140.

37 Loke, "Mothering and Governing."

38 Leslie Sanchez, "Palin is a VP for the rest of us," CNN, September 4, 2008, http://articles.cnn.com/2008–09–04/politics/sanchez.palin_1_sarah-palin-life-choices-life-support?_s=PM:POLITICS.

39 Sam Harris, "When Atheists Attack," *Newsweek* (September 29, 2008), http://www.newsweek.com/id/160080.

40 Lindsey Palmer, "The Debut of the Hockey Mom," *Redbook* (October 2008).

41 Ibid.

42 Ibid.

43 Sarah Palin, *Going Rogue: An American Life* (New York: Harper, 2009), 51.

44 Adrienne Gaines, "Evangelical Voters Energized by McCain VP Pick," *Charisma* (September 2, 2008), http://www.charismamag.com/index.php/news-old/19520.

45 J. Lee Grady, "Sarah Palin and the Deborah Anointing," *Fire in My Bones* blog (September 10, 2008).

46 Rich Morin and Paul Taylor, "Revisiting the Mommy Wars: Politics, Gender and Parenthood," Pew Research Center (September 15, 2008), http://pewresearch.org/pubs/950/mommy-wars.

47 Donald Mathews and Jane Sharon DeHart, *Sex, Gender and the Politics of ERA* (New York: Oxford University Press, 1992); Jane Mansbridge, *Why We Lost the ERA* (Chicago, IL: University of Chicago Press, 1986).

48 Marilyn Quayle (speech given at the Republican National Convention, Houston, TX, August 19, 1988).

49 Maria Shriver and the Center for American Progress, *The Shriver Report: A Women's Nation Changes Everything*, eds. Heather Boushey and Ann O'Leary (2009).

50 Liza Mundy, "Women, Money and Power," *Time* (March 26, 2012), 28–34.

51 Kristin Luker, *Abortion and the Politics of Motherhood* (Berkeley: University of California Press, 1984); Rebecca Klatch, *Women of the New Right* (Philadelphia, PA: Temple University Press, 1987).

52 R. Albert Mohler Jr., "Palin Can Serve Family and Country," *The Washington Post* "On Faith" blog (September 5, 2008), http://newsweek.washingtonpost.com/onfaith/panelists/r_albert_mohler_jr/2008/09/a_tale_of_two_offices.html.

53 Ibid.

54 Karen Parrish, letter to the editor, *Charisma,* November 2008.

55 Anna Sofia and Elizabeth Botkin, "Q&A Regarding Our Position on Sarah Palin," *Visionary Daughters* website (October 19, 2008), http://visionarydaughters.com/category/female-magistrates.

56 Molly Worthen, "Housewives of God," *New York Times Magazine* (November 12, 2010).

57 Ibid.

58 Amanda Fortini, "The 'Bitch' and the 'Ditz': How the Year of the Woman Reinforced the Two Most Pernicious Sexist Stereotypes and Actually Set Women Back," *New York* (November 16, 2008), http://www.nymag.com/news/politics/nationalinterest/52184.

59 Sandra Sobieraj Westfall, "John McCain and Sarah Palin on Shattering the Glass Ceiling," *People* (August 29, 2008).

60 Julia Baird, "From Seneca Falls to Sarah Palin," *Newsweek* (September 22, 2008).

61 Ibid.

62 Ibid.

63 For example, Jodi Kantor and Rachel Swarns, "A New Twist in the Debate on Mothers," *New York Times* (September 2, 2008), A1; Ruth Marcus, "Palin Hits the Motherload," *The Washington Post* (September 10, 2008); Katherine Marsh, "Whine Not: The Working Mothers' Case against Sarah Palin," *The New Republic* (September 24, 2008); Michelle Cottle, "Shattered," *New Republic* (September 24, 2008); Anna Quindlen, "Can You Say Sexist?" *Newsweek* (September 15, 2008), http://www.newsweek.com/id/157543.

64 Gaines, "Evangelical Voters Energized by McCain VP Pick."

65 Andrew Malcom, "James Dobson, Barack Obama among Those Reacting to Pregnancy of Sarah Palin's Daughter," *Los Angeles Times* "Top of the Ticket" blog (September 1, 2008).

66 Ibid.

67 Hanna Rosin, "What Scarlet Letter?" *Slate* (September 4, 2008), http://www.slate.com/articles/double_x/xxfactor_xxtra/2008/09/what_scarlet_letter.html.

68 Ibid.

69 John Harris and Beth Frerking, "Clinton Aids: Palin Treatment Sexist," *Politico* (September 3, 2008), http://www.politico.com/news/stories/0908/13129.html.

70 Ibid.

71 Ibid.

72 Marsh, "Whine Not."

73 Cottle, "Shattered."

74 Kantor and Swarns, "A New Twist."

75 Emily Bazelon and Dahlia Lithwick, "Questions for a Superhuman Mom," *Slate* (September 2, 2008).

76 Ibid.

77 "Parsing Palin," *Slate* (September 4, 2008), http://www.slate.com/articles/news_and_politics/the_chat_room/2008/09/parsing_palin.single.html.

78 Nancy Gibbs, "Parent Trap: Sarah Palin's Complicated Life Story Speaks to the Agonizing Choices that Women Face," *Time* (September 15, 2008).

79 Ximena Tagle, "Mail Call and Corrections," *Newsweek* (September 22, 2008), http://www.thedailybeast.com/newsweek/2003/08/17/mail-call-and-corrections.html.

80 Karen Tumulty, "Maxed-Out Moms," *Time* (September 29, 2008): 42–44.

81 Rebecca Traister, "Palin, Pregnancy and the Presidency," *Salon* (September 1, 2008), http://www.salon.com/2008/09/01/palin_baby/.

82 E. J. Dionne Jr., "Clinton Swipes the GOP's Lyrics: The Democrat as Liberal Republican," *The Washington Post* (July 21, 1996): C1.

83 Susan J. Carroll and Richard Logan Fox, *Gender and Elections* (New York: Cambridge University Press, 2006), 93–94.

84 Jay Weiner, "She's Now a Household Phrase, but What Is a Hockey Mom?" *MinnPost* (September 5, 2008), http://www.minnpost.com/stories/2008/09/05/3407/shes_now_household_phrase_but_whats_a_hockey_mom.

85 Jacob Leibenluft, "Hockey Moms vs. Soccer Moms," *Slate* (September 4, 2008).

86 Tina Kelley, "Soccer Moms Welcome their Hockey-Loving Sisters to the Political Arena," *New York Times* (September 7, 2008).
87 Michelle Obama (speech given in Milwaukee, WI, February 18, 2008).
88 Evan Thomas, "Alienated in the U.S.A," *Daily Beast* (March 12, 2008) http://www.thedailybeast.com/newsweek/2008/03/12/alienated-in-the-u-s-a.html.

Chapter 5

1 Fred Barnes, "The Most Popular Governor: Alaska's Sarah Palin is the GOP's Newest Star," *Weekly Standard* (July 16, 2007).
2 Jim Carlton, "Profile of Alaska's Sarah Palin: Governor, Reformer, Mother," *Wall Street Journal* (September 24, 2008).
3 Quoted in Libby Copeland, "Shooting from the Hip, with a Smile to Boot," *The Washington Post* (October 1, 2008).
4 Troy Patterson, "The Sarah Palin Show," *Slate* (September 2, 2008).
5 Maureen Dowd, "Vice in Go-Go Boots?" *New York Times* (August 31, 2008).
6 Frank DeFord, *There She Is: The Life and Times of Miss America* (New York: Viking Press, 1971); Elwood Watson and Darcy Martin, "Introduction," in *"There She Is, Miss America:" The Politics of Sex, Beauty and Race*, ed. Elwood Watson and Darcy Martin (New York: Palgrave MacMillan, 2004), 1–23.
7 Watson and Martin, *"There She Is."*
8 Deborah Siegel, *Sisterhood Interrupted* (New York: Palgrave MacMillan, 2007), 47–48.
9 Ruth Rosen, *The World Split Open* (New York: Penguin, 2006), 159–160.
10 Ibid.
11 Christine R. Yano, *Crowning the Nice Girl: Gender, Ethnicity, and Culture in Hawaii's Cherry Blossom Festival* (Honolulu: University of Hawaii Press, 2006), 14.
12 Sarah Banet-Weiser, *The Most Beautiful Girl in the World: Beauty Pageants and National Identity* (Berkeley: University of California Press, 1999); Watson and Martin, *"There She Is,"* 11–16.
13 Watson and Martin, *"There She Is"* 14–16.
14 Yano, *Crowning the Nice Girl*, 16.
15 The class-based appeal of beauty pageants can be seen as reaching even deeper into the working class/lower middle class in the twenty-first century. See, for example, the popularity of The Learning Channel's reality-based television show *Toddlers and Tiaras*, which profiles little girls (typically ages three to eight) who compete in regional beauty contests. The contestants and their mothers are almost always from non-wealthy, working-class backgrounds and often state quite explicitly that the cash prizes in these pageants are a primary motivation for entering them. The transformation of these "toddlers" into hyper-sexualized, elaborately coiffed, and made-up beauty queens is both fascinating and disturbing, which is surely part of the show's appeal. The transformation of these ordinary little girls into pageant contestants clearly demonstrates the norms of ultimate femininity, and how that femininity can be carefully contrived and performed. However, the contrast between their everyday realities and the glitz of their pageant gowns, makeup, and manners also highlights the class aspirations inherent in these pageants. They are a way of physically transcending the gulf between the "Wal-Mart aesthetic" of their lives (small, plain, rural homes; older cars; the nondescript jeans and sweatshirts worn by the mothers; even the low-budget chain hotel meeting rooms the pageants are held in) and the glamorous celebrity aesthetic of the oversize crowns studded with sparkling crystals, the taffeta and sequined gowns, and exaggerated paparazzi-ready smiles.

16 Mary Anne Schofield, "Miss America, Rosie the Riveter, and World War II," in *"There She Is, Miss America:" The Politics of Sex, Beauty and Race*, ed. Elwood Watson and Darcy Martin (New York: Palgrave MacMillan, 2004), 53–66; 59.
17 Schofield, "Miss America," 60–61.
18 Bill Tancer, "Searching for Sarah Palin's 'Hot Photos,'" *Time* (September 2, 2008).
19 Ibid.
20 Charlotte Hilton Andersen, "McCain Plays the MILF Card—Will It Work?" *The Huffington Post* (September 29, 2008) http://www.huffingtonpost.com/charlotte-hilton-andersen/mccain-plays-the-milf-car_b_130288.html.
21 Ann Hulbert, Rachael Larimore, and Emily Yoffe, "Parsing Palin: XX Factor Bloggers Take Readers' Questions about the Republican Vice-Presidential Nominee and Her Speech" (transcript posted September 4, 2008), http://www.slate.com/articles/news_and_politics/the_chat_room/2008/09/parsing_palin.html.
22 David Plotz, "I Dream About Sarah Palin. Do You?" *Slate* (September 9, 2008).
23 Abby Callard and David Plotz, "Your Dreams (and Nightmares) About Sarah Palin," *Slate* (September 12, 2008).
24 Evan Thomas and Karen Beslau, "McCain's Mrs. Right: Gov. Sarah Palin Came Out of Nowhere to Win the John McCain Veep Sweepstakes. Well, Not Quite Nowhere," *Newsweek* (September 8, 2008), 24.
25 Ibid.
26 Ibid. (italics added).
27 Joshua Alston, "Why Obama Needs a Tina Fey," *Newsweek* (November 3, 2008), 68.
28 Bruce Horowitz, "Palin Has Created Quite a Stir," *USA Today* (September 3, 2008); Gigi Stone, "Palin's Spec-tacular Fashion Statement," *Good Morning America* (September 7, 2008).
29 Ibid.
30 Ellen Byron, Jennifer Saranow, and Rachel Dodes, "Palin's Style Sparks a Buying Frenzy, and Fashion Firms Rush to Cash In," *Wall Street Journal* (September 12, 2008).
31 Ibid.
32 Ibid.
33 Ibid.
34 Linda Witt, Karen M. Paget, and Glenna Matthews, *Running as a Woman: Gender and Power in American Politics* (New York: Free Press, 1994), 56.
35 Ibid., 59.
36 Quoted in Witt, Paget, and Matthews, *Running as a Woman*, 59–60.
37 Sean Aday and James Devitt, "Style over Substance: Newspaper Coverage of Elizabeth Dole's Presidential Bid," *International Journal of Press/Politics* 6, no. 2 (2001): 52–73.
38 Karrin Vasby Anderson and Kristina Horn Sheeler, *Governing Codes: Gender, Metaphor and Political Identity* (New York: Lexington Books, 2005).
39 Copeland, "Shooting from the Hip."
40 Ibid.
41 Ibid.
42 Kim Severson, "The Spotlight Arrives, to Some Unease, in a State that Savors Its Isolation," *New York Times* (August 31, 2008).
43 cfarnham, "U.S. Public Stupified by Palin's 'Sexy Librarian' Look" (September 9, 2008) http://www.zimbio.com/2008+Presidential+Candidates/articles/11586/Public+Stupified+Palin+Sexy+Librarian+look.
44 Thomas and Beslau, "McCain's Mrs. Right."
45 Donny Deutch, "The Big Idea," CNBC (September 4, 2008).
46 Tom Perrotta, "The Sexy Puritan," *Slate* (September 26, 2008), http://www.slate.com/id/2200814/.
47 Kathleen Parker, "Palin Problem," *National Review Online* (September 26, 2008).

48 Ibid.

49 Dahlia Lithwick, "The Downsides of Diversity," *Slate* (September 27, 2008).

50 Ibid.

51 Katie Baker, "Cracking the Highest Glass Ceiling," *Newsweek* (October 6, 2008), 7.

52 Hero Builders website, http://www.herobuilders.com/08.htm.

53 Jeanne Cumming, "RNC Shells Out $150K for Palin Fashion," *Politico* (October 21, 2008), http://www.politico.com/news/stories/1008/14805.html.

54 Ryan Tate, "Sarah Palin's $150,000 Fashion Spree," *Gawker* (October 21, 2008), http://gawker.com/5066894/sarah-palins-150000-fashion-spree; Sarah Hepola, "Sarah Palin, $150,000 Fashionista," *Salon* (October 22, 2008), http://www.salon.com/2008/10/22/palin_wardrobe/; "Who Requested Sarah Palin's $150,000 Makeover?" *Day to Day* (October 23, 2008), http://www.npr.org/templates/story/story.php?storyId=96032122; Stephen M. Silverman, "Republicans Spent $150,000 on Sarah Palin's Wardrobe," *People* (October 22, 2008), http://www.people.com/people/article/0,,20234976,00.html.

55 Todd J. Gillman, "Letterman's Top 10 List: Sarah Palin and Her $150,000 Wardrobe," *Dallas Morning News* (October 27, 2008), http://trailblazersblog.dallasnews.com/archives/2008/10/lettermans-top-10-list-sarah-p.html.

56 "Campbell Brown," CNN (October 22, 2008).

57 Tahman Bradley, "Campbell Brown: Stop Covering Palin's Wardrobe Controversy; Women Are Unfairly Held to Higher Standard on Appearance," ABC News *Political Punch* website (October 23, 2008), http://abcnews.go.com/blogs/politics/2008/10/campbell-brown/.

58 Kate Betts, "Sarah Palin's $150,000 Crime against Fashion," *Time* (October 23, 2008), http://www.time.com/time/politics/article/0,8599,1853529,00.html.

59 Robin Givhan, "After a $150,000 Makeover, Sarah Palin has an Image Problem," *The Washington Post* (October 23, 2008).

60 Robin Abcarian and Kate Linthicum, "A Political Fashion Do or Don't?" *Los Angeles Times* (October 23, 2008).

61 *The View*, ABC (October 22, 2008).

62 Betts, "Crime against Fashion."

63 Givhan, "Image Problem."

64 Michael Isikoff and Suzanne Smalley, "Not the Change They Wanted," *Newsweek* (November 3, 2008), 8.

65 Ibid.

66 *Saturday Night Live: Primetime Election Special*, NBC (aired October 23, 2008).

67 Kate Snow and Imtiyaz Delawala, "Palin a Diva: Ruffled Feathers in McCain Camp," ABC News *Political Radar* blog (October 25, 2008), http://blogs.abcnews.com/politicalradar/2008/10/palin-a-diva-ru.html; Dana Bash, Peter Hamby, and John King, "Palin's 'Going Rogue,' McCain Aide Says," *CNN Politics* (October 25, 2008), http://articles.cnn.com/2008-10-25/politics/palin.tension.

68 Snow and Delawala, "Palin a Diva"; Bash, Hamby, and King, "Palin's 'Going Rogue.'"

69 *Saturday Night Live*, NBC (aired November 1, 2008).

70 Ibid.

Chapter 6

1 Sarah Palin (speech given at the Vice-Presidential Announcement Convention, Dayton, OH, August 29, 2008), transcript available at http://www.npr.org/templates/story/story.php?storyId=94118910.

2 Katie Couric interview with Sarah Palin, CBS News, (aired September 30, 2008).

3 Susanna Schrobsdorff, "Sister, Sister: What Some of America's Smartest, Most Successful Women Have to Say about Sarah Palin, Hillary Clinton and the Meaning of the Word 'Feminist' in 2008," *Newsweek* (October 9, 2008), http://www.newsweek.com/id/163219.

4 Michelle Cottle, "Shattered," *New Republic* (September 24, 2008).

5 Anna Quindlen, "Can You Say Sexist?" *Newsweek* (September 15, 2008), http://www.newsweek.com/id/157543.

6 Amanda Fortini, "The 'Bitch' and the 'Ditz': How the Year of the Woman Reinforced the Two Most Pernicious Sexist Stereotypes and Actually Set Women Back," *New York* (November 16, 2008), http://www.nymag.com/news/politics/nationalinterest/52184; *US Weekly* cover (September 3, 2008); *People* cover (September 22, 2008).

7 Katha Pollitt, "Lipstick on a Wing Nut," *Nation* (September 29, 2008).

8 Rory Dicker, *Catching a Wave: Reclaiming Feminism for the 21st Century* (Boston, MA: Northeastern University Press, 2003), 10.

9 Rebecca Walker, *To Be Real: Telling the Truth and Changing the Face of Feminism* (New York: Anchor Books, 1995), xxxiv.

10 Gina Dent, "Missionary Position," in *To Be Real: Telling the Truth and Changing the Face of Feminism*, ed. Rebecca Walker (New York: Anchor Books, 1995), 61–75.

11 Ibid., 74.

12 Barbara Findlen, *Listen Up: Voices from the Next Feminist Generation* (Emeryville, CA: Seal Press, 2001); Rebecca Walker, *To Be Real*.

13 Dicker, *Catching a Wave*, 12.

14 Rosalind Gill, *Gender and the Media* (Cambridge, UK: Polity, 2007).

15 Ibid.

16 Jennifer Baumgardner and Amy Richards, *Manifesta: Young Women, Feminism, and the Future* (New York: Farrar, Straus, and Giroux, 2000), 136.

17 Ibid., 137.

18 Ibid., 141.

19 Ibid., 163.

20 Gill, *Gender and the Media*, 269.

21 Kathleen Deveny, "Confessions of a Secret Sarah Admirer," *Newsweek* (September 15, 2008).

22 Robin Abcarian, "Insiders See 'New Feminism,'" *Los Angeles Times* (September 4, 2008); "Sarah Palin: New Face of Feminism?" *All Things Considered*, National Public Radio (September 7, 2008), transcript available at http://www.npr.org/templates/transcript/transcript.php?storyId=94369835.

23 Tammy Bruce, "A Feminist's Argument for McCain's VP," *San Francisco Chronicle* (September 7, 2008), http://www.realclearpolitics.com/articles/2008/09/a_feminists_argument_for_mccai.html.

24 Ibid.

25. Kate Kaye, *Campaign '08: A Turning Point for Digital Media* (Create Space, 2009).

26 Ibid.

27 Ibid.

28 Barbara Lippert, "Analysis: Feminism's Next Wave," *Adweek* (September 8, 2008), http://www.adweek.com/news/advertising-branding/analysis-feminisms-next-wave-96940.

29 Kate Barrett, "Palin's Switcheroo on Feminism," *ABC News* blog (October 24, 2008), http://www.abcnews.go.com/blogs/politics/2008/10/palins-switcher.

30 Karin Agness, "Sarah Palin: A Liberated Woman," *TownHall.com* (September 7, 2008), http://townhall.com/columnists/karinagness/2008/09/07/sarah_palin_a_liberated_woman/page/full/.

31 Ibid.

32 Ibid.

33 Elaine Lafferty, "Sarah Palin's a Brainiac," *Daily Beast* (October 27, 2008).
34 Ibid.
35 Ibid.
36 Angela McRobbie, *The Aftermath of Feminism: Gender, Culture and Social Change* (Thousand Oaks, CA: Sage, 2009), 1–8.
37 Ibid; Rosalind Gill and Christina Scharff, *New Femininities: Postfeminism, Neoliberalism and Subjectivity* (New York: Palgrave Macmillan, 2011).
38 Shelley Budgeon, "The Contradictions of Successful Femininity: Third–Wave Feminism, Postfeminism and 'New' Femininities" in *New Femininities: Postfeminism, Neoliberalism and Subjectivity*, ed. Rosalind Gill and Christina Scharff (New York: Palgrave Macmillan, 2011), 281.
39 Gill, *Gender and the Media*, 255.
40 Ibid., 258.
41 See original 1918 photo online at http://old-photos.blogspot.com/2010/02/white-house-protest.html; see 2008 version available at http://www.mindsay.com/comments/ubu13/mr_mccain_americas_women_have_not_waited_232_years_for_sarah_palin.mws.
42 Harris & Ewing, 1917 photograph from "The Women of Protest" collection, photographs of the National Women's Party, Library of Congress, available at http://memory.loc.gov/ammem/collections/suffrage/nwp/.
43 Sarah Seltzer, "A Feminist Appalled by Palin," *Huffington Post* (August 29, 2008), http://www.huffingtonpost.com/sarah-seltzer/a-feminist-appalled-by-pa_b_122489.html.
44 Megan Carpentier, "Sarah Palin: When Choosing a Woman Might Not Be Choosing for Women," *Jezebel* (September 29, 2008), http://jezebel.com/5043669/sarah-palin-when-choosing-a-woman-might-not-be-choosing-for-women.
45 Ibid.
46 Gloria Steinem, "Wrong Woman, Wrong Message," *New York Times* (September 4, 2008).
47 Ibid.
48 Ibid.
49 Eve Ensler, "Drill, Drill, Drill," *Huffington Post* (September 8, 2008).
50 Cintra Wilson, "Pissed About Palin," *Salon.com* (September 10, 2008).
51 Ibid.
52 Beverly Davis, "Palin Pregnancy: Mother Daughter Interrupted," *Huffington Post* (September 2, 2008).
53 Joan Williams, "Is Sarah Palin Working Mother of the Year?" *Huffington Post* (September 5, 2008).
54 Lippert, "Analysis: Feminism's Next Wave."
55 Abcarian, "Insiders See 'New Feminism.'"
56 "Marie Wilson on Palin, Women's Progress In Politics," News and Notes, National Public Radio (September 4, 2008), transcript available at http://www.wbur.org/npr/94276947/marie-wilson-on-palin-womens-progress-in-politics.
57 Rebecca Traister, "Zombie Feminists of the RNC," *Salon.com* (September 11, 2008), http://www.salon.com/2008/09/11/zombie_feminism.
58 Julia Hoppock, "Women against Sarah Palin Speak Out," *ABC News* Political Radar blog (September 11, 2008), http://abcnews.go.com/blogs/politics/2008/09/women-against-s/.
59 Marcia G. Yerman, "Women Respond to Palin: Part One," *Huffington Post* (September 15, 2008).
60 Ibid.
61 John Heileman, "The Sixty-Day War," *New York* (September 5, 2008), http://www.nymag.com/news/politics/49961.

62 John F. Harris and Beth Frerking, "Clinton Aides: Palin Treatment Sexist," *Politico* (September 3, 2008).

63 Anna Quindlen, "Can You Say 'Sexist'?" *Newsweek* (September 15, 2008).

64 Abcarian, "Insiders See 'New Feminism.'"

65 Quindlen, "Can You Say 'Sexist'?"

66 See photo at http://blog.news-record.com/staff/jrblog/2008/10/_supporters_wat. shtml.

67 Nico Pitney, "Palin Misquotes Albright: Place in Hell Reserved for Women Who Don't Support Other Women," *Huffington Post* (October 5, 2008), http://www. huffingtonpost.com/2008/10/05/palin-misquotes-albright_n_131967.html.

68 Kathleen Parker, "Palin Problem," *National Review* (September 26, 2008).

69 Rebecca Traister, "The Sarah Palin Pity Party," *Salon.com* (September 30, 2008), http://www.salon.com/mwt/feature/2008/09/30/palin_pity/print.html.

70 Bernadette Barker-Plummer, "Reading Sarah Palin," *Flow TV* (8.10) (October 18, 2008), http://flowtv.org/2008/10/reading-sarah-palin-bernadette-barker-plummer-university-of-san-francisco/.

71 Quindlen, "Can You Say 'Sexist'?"

72 Ibid.

73 Julia Baird, "From Seneca Falls to … Sarah Palin?" *Newsweek* (September 22, 2008).

74 An early October public opinion report by the Pew Research Center showed women's enthusiasm for Palin generally cooling. During the first week of September, 52 percent of women said she was qualified to be president, but by the end of September, only 34 percent felt she was qualified—an 18 percent drop, and 6 percentage points lower than men's assessment of the governor's readiness.

75 Ibid.

76 Daniel Henninger, "What's So Special about Sarah?" *Wall Street Journal* (September 4, 2008).

77 Ibid.

78 "McCain VP Pick: A New Day for Feminism," NPR News interview with Serrin Foster, president of Feminists for Life (September 1, 2008), transcript available at http://www.npr.org/templates/story/story.php?storyId=94169777.

79 Barbara Amiel, "What Mrs. Palin Could Learn from Mrs. T.," *Wall Street Journal* (September 5, 2008).

80 Victor Davis Hanson, "What Was Feminism?" *National Review Online* (September 11, 2008).

81 Henninger, "What's So Special."

82 Belinda Luscombe, "Why Some Women Hate Sarah Palin," *Time* (October 2, 2008), http://www.time.com/time/politics/article/0,8599,1846832,00.html.

83 Mary Grabar, "The Harpies Are Out to Get Sarah Palin," *Townhall.com* (August 31, 2008), http://townhall.com/columnists/marygrabar/2008/08/31/the_harpies_are_out_to_get_sarah_palin/page/full/.

84 Ibid.

85 Ibid.

86 Cathy Young, "A Great Moment for Women," *Boston Globe* (September 12, 2008).

87 Ibid.

88 Suzanne Fields, "A Face-Off for the Future," *Washington Times* (September 19, 2008).

89 Belinda Luscombe, "Heeling Power," *Time* (October 13, 2008), 63–64.

90 Ibid.

91 Juliet Eilperin, "Palin Displays Her Feminist Side," *The Washington Post* political blog "The Trail" (October 21, 2008).

92 Larry Rohter, "Palin Criticizes Obama as Faux Feminist," *New York Times* political blog "The Caucus" (October 21, 2008), http://thecaucus.blogs.nytimes.com/2008/10/21/palin-criticizes-obama-as-faux-feminist/.

93 Eilperin, "Palin Displays."

94 Ibid.

95 Judith Warner, "The Mirrored Ceiling," *New York Times* (September 4, 2008).

96 Ibid.

97 Dicker, *Catching a Wave*, 17.

98 Traister, "Zombie Feminists of the RNC."

99 Ibid.

100 Alessandra Stanley, "On 'SNL' It's the Real Sarah Palin, Looking Like a Real Entertainer," *New York Times* (October 20, 2008).

101 Ibid.

102 Emily Bazelon, "Palin Does SNL," The XX Factor, *Slate* (October 19, 2008), http://img.slate.com/blogs/blogs/xxfactor/archive/2008/10/19.aspx.

103 Melinda Henninger, "Anyway, She Looked Good …," The XX Factor, *Slate* (October 20, 2008), http://img.slate.com/blogs/blogs/xxfactor/archive/tags/Sarah+Palin+SNL/default.aspx.

104 Maureen Sullivan, "What, If Any of This, Is Justified?" The XX Factor, *Slate* (October 20, 2008), http://img.slate.com/blogs/blogs/xxfactor/archive/tags/Sarah+Palin+SNL/default.aspx.

105 Rachael Larimore, "Palin, SNL, and the T-Shirts that Really Bother Me," The XX Factor, *Slate* (October 20, 2008), http://img.slate.com/blogs/blogs/xxfactor/archive/tags/Sarah+Palin+SNL/default.aspx.

106 Ibid.

107 Emily Bazelon, "The Un-Hillary: Why Watching Sarah Palin is Agony for Women," *Slate* (October 1, 2008), http://www.slate.com/articles/double_x/xxfactor_xxtra/2008/10/the_unhillary.html.

108 Fortini, "The 'Bitch' and the 'Ditz.'"

Chapter 7

1 Robert Harriman, *Political Style: The Artistry of Power* (Chicago, IL: University of Chicago Press, 1995).

2 Jennifer Lobasz, "The Woman in Peril and the Ruined Woman," *Journal of Women, Politics & Policy* (2008): 305–334.

3 Anne Kornblut, *Notes from a Cracked Ceiling: Hillary Clinton, Sarah Palin, and What it Will Take for a Woman to Win* (New York: Crown, 2009).

4 Rebecca Traister, *Big Girls Don't Cry* (New York: Free Press, 2010), 287.

5 Janis Edwards, "The 2008 Gendered Campaign and the Problem with Hillary Studies," *Rhetoric and Public Affairs* 14, no. 1 (2011): 157.

6 Ibid.; Nichola D. Gutgold, *Almost Madam President* (Lanham, MD: Lexington Books, 2009); Regina Lawrence and Melody Rose, *Hillary Clinton's Race for the White House: Gender Politics and the Media on the Campaign Trail* (Boulder, CO: Lynne Rienner Publishers, 2010); Ted Sheckels, ed., *Cracked but not Shattered: Hillary Rodham Clinton's Unsuccessful Campaign for President* (Lanham, MD: Lexington Books, 2009); Anne Kornblut, *Notes from a Cracked Ceiling: Hillary Clinton, Sarah Palin, and What It Will Take for a Woman to Win* (New York: Crown, 2009).

7 Ibid., 166.

8 Ibid.

9 Diana B. Carlin and Kelly L. Winfrey, "Have You Come a Long Way, Baby? Hillary Clinton, Sarah Palin and Sexism in the 2008 Campaign Coverage," *Communication Studies* 60, no. 4 (September–October 2009): 326–343.

10 Ruth LaFerla, "For Female Candidates, Conservative Clothes are Trendy," *New York Times* (October 21, 2010), under "Ruth LaFerla, Fashion" http://www.nytimes.com/2010/10/21/fashion/21IMAGE.html?_r=3&ref=style (accessed March 25, 2012).

11 Ibid.
12 Ann C. McGinley, "Hillary Clinton, Sarah Palin, and Michelle Obama: Performing Gender, Race and Class on the Campaign Trail," *Scholarly Works* (paper 171): 721, http://scholars.law.unlv.edu/facpub/171 (accessed July 27, 2011).
13 Megan Garber, "Strike a Pose—Rogue (Rogue, Rogue …)," *Columbia Journal Review* (November 16, 2009), http://www.cjr.org/campaign_desk/strike_a_poserogue_rogue_rogue.php?page=all (accessed March 25, 2012).
14 Ibid.
15 Regina G. Lawrence and Melody Rose, *Hillary Clinton's Race for the White House: Gender Politics and the Media on the Campaign Trail* (Boulder, CO: Lynne Rienner, 2010), 221–222.
16 Amanda Fortini, "The 'Bitch' and the 'Ditz': How the Year of the Woman Reinforced the Two Most Pernicious Sexist Stereotypes and Actually Set Women Back," *New York Magazine* (November 16, 2008), under "Politics, The 'Bitch' and the 'Ditz'," http://nymag.com/news/politics/nationalinterest/52184/(accessed March 25, 2012).
17 Ibid.
18 Philip Rucker and Eli Saslow, "Sarah Palin to Resign as Alaska Governor, Citing Probes and Family Needs," *The Washington Post* (July 4, 2009), under "Politics, Sarah Palin" http://www.washingtonpost.com/wp-dyn/content/article/2009/07/03/AR2009070301738.html (accessed March 25, 2012).
19 Sarah Palin, "Resignation Speech" (speech, Wasilla, AK, July 4, 2009): full text of speech found at http://www.huffingtonpost.com/2009/07/03/sarah-palin-resignation-s_n_225557.html (accessed March 25, 2012).
20 See as examples: "Conservatives Taken Aback by Palin's Decision to Resign," *CNN.com* (July 5, 2009), under "CNN Politics" http://articles.cnn.com/2009–07–05/politics/palin.reaction_1_sarah–palin–rove–alaska–gov/2?_s=PM:POLITICS (accessed March 25, 2012); Sean Cockerham, "Palin's Resignation Shocks Alaska, Nation," *Anchorage Daily News* (July 3, 2009), under "2009, Palin's Resignation" http://www.adn.com/2009/07/03/852419/palins-resignation-shocks-alaska.html (accessed March 25, 2012); Susan Davis, "Palin's Resignation: Shrewd Move or Political Suicide?" *Wall Street Journal* (July 3, 2009), under "Politics, Sarah Palin Resignation" http://blogs.wsj.com/washwire/2009/07/03/palins-resignation-shrewd-move-or-political-suicide/(accessed March 25, 2012); Lorenzo Benet, "Sarah Palin Resigns as Alaska Governor," *People* (July 3, 2009), under "2009, Palin Resigns" http://www.people.com/people/article/0,,20289436,00.html (accessed March 25, 2012).
21 Davis, "Palin's Resignation: Shrewd Move or Political Suicide?".
22 Sarah Palin (message to supporters), quoted at http://articles.cnn.com/2009–07–05/politics/palin.reaction_1_sarah-palin-rove-alaska-gov/2?_s=PM:POLITICS (accessed March 25, 2012).
23 "Conservatives Taken Aback by Palin's Decision to Resign," *CNNPolitics.com* (July 6, 2009), http://www.cnn.com/2009/POLITICS/07/05/palin.reaction/index.html?iref=allsearch (accessed April 4, 2012).
24 In a May 2011 post by AKMuckraker on *Huffington Post* regarding "The Tragedy of Sarah Palin" *Atlantic* article.
25 Michael Nelson, *PS: Political Science and Politics* 21, no. 4 (Autumn 1988): 865.
26 Sarah Palin, "2010 Susan B. Anthony List Speech" (speech, Washington, DC, May 14, 2010): full video of speech found at http://www.c-spanvideo.org/program/293509-1 (accessed March 24, 2012).
27 Sarah Palin (speech at Annual NRA Meeting, May 14, 2010), as quoted at www.foxnews.com/politics/2010/05/14/palin-tells-womens-group-washington-beware-mama-grizzlies/?test=latestnews#ixzz1q4nnjKMD (accessed March 24, 2012).
28 See for example: Amy Gardner, "Palin Pushes Abortion Foes to Form 'Conservative, Feminist Identity'," *The Washington Post* (May 15, 2010), under "Nation,

2010, Palin" http://www.washingtonpost.com/wp-dyn/content/article/2010/05/15/AR2010051500002.html (accessed March 24, 2012).

29 Palin, "Susan B. Anthony," as quoted by Andy Barr, "Palin Praises 'Mama Grizzlies,'" *Politico* (May 14, 2010), under "Palin Praises 'Mama Grizzlies'" http://dyn.politico.com/printstory.cfm?uuid=97AF494F-18FE-70B2-A82B770147C64499 (accessed March 24, 2012).

30 Palin, "Susan B. Anthony."

31 Ibid.

32 Jessica Valenti, "Opinion: The Fake Feminism of Sarah Palin," *The Washington Post* (May 30, 2010), under "Politics, 2010, Fake Feminism" http://www.washingtonpost.com/wp-dyn/content/article/2010/05/28/AR2010052802263.html?sid%3DST2010060501883&sub=AR (accessed March 24, 2012).

33 Kathryn Jean Lopez, "Sarah Palin: A Feminist in the Pro-Life Tradition," *National Review Online* (May 24, 2010), under "Sarah Palin: A Feminist in the Pro-Life Tradition" http://www.nationalreview.com/articles/229811/sarah-palin-feminist-pro-life-tradition/kathryn-jean-lopez (accessed March 24, 2012).

34 Lori Ziganto, "Taking Feminism Back: Sarah Palin Endorses Nikki Haley for SC Governor," *News Real Blog* (May 14, 2010), under "2010, Taking Feminism Back" http://www.newsrealblog.com/2010/05/14/taking-feminism-back-sarah-palin-endorses-nikki-haley-for-sc-governor/(accessed March 24, 2012).

35 Valenti, "Opinion."

36 Stephanie Schriock as quoted by Jennifer Barber, "Inside the Beltway," *Washington Times* (May 17, 2010), under "2010, May, Inside the Beltway" http://www.washingtontimes.com/news/2010/may/17/inside-the-beltway-25884695/(accessed March 25, 2012).

37 Tasha N. Dubriwny, "First Ladies and Feminism: Laura Bush as Advocate for Women's and Children's Rights," *Women's Studies in Communication* 28 (2005).

38 Melody Rose, "Pro-Life, Pro-Woman? Frame Extension in the American Abortion Movement," *Journal of Women, Politics & Policy* 32, no. 1 (2011): 1–27.

39 Meghan Daum, "Sarah Palin, Feminist," *Los Angeles Times* (May 20, 2010), under "Collections, Women's Rights" http://articles.latimes.com/2010/may/20/opinion/la-oe-0520-daum-fword-20100520 (accessed March 24, 2012). See also Meghan Daum interview at http://www.npr.org/templates/story/story.php?storyId=127092813 (accessed April 2, 2012).

40 Ross Douthat, "No Mystique about Feminism," *New York Times* (June 13, 2010), under "2010, Opinion, Editorials" http://www.nytimes.com/2010/06/14/opinion/14douthat.html (accessed April 2, 2012).

41 R. Marie Griffith, as quoted in Sean Alfano, "Sarah Palin Viewed as a Modern-Day Prophet to Evangelicals, Newsweek Profile Suggests," *New York Daily News.com* (June 11, 2010), under "NYDN Home, Collections, Sarah Palin" http://articles.nydailynews.com/2010-06-11/news/27066946_1_sarah–palin-early-feminists-cecile-richards (accessed April 6, 2012).

42 Lisa Miller, "Hear Them Growl: Sarah Palin Says a New Crop of Conservative Women Will 'Rise Up' to Protect Their Cubs. But Will They?" *Daily Beast* (September 27, 2010), under "News, 2010, October, Mama Grizzly" http://www.thedailybeast.com/newsweek/2010/09/27/what-does-mama-grizzly-really-mean.print.html (accessed March 25, 2012).

43 "Campaign 2010: The Politics of Palin," *The Washington Post* (updated November 22, 2010), http://www.washingtonpost.com/wp-srv/special/politics/palin_tracker/ (accessed March 24, 2012).

44 Ibid.

45 SarahPac.com, "Sarah Palin—'Mama Grizzlies'," under "Sarah Palin—Mama Grizzlies" (July 8, 2010), http://www.youtube.com/watch?v=oF-OsHTLfxM (accessed March 25, 2012).

46 Sarah Palin, *America by Heart: Reflections on Family, Faith, and Flag* (New York: Harper Collins, 2010).

47 Dr. Peggy Drexler, "Hot Women of the Republic Right," *Huffington Post* Huff Post Women Blog (August 10, 2011), http://www.huffingtonpost.com/peggy-drexler/hot-women-of-the-republic_b_923236.html (accessed March 25, 2012).

48 See *Newsweek* (October 4, 2010), http://tpmlivewire.talkingpointsmemo.com/2010/09/newsweek-cover-story-explores-the-mama-grizzly-phenomenon.php (accessed April 5, 2012).

49 Quoted in Howard Kurtz, "Should We Blame Sarah Palin for Gabrielle Giffords' Shooting?" *Newsweek* (January 8, 2011), under "U.S. Politics, Gabrielle Giffords and Sarah Palin" http://www.thedailybeast.com/articles/2011/01/08/gabrielle-giffords-shooting-dont-blame-sarah-palin.html (accessed March 25, 2012).

50 John Berman, "Sarah Palin's 'Crosshairs' Ad Dominates Gabrielle Giffords Debate," *ABC News* (January 9, 2011), under "Politics, Palin and Gifford" http://abcnews.go.com/Politics/sarah-palins-crosshairs-ad-focus-gabrielle-giffords-debate/story?id=12576437#.T259wtVbKuI (accessed March 24, 2012).

51 See Sarah Palin twitter comment at http://twitpic.com/3ofie7/full (accessed March 24, 2012).

52 Berman, "Palin's 'Crosshairs' Ad."

53 Emanuel Cleaver as quoted by Heidi Przybyla, "Giffords Shooting in Arizona May Cool U.S. Political Rhetoric, Hurt Palin," *Bloomberg* (January 10, 2011), under "News, U.S. Politics, Giffords" http://www.bloomberg.com/news/2011-1-09/lawmakers-urge-end-to-political-rhetoric-after-tucson-shootings.html (accessed March 25, 2012).

54 Paul Krugman, "Assassination Attempt in Arizona," *New York Times* (January 8, 2011), under "Opinion, Conscience of a Liberal, Assassination Attempt in Arizona," http://krugman.blogs.nytimes.com/2011/01/08/assassination-attempt-in-arizona/(accessed March 25, 2012).

55 *Newsweek* (October 4, 2010).

56 See as examples of debate: Jeff Muskus, "Sarah Palin's PAC Puts Gun Sights on Democrats She's Targeting in 2010," *Huffington Post* (January 9, 2011), under "Politics" http://www.huffingtonpost.com/2010/03/24/sarah-palins-pac-puts-gun_n_511433.html; Alissa Walker, "Crosshairs and Targets: Innocent Symbols or Incendiary Iconography?" *Good News* (January 8, 2011), under "News, Politics" http://www.good.is/post/palin-s-crosshairs-map-targeted-shot-arizona-congressperson/; Dan Balz, "Palin Caught in Crosshairs Map Controversy after Tucson Shootings," *The Washington Post* (January 10, 2011), under "In The News, Politics" http://www.washingtonpost.com/wp-dyn/content/article/2011/01/10/AR2011011006653.html; Alexander Mooney, "Palin: 'I am Not Going to Shut Up'," CNN (January 18, 2011), under "Videos, Palin" http://ac360.blogs.cnn.com/2011/01/18/palin-i-am-not-going-to-shut-up/?iref=allsearch; James Taranto, "'We Don't Have Proof Yet': Violent Fantasy Goes Mainstream on the Left," *Wall Street Journal* (January 10, 2011), under "Opinion, Proof" http://online.wsj.com/article/SB10001424052748703667904576072840602094576.html (all accessed March 24, 2012).

57 Lisa Miller, "Hear Them Growl: Sarah Palin Says a New Crop of Conservative Women Will 'Rise Up' to Protect Their Cubs. But Will They?" *Daily Beast* (September 27, 2010), under "U.S. Politics, Palin" http://www.thedailybeast.com/newsweek/2010/09/27/what-does-mama-grizzly-really-mean.print.html (accessed March 25, 2012).

58 Chris Cilizza, "Why Michelle Bachmann is No Sarah Palin," *The Washington Post* (June 6, 2011), under "Blogs, The Fix, 2011, Bachmann" http://www.washingtonpost.com/blogs/the-fix/post/why-michele-bachmann-is-no-sarah-palin/2011/06/28/AGG5ADpH_blog.html (accessed March 31, 2012).

59 Toby Harnden, "Sarah Palin and Michele Bachmann Head for 2012 Cat Fight," *Telegraph Online* (June 8, 2011), under "World News, Bachmann" http://www.telegraph.co.uk/news/worldnews/sarah-palin/8564344/Sarah-Palin-and-Michele-Bachmann-head-for-2012-cat-fight.html (accessed April 4, 2012).

60 Libby Copeland, "Sarah Palin's Improbable Gift to Women," *Slate.com* (October 5, 2011), under "Doublex, Palin" http://www.slate.com/articles/double_x/doublex/2011/10/sarah_palin_not_running_in_2012_palin_won_t_be_the_first_woman_p.html (accessed March 25, 2012).

BIBLIOGRAPHY

Abcarian, Robin. "Insiders See 'New Feminism.'" *Los Angeles Times*, September 4, 2008.

Abcarian, Robin and Kate Linthicum. "A Political Fashion Do or Don't?" *Los Angeles Times*, October 23, 2008.

Abramson, Paul R., John H. Aldrich, and David W. Rohde. *Change and Continuity in the 2008 Elections*. Washington, DC: CQ Press, 2010.

Aday, Sean and James Devitt. "Style Over Substance: Newspaper Coverage of Elizabeth Dole's Presidential Bid." *International Journal of Press/Politics* 6, no. 2 (2001): 52–73.

Addams, Jane. "Why Women Should Vote." *Modern History Sourcebook*, 1915. http://www.fordham.edu/halsall/mod/1915janeadams-vote.html (accessed March 24, 2012).

Agness, Karin. "Sarah Palin: A Liberated Woman." *TownHall.com*, September 7, 2008. http://townhall.com/columnists/karinagness/2008/09/07/sarah_palin_a_liberated_woman/page/full/ (accessed March 25, 2012).

Alston, Joshua. "Why Obama Needs a Tina Fey." *Newsweek*, November 3, 2008.

"American Experience Episode: Reagan." PBS. http://www.pbs.org/wgbh/americanexperience/features/general-article/reagan-quotes/ (accessed April 4, 2012).

American National Election Studies. *The ANES Guide to Public Opinion and Electoral Behavior*. http://www.electionstudies.org/nesguide/toptable/tab5a_5.htm (accessed March 3, 2012).

Amiel, Barbara. "What Mrs. Palin Could Learn from Mrs. T." *Wall Street Journal*, September 5, 2008.

Ammerman, Nancy T. "American Evangelicals in American Culture: Continuity and Change." In *Evangelicals and Democracy in America, volume I*, eds, Steven Brint and Jean Reith Schroedel. New York: Russell Sage Foundation, 2009.

Andersen, Charlotte Hilton. "McCain Plays the MILF Card—Will It Work?" *Huffington Post*, September 29, 2008. http://www.huffingtonpost.com/charlotte-hilton-andersen/mccain-plays-the-milf-car_b_130288.html (accessed April 2, 2012).

Anderson, Julie, dir. *Mr. Conservative: Goldwater on Goldwater*. DVD. New York: Zeitgeist Films, 2007.

Anderson, Karrin Vasby. "Framing Gender: Pioneers, Beauty Queens, and Unruly Women." *Communication Currents*, special edition of the National Communication Association (October 2008). http://www.natcom.org/CommCurrentsArticle. aspx?id=1083 (accessed March 18, 2012).

Anderson, Karrin Vasby and Kristina Horn Sheeler. *Governing Codes: Gender, Metaphor, and Political Identity*. Lanham, MD: Lexington Books, 2005.

"Anna Wintour Takes Hillary Clinton to Task." *Huffington Post*, March 28, 2008. http://www.huffingtonpost.com/2008/01/18/anna-wintour-takes-hillar_n_82132.html (accessed April 1, 2012).

Atkins-Sayre, Wendy. "Governor Mom: Jane Swift and the Body Politic." In *Gender and Political Communication in America: Rhetoric, Representation, and Display*, Janis L. Edwards ed., 129–148. Lanham, MD: Lexington Books, 2009.

Bailey, Sarah Pulliam. "McCain picks Alaska Gov. Sarah Palin for VP." *Christianity Today* Politics Blog, August 29, 2008.

Baird, Julia. "From Seneca Falls to … Sarah Palin?" *Newsweek*, September 22, 2008. http://www.thedailybeast.com/newsweek/2008/09/12/from-seneca-falls-to-sarah-palin.html (accessed March 9, 2012).

Baker, Katie. "Cracking the Highest Glass Ceiling." *Newsweek*, October 6, 2008.

Banet-Weiser, Sarah. *The Most Beautiful Girl in the World: Beauty Pageants and National Identity*. Berkeley: University of California Press, 1999.

Barbara Lee Family Foundation. *Cracking the Code: Political Intelligence for Women Running for Governor*. Brookline, MA: Barbara Lee Family Foundation, 2004.

Barbara Lee Family Foundation. *Positioning Women to Win*. Brookline, MA: Barbara Lee Family Foundation, 2007.

Barber, Jennifer. "Inside the Beltway." *Washington Times*, May 17, 2010. http://www.washingtontimes.com/news/2010/may/17/inside-the-beltway-25884695/ (accessed March 25, 2012).

Barholet, Jeffrey and Karen Breslau. "An Apostle of Alaska." *Newsweek*, September 15, 2008.

Barker-Plummer, Bernadette. "Reading Sarah Palin." *Flow TV* 8.10, October 18, 2008. http://flowtv.org/2008/10/reading-sarah-palin-bernadette-barker-plummer-university-of-san-francisco/ (accessed December 3, 2008).

Barnes, Bart. "Barry Goldwater, GOP Hero, Dies." *The Washington Post*, May 30, 1998. http://www.washingtonpost.com/wp-srv/politics/daily/may98/goldwater_dead_at_89 (accessed June 7, 2011).

Barnes, Fred. "The Most Popular Governor: Alaska's Sarah Palin is the GOP's Newest Star." *Weekly Standard*, July 16, 2007. http://www.weeklystandard.com/Content/Public/Articles/000/000/013/851orcjq.asp (accessed March 17, 2009).

Barrett, Kate. "Palin's Switcheroo on Feminism." *ABC News*, October 24, 2008. http://www.abcnews.go.com/blogs/politics/2008/10/palins-switcher (accessed March 24, 2012).

Bash, Dana, Peter Hamby, and John King. "Palin's 'Going Rogue,' McCain Aide Says." CNN, October 25, 2008. http://articles.cnn.com/2008-10-25/politics/palin.tension (accessed March 25, 2012).

Baumgardner, Jennifer and Amy Richards. *Manifesta: Young Women, Feminism, and the Future*. New York: Farrar, Straus, and Giroux, 2000.

Baumgartner, Frank R., Suzanna Linn, and Amber E. Boydstun. "The Decline of the Death Penalty: How Media Framing Changed Capital Punishment in America."

In *Winning with Words: The Origins & Impact of Political Framing*, Brian F. Schaffner and Patrick J. Sellers eds., 159–184. New York: Routledge, 2010.

Bazelon, Emily. "The Un-Hillary: Why Watching Sarah Palin is Agony for Women." *Slate*, October 1, 2008. http://www.slate.com/articles/double_x/xxfactor_xxtra/2008/10/the_unhillary.html (accessed March 25, 2012).

Bazelon, Emily. "Palin Does SNL." The XX Factor, *Slate*, October 19, 2008. http://img.slate.com/blogs/blogs/xxfactor/archive/2008/10/19.aspx (accessed March 25, 2012).

Bazelon, Emily and Dahlia Lithwick. "Questions for a Superhuman Mom." *Slate*, September 2, 2008.

Beail, Linda and Rhonda S. Kinney. "Gender and the Study of the Presidency." Paper presented at the annual meeting of the American Political Science Association, San Francisco, CA, September 1996.

Bem, Sandra. "The Measurement of Psychological Androgyny." *Journal of Clinical and Consulting Psychology* 42 (1974): 155–162.

Berman, John. "Sarah Palin's 'Crosshairs' Ad Dominates Gabrielle Giffords Debate." *ABC News*, January 9, 2011. http://abcnews.go.com/Politics/sarah-palins-crosshairs-ad-focus-gabrielle-giffords-debate/story?id=12576437#.T259wtVbKuI (accessed March 24, 2012).

Betts, Kate. "Sarah Palin's $150,000 Crime against Fashion." *Time*, October 23, 2008. http://www.time.com/time/politics/article/0,8599,1853529,00.html (accessed April 2, 2012).

Bingham, Clara. "The Women on the Hill." *Vogue*, August, 1993.

Boxer, Barbara and Nicole Boxer. *Strangers in the Senate: Politics and the New Revolution of Women in America*. Washington, DC: National Press Books, 1994.

Bradley, Tahman. "Campbell Brown: Stop Covering Palin's Wardrobe Controversy; Women Are Unfairly Held to Higher Standard on Appearance." *ABC News*, October 23, 2008. http://abcnews.go.com/blogs/politics/2008/10/campbell-brown/ (accessed March 24, 2012).

Brooks, David. "What the Palin Pick Says." *New York Times*, September 2, 2008.

Broverman, Inge et al. "Sex-Role Stereotypes: A Current Appraisal." *Journal of Social Issues* 28 (1972): 59–78.

Bruce, Tammy. "A Feminist's Argument for McCain's VP." *San Francisco Chronicle*, September 7, 2008. http://www.realclearpolitics.com/articles/2008/09/a_feminists_argument_for_mccai.html (accessed March 24, 2012).

Budgeon, Shelley. "The Contradictions of Successful Femininity: Third-Wave Feminism, Postfeminism and 'New' Femininities." Quoted in Rosalind Gill and Christina Scharff, *New Femininities: Postfeminism, Neoliberalism and Subjectivity*. Basingstoke, UK: Palgrave Macmillan, 2011.

Bumiller, Elisabeth and Michael Cooper. "Advisers Say Conservative Ire Pushed McCain Away From Picking Lieberman." *New York Times*, August 31, 2008.

Burrell, Barbara. *A Woman's Place is in the House: Campaigning for Congress in the Feminist Era*. Ann Arbor: The University of Michigan Press, 1994.

Burrell, Barbara. *Public Opinion, The First Ladyship and Hillary Rodham Clinton*. New York: Routledge, 2001.

Bush, George W. "State of the Union." Speech delivered to Congress at Washington, DC, January 28, 2003. http://www.americanrhetoric.com/speeches/stateoftheunion2003.html (accessed April 5, 2012).

Byron, Ellen, Jennifer Saranow, and Rachel Dodes. "Palin's Style Sparks a Buying Frenzy, and Fashion Firms Rush to Cash In." *Wall Street Journal*, September 12, 2008.

Callard, Abby and David Plotz. "Your Dreams (and Nightmares) About Sarah Palin." *Slate*, September 12, 2008.

"Campaign 2010: The Politics of Palin." *The Washington Post*, last updated November 22, 2010. http://www.washingtonpost.com/wp-srv/special/politics/palin_tracker/ (accessed March 24, 2012).

Capra, Frank, dir. *Mr. Smith Goes to Washington*. DVD. Culver City, CA: Columbia Pictures Corporation, 1939.

Carlin, Diana B. and Kelly L. Winfrey. "Have You Come a Long Way, Baby? Hillary Clinton, Sarah Palin and Sexism in the 2008 Campaign Coverage." *Communication Studies* 60, no. 4 (September–October 2009): 326–343.

Carlton, Jim. "Profile of Alaska's Sarah Palin: Governor, Reformer, Mother." *Wall Street Journal*, September 24, 2008.

Carpentier, Megan. "Sarah Palin: When Choosing A Woman Might Not Be Choosing For Women." *Jezebel*, August 29, 2008. http://jezebel.com/5043669/sarah-palin-when-choosing-a-woman-might-not-be-choosing-for-women (accessed April 2, 2012).

Carroll, Susan J. "Security Moms and Presidential Politics." In *Voting the Gender Gap*, Lois Duke Whitaker ed., 75–90. Urbana: University of Illinois Press, 2008.

Carroll, Susan J. "Voting Choices: The Politics of the Gender Gap." In *Gender and Elections: Shaping the Future of American Politics*, 2nd edition, Susan J. Carroll and Richard L. Fox eds, 125–128. New York: Cambridge University Press, 2010.

Carroll, Susan J. and Kelly Dittmar. "The 2008 Candidacies of Hillary Clinton and Sarah Palin: Cracking the Highest, Hardest Glass Ceiling." In *Gender and Elections: Shaping the Future of American Politics*, Susan J. Carroll and Richard L. Fox eds. New York: Cambridge University Press, 2010.

Carroll, Susan J. and Richard Logan Fox. *Gender and Elections*. New York: Cambridge University Press, 2006.

Center for the American Woman and Politics (CAWP). "The Gender Gap: Voting Choices in Presidential Elections." CAWP, Eagleton Institute for Politics, Rutgers University, 2008. http://www.cawp.rutgers.edu/fast_facts/voters/documents/GGPresVote.pdf (accessed March 24, 2012).

cfarnham. "U.S. Public Stupified by Palin's 'Sexy Librarian' Look." September 9, 2008. http://www.zimbio.com/2008+Presidential+Candidates/articles/11586/Public+Stupified+Palin+Sexy+Librarian+look (accessed March 25, 2012).

Chong, Dennis and James N. Druckman. "Identifying Frames in Political News." In *Sourcebook for Political Communication Research: Methods, Measures, and Analytical Techniques*, Erik P. Bucy and R. Lance Holbert eds., 238–267. New York: Routledge, 2010.

Clift, Eleanor and Tom Brazaitis. *Madame President: Women Blazing the Leadership Trail*. New York: Routledge, 2003.

Continetti, Matthew. "Two-Front Republicans." *New York Times*, August 30, 2008.

Cooper, Michael and Elisabeth Bumiller. "Alaskan is McCain's Choice; First Woman on the G.O.P. Ticket." *New York Times*, August 30, 2008.

Copeland, Libby. "Shooting from the Hip, With a Smile to Boot." *The Washington Post*, October 1, 2008. http://www.washingtonpost.com/wpsrv/artsandliving/style/features/2008/rhetoric/gallery.html (accessed March 9, 2012).

Copeland, Libby. "Sarah Palin's Improbable Gift to Women." *Slate*, October 5, 2011. http://www.slate.com/articles/double_x/doublex/2011/10/sarah_palin_not_running_in_2012_palin_won_t_be_the_first_woman_p.html (accessed March 25, 2012).

Cornog, Evan. *The Power and the Story: How the Crafted Presidential Narrative has Determined Political Success from George Washington to George W. Bush.* New York: Penguin, 2004.

Cottle, Michelle. "Shattered." *The New Republic,* September 24, 2008.

Crenshaw, Kimberle. "Whose Story Is It, Anyway? Feminist and Anti-Racist Appropriations of Anita Hill." In *Race-ing Justice, En-Gendering Power: Essays on Anita Hill, Clarence Thomas, and the Construction of Social Reality,* Toni Morrison ed., 402–420. New York: Pantheon, 1992.

Critchlow, Donald T. and Nancy MacLean. *Debating the American Conservative Movement: 1945 to the Present.* Lanham, MD: Rowman & Littlefield, 2009.

Cronin, Thomas E. and Michael A. Genovese. *The Paradoxes of the American Presidency,* 3rd edition. New York: Oxford University Press, 2010.

Cumming, Jeanne. "RNC Shells Out $150K for Palin Fashion." *Politico,* October 21, 2008. http://www.politico.com/news/stories/1008/14805.html (accessed March 24, 2012).

Daum, Meghan. "Sarah Palin, Feminist." *Los Angeles Times,* May 20, 2010. http://articles.latimes.com/2010/may/20/opinion/la-oe-0520-daum-fword-20100520 (accessed March 24, 2012).

Davis, Beverly. "Palin Pregnancy: Mother Daughter Interrupted." *Huffington Post,* September 2, 2008.

Davis, Susan. "Palin's Resignation: Shrewd Move or Political Suicide?" *Wall Street Journal,* July 3, 2009. http://blogs.wsj.com/washwire/2009/07/03/palins-resignation-shrewd-move-or-political-suicide/ (accessed March 25, 2012).

Day to Day. "Who Requested Sarah Palin's $150,000 Makeover?" *Day to Day,* October 23, 2008. http://www.npr.org/templates/story/story.php?storyId=96032122 (accessed April 2, 2012).

DeFord, Frank. *There She Is: The Life and Times of Miss America.* New York: Viking Press, 1971.

Delli Carpini, Michael X., and Bruce A. Williams. "Constructing Public Opinion: The Uses of Fictional and Nonfictional Television in Conversations about the Environment." In *The Psychology of Political Communication,* Ann N. Crigler ed., 149–176. Ann Arbor: University of Michigan Press, 1996.

Dent, Gina. "Missionary Position." Quoted in Rebecca Walker, *To Be Real: Telling the Truth and Changing the Face of Feminism.* New York: Anchor Books, 1995.

Deutch, Donny. "The Big Idea." CNBC, September 4, 2008.

Deveny, Kathleen. "Confessions of a Secret Sarah Admirer." *Newsweek,* September 15, 2008.

Dicker, Rory. *Catching a Wave: Reclaiming Feminism for the 21st Century.* Boston, MA: Northeastern University Press, 2003.

Dionne, E. J., Jr. "Clinton Swipes the GOP's Lyrics: the Democrat as Liberal Republican." *The Washington Post,* July 21, 1996.

Dolan, Kathleen. "The Impact of Candidate Sex on Evaluations of Candidates for the U.S. House of Representatives." *Social Science Quarterly* 85 (2004): 206–217.

Dolan, Kathleen. "Do Women Candidates Play to Gender Stereotypes? Do Men Candidates Play to Women? Candidate Sex and Issues Priorities on Campaign Websites." *Political Research Quarterly* 58 (2005): 31–44.

Douthat, Ross. "No Mystique about Feminism." *New York Times,* June 13, 2010. http://www.nytimes.com/2010/06/14/opinion/14douthat.html (accessed April 2, 2012).

Dowd, Maureen. "Can Hillary Cry Her Way Back to the White House?" *New York Times,* January 9, 2008. http://www.nytimes.com/2008/01/09/opinion/08dowd.html?pagewanted=all (accessed March 24, 2012).

Dowd, Maureen. "Vice in Go-Go Boots?" *New York Times,* August 31, 2008.

Druckman, James N. "Competing Frames in a Political Campaign." In *Winning with Words: The Origins & Impact of Political Framing*, Brian F. Schaffner and Patrick J. Sellers eds., 101–120. New York: Routledge, 2010.

Duerst-Lahti, Georgia. "Presidential Elections: Gendered Space and the Case of 2008." In *Gender and Elections: Shaping the Future of American Politics*, 2nd edition, Susan J. Carroll and Richard L. Fox eds., 11–37. New York: Cambridge University Press, 2010.

Dye, Jane Lawler. "Fertility of American Women: 2008." U.S. Census Bureau, November 2010. http://www.census.gov/prod/2010pubs/p20-563.pdf (accessed April 2, 2012).

Edwards, Janis L. "The 2008 Gendered Campaign and the Problem with Hillary Studies." *Rhetoric and Public Affairs* 14, no. 1 (Spring 2011): 155–168.

Eilperin, Juliet. "Palin Displays Her Feminist Side." *The Washington Post* political blog "The Trail," October 21, 2008.

Ensler, Eve. "Drill, Drill, Drill." *Huffington Post*, September 8, 2008.

Ertelt, Steven. "More Pro-life Reaction to John McCain Picking Abortion Opponent Sarah Palin." *LifeNews.com*, August 29, 2008.

Falk, Erika. *Women for President: Media Bias in Eight Campaigns*. Urbana: University of Illinois Press, 2008.

Farber, David. *The Rise and Fall of Modern American Conservatism: A Short History*. Princeton, NJ: Princeton University Press, 2010.

Fields, Suzanne. "A Face-Off for the Future." *Washington Times*, September 19, 2008.

Findlen, Barbara. *Listen Up: Voices from the Next Feminist Generation*. Emeryville, CA: Seal Press, 2001.

Fortini, Amanda. "The 'Bitch' and the 'Ditz': How the Year of the Woman Reinforced the Two Most Pernicious Sexist Stereotypes and Actually Set Women Back." *New York Magazine*, November 16, 2008. http://nymag.com/news/politics/nationalinterest/52184/ (accessed March 25, 2012).

Foster, Serrin. "McCain VP Pick: A New Day for Feminism." Interview with Serrin Foster by Deborah Amos. NPR, September 1, 2008. http://www.npr.org/templates/story/story.php?storyId=94169777 (accessed April 2, 2012).

Fridkin Kim and Patrick Kenney. "The Role of Gender Stereotypes in U.S. Senate Campaigns." *Politics & Gender* 5 (2009): 301–324.

Gaines, Adrienne. "Evangelical Voters Energized by McCain VP Pick." *Charisma*, September 2, 2008. http://www.charismamag.com/indez.php/news-old/19520 (accessed March 24, 2012).

Gallup, Inc. "Confidence in Institutions." http://www.gallup.com/poll/1597/Confidence-Instituions.aspx?version=print (accessed March 3, 2012).

Gallup, Inc. "Trust in Government." http://www.gallup.com/poll/5392/trustgovernment.aspx?version=print (accessed March 3, 2012).

Gerzai, Vanessa. "Where to Now? Women's Leadership Needs New Direction." *The Washington Post*, March 15, 2009. http://www.washingtonpost.com/wp-dyn/content/article/2009/03/06/AR2009030601712.html (accessed April 2, 2012).

Gibbs, Nancy. "Parent Trap: Sarah Palin's Complicated Life Story Speaks to the Agonizing Choices that Women Face." *Time*, September 15, 2008.

Gilgoff, Dan. "God-o-Meter Q&A with Sarah Palin's Biographer" (interview with Kaylene Johnson). *Christianity Today* Politics blog, September 3, 2008.

Gill, Rosalind. *Gender and the Media*. Cambridge, UK: Polity, 2007.

Gill, Rosalind and Christina Scharff. *New Femininities: Postfeminism, Neoliberalism and Subjectivity*. New York: Palgrave Macmillan, 2011.

Gillman, Todd J. "Letterman's Top 10 List: Sarah Palin and Her $150,000 Wardrobe." *Dallas Morning News*, October 27, 2008. http://trailblazersblog.dallasnews.com/archives/2008/10/lettermans-top-10-list-sarah-p.html (accessed April 2, 2012).

Givhan, Robin. "After a $150,000 Makeover, Sarah Palin Has an Image Problem." *The Washington Post*, October 23, 2008.

Goldberg, Michelle. "3 a.m. for Feminism." *The New Republic*, June 6, 2008.

Goldwater, Barry. "Presidential Nomination Acceptance Speech." Speech given at the 28th Republican National Convention, San Francisco, CA, July 15, 1964.

Gordon, Linda. "Putting Children First: Women, Maternalism and Welfare in the Early Twentieth Century." In *U.S. History as Women's History: New Feminist Essays*, Linda K. Kerber, Alice Kessler-Harris, and Kathryn Kish Sklar eds. Chapel Hill: University of North Carolina Press, 1995.

Grabar, Mary. "The Harpies Are Out to Get Sarah Palin." *Townhall.com*, August 31, 2008. http://townhall.com/columnists/marygrabar/2008/08/31/the_harpies_are_out_to_get_sarah_palin/page/full/ (accessed March 24, 2012).

Grady, J. Lee. "Sarah Palin and the Deborah Anointing." *Fire in My Bones* blog, September 10, 2008.

Hanson, Victor Davis. "What Was Feminism?" *National Review Online*, September 11, 2008.

Harper, Jennifer. "'Gender Bias' Did in Clinton?" *Washington Times*, June 6, 2008.

Harriman, Robert. *Political Style: The Artistry of Power*. Chicago, IL: University of Chicago Press, 1995.

Harris, John and Beth Frerking. "Clinton Aids: Palin Treatment Sexist." *Politico*, September 3, 2008. http://www.politico.com/news/stories/0908/13129.html (accessed March 24, 2012).

Harris, Sam. "When Atheists Attack." *Newsweek,* September 29, 2008. http://www.newsweek.com/id/160080 (accessed March 25, 2012).

Hartley, Lesa Major and Renita Coleman. "The Intersection of Race and Gender in Election Coverage: What Happens When the Candidates Don't Fit the Stereotypes?" *The Howard Journal of Communications* 19 (2008): 315–333.

Hayden, Sara. "Negotiating Femininity and Power in the Early Twentieth Century West: Domestic Ideology and Feminine Style in Jeanette Rankin's Suffrage Rhetoric." *Communication Studies* 50, no. 2 (1999), 83–102.

Hayes, Danny. "When Gender and Party Collide: Stereotyping in Candidate Trait Attribution." *Politics & Gender* 7 (2011): 133–165.

Heileman, John. "The Sixty-Day War." *New York Magazine*, September 15, 2008. www.nymag.com/news/politics/49961 (accessed April 1, 2012).

Heileman, John and Mark Halperin. *Game Change: Obama and the Clintons, McCain and Palin, and the Race of a Lifetime*. New York: Harper Collins, 2010.

Heith, Diane J. "The Lipstick Watch: Media Coverage, Gender, and Presidential Campaigns." In *Anticipating Madam President*, Robert P. Watson and Ann Gordon eds., 123–130. Boulder, CO: Lynne Rienner, 2003.

Henninger, Daniel. "What's So Special about Sarah?" *Wall Street Journal*, September 4, 2008. http://online.wsj.com/article/SB122048635407597177.html?KEYWORDS=Daniel+Henninger (accessed April 1, 2012).

Henninger, Melinda. "Anyway, She Looked Good ... ." The XX Factor, *Slate*, October 20, 2008. http://img.slate.com/blogs/blogs/xxfactor/archive/tags/Sarah+Palin+SNL/default.aspx (accessed March 20, 2012).

Hepola, Sarah. "Sarah Palin, $150,000 Fashionista." *Salon.com*, October 22, 2008. http://www.salon.com/2008/10/22/palin_wardrobe/ (accessed March 25, 2012).

Hero Builders. http://www.herobuilders.com/08.htm (accessed April 2, 2012).

Hernandez, Daisy, and Bushra Rehman, eds. *Colonize This! Young Women of Color on Today's Feminism*. Emeryville, CA: Seal Press, 2002.

Herrnson, Paul S., Celeste Lay, and Atiya Stokes. "Women Running 'As Women': Candidate Gender, Campaign Issues, and Voter Targeting Strategies." *Journal of Politics* 65 (2003): 244–255.

Hilley, Joe. *Sarah Palin: A New Kind of Leader* (with foreword by Charles Colson), Grand Rapids, MI: Zondervan October 2008.

Hoppock, Julia. "Women Against Sarah Palin Speak Out." *ABC News*, September 11, 2008. http://abcnews.go.com/blogs/politics/2008/09/women-against-s/ (accessed April 2, 2012).

Horowitz, Bruce. "Palin Has Created Quite a Stir." *USA Today*, September 3, 2008. http://blogs.abcnews.com/politicalradar/2008/10/palin-a-diva-ru.html (accessed March 25, 2012).

Huddy, Leonie and Nayda Terkildsen. "Gender Stereotypes and the Perception of Male and Female Candidates." *American Journal of Political Science* 37 (1993): 99–147.

Hulbert, Ann, Rachael Larimore, and Emily Yoffe. "Parsing Palin: XX Factor Bloggers Take Readers' Questions about the Republican Vice-Presidential Nominee and Her Speech." *Slate*, September 4, 2008. http://www.slate.com/articles/news_and_politics/the_chat_room/2008/09/parsing_palin.html (accessed March 25, 2012).

Isikoff, Michael and Suzanne Smalley. "Not the Change They Wanted." *Newsweek*, November 3, 2008.

Iyengar, Shanto. *Is Anyone Responsible? How Television Frames Political Issues*. Chicago, IL: University of Chicago Press, 1991.

Iyengar, Shanto and Donald Kinder. *News That Matters: Television and American Opinion*. Chicago, IL: University of Chicago Press, 1987.

Jamieson, Kathleen Hall. *Beyond the Double Bind*. New York: Oxford University Press, 1995.

Jamieson, Kathleen Hall, ed. *Electing the President, 2008: The Insiders' View*. Philadelphia: University of Pennsylvania Press, 2009.

Johnson, Kaylene. "America, Meet Sarah Palin." *CNN Politics.com*, September 3, 2008. http://www.cnn.com/2008/POLITICS/09/02/kaylene.johnson.palin/?iref=hpmostpop (accessed April 5, 2012).

Johnson, Kirk and Kim Severson. "Bible is Palin's Professional Guide, Friends and Pastors Say." *New York Times*, September 7, 2008.

Johnson, Susan Lee. "'A Memory Sweet to Soldiers': The Significance of Gender in the History of the 'American West.'" *Western Historical Quarterly* 24, no. 4 (November 1993): 495–517. http://www.jstor.org/stable/970703 (accessed March 6, 2011).

Jones, Jeffrey P. *Entertaining Politics: Satiric Television and Political Engagement*. 2nd edition. Lanham, MD: Rowman & Littlefield, 2010.

Kahn, Kim Fridkin. *The Political Consequences of Being a Woman: How Stereotypes Influence the Conduct and Consequences of Political Campaigns*. New York: Columbia University Press, 1996.

Kaid, Lynda Lee, Sandra L. Myers, Val Pipps, and Jan Hunter. "Sex Role Perceptions and Televised Political Advertising: Comparing Male and Female Candidates." *Women & Politics* 4, no. 4, (1984): 41–53.

Kantor, Jodi. "Gender Issue Lives On as Clinton's Bid Wanes." *New York Times*, May 19, 2008.

Kantor, Jodi and Rachel Swarns. "A New Twist in the Debate on Mothers." *New York Times*, September 2, 2008.

Kaye, Kate. *Campaign '08: A Turning Point for Digital Media*. Create Space, 2009.

Kaye, Randi. "Pastor: GOP May Be Downplaying Palin's Religious Beliefs." *CNN Politics* Online, September 8, 2008. http://articles.cnn.com/2008-09-08/politics/palin. pastor_1_meghan-stapleton-wasilla-bible-church-sarah-palin?_s=PM:POLITICS (accessed March 25, 2012).

Kelley, Tina. "Soccer Moms Welcome Their Hockey-Loving Sisters to the Political Arena." *New York Times*, September 7, 2008.

Kenski, Kate, Bruce W. Hardy, and Kathleen Hall Jamieson. *The Obama Victory: How Media, Money and Message Shaped the 2008 Election* (for Kindle). New York: Oxford University Press, 2010.

Kerber, Linda. *Women of the Republic*. Chapel Hill: University of North Carolina Press, 1980.

King, David C. and Richard E. Matland. "Sex and the Grand Old Party: An Experimental Investigation of the Effect of Candidate Sex on Support for a Republican Candidate." *American Politics Research* 31 (2003): 595–612.

Klatch, Rebecca. *Women of the New Right*. Philadelphia, PA: Temple University Press, 1987.

Kornblut, Anne E. *Notes from the Cracked Ceiling: Hillary Clinton, Sarah Palin, and What It Will Take for a Woman to Win*. New York: Crown Publishing, 2009.

Krugman, Paul. "Assassination Attempt in Arizona." *New York Times*, January 8, 2011. http://krugman.blogs.nytimes.com/2011/01/08/assassination-attempt-in-arizona/ (accessed March 25, 2012).

Kurtz, Howard. "Should We Blame Sarah Palin for Gabrielle Giffords' Shooting?" *Newsweek*, January 8, 2011. http://www.thedailybeast.com/articles/2011/01/08/ gabrielle-giffords-shooting-dont-blame-sarah-palin.html (accessed March 25, 2012).

LaFerla, Ruth. "For Female Candidates, Conservative Clothes are Trendy." *New York Times*, October 21, 2010. http://www.nytimes.com/2010/10/21/fashion/21IMAGE. html?_r=3&ref=style (accessed March 25, 2012).

Lafferty, Elaine. "Sarah Palin's a Brainiac." *Daily Beast*, October 27, 2008.

Laird, Rebecca. *Ordained Women in the Church of the Nazarene: The First Generation*. Kansas City, KS: Nazarene Publishing House, 1993.

Lakoff, George. *The Political Mind: Why You Can't Understand 21st Century American Politics with an 18th Century Brain*. New York: Viking Publishers, 2008.

Larimore, Rachael. "Palin, SNL, and the T-Shirts that Really Bother Me." The XX Factor, *Slate*, October 20, 2008. http://img.slate.com/blogs/blogs/xxfactor/archive/ tags/Sarah+Palin+SNL/default.aspx (accessed March 24, 2012).

Lawless, Jennifer. "Women, War and Winning Elections: Gender Stereotyping in the Post-September 11 Era." *Political Research Quarterly* 57 (2004): 479–490.

Lawrence, Regina G. and Melody Rose. *Hillary Clinton's Race for the White House: Gender Politics and the Media on the Campaign Trail*. Boulder, CO: Lynne Rienner, 2010.

Lebsock, Suzanne. "Women and American Politics, 1880–1920." In *Women, Politics and Change*, edited by Louise A. Tilly and Patricia Gurin. New York: Russell Sage, 1992.

Leeper, Mark S. "The Impact of Prejudice on Female Candidates: An Experimental Look at Voter Inference." *American Politics Quarterly* 19 (1991): 248–261.

Leibenluft, Jacob. "Hockey Moms vs. Soccer Moms." *Slate*, September 4, 2008.

Levin, Yuval. "The Meaning of Sarah Palin." *Commentary Magazine* (February 2009): 15–19.

Lippert, Barbara. "Analysis: Feminism's Next Wave." *Adweek*, September 8, 2008. http://www.adweek.com/news/advertising-branding/analysis-feminisms-next-wave-96940 (accessed April 2, 2012).

Lithwick, Dahlia. "The Downsides of Diversity." *Slate*, September 27, 2008.

Lobasz, Jennifer. "The Woman in Peril and the Ruined Woman." *Journal of Women, Politics & Policy* (2008): 305–334.

Loke, Jaime, Dustin Harp, and Ingrid Bachmann. "Mothering and Governing." *Journalism Studies* 28 (2010): 205–220.

Lopez, Kathryn Jean. "Sarah Palin: A Feminist in the Pro-Life Tradition." *National Review Online*, May 24, 2010. http://www.nationalreview.com/articles/229811/sarah-palin-feminist-pro-life-tradition/kathryn-jean-lopez (accessed March 24, 2012).

Luker, Kristin. *Abortion and the Politics of Motherhood*. Berkeley: University of California Press, 1984.

Luscombe, Belinda. "Why Some Women Hate Sarah Palin." *Time*, October 2, 2008. http://www.time.com/time/politics/article/0,8599,1846832,00.html (accessed March 24, 2012).

Luscombe, Belinda. "Heeling Power." *Time*, October 13, 2008.

Maher, Jane Maree and Lise Saugeres. "To Be or Not to Be? Women Negotiating Cultural Representations of Mothering." *Journal of Sociology* 43, no. 1 (2007): 5–21.

Malcom, Andrew. "James Dobson, Barack Obama among Those Reacting to Pregnancy of Sarah Palin's Daughter." *Los Angeles Times* "Top of the Ticket" blog, September 1, 2008.

Mansbridge, Jane. *Why We Lost the ERA*. Chicago, IL: University of Chicago Press, 1986.

Marcus, Ruth. "Palin Hits the Motherload." *The Washington Post*, September 10, 2008.

"Marie Wilson on Palin, Women's Progress in Politics." News and Notes, *National Public Radio*, September 4, 2008. http://www.wbur.org/npr/94276947/marie-wilson-on-palin-womens-progress-in-politics (accessed March 25, 2012).

Marsh, Katherine. "Whine Not: The Working Mothers' Case against Sarah Palin." *The New Republic*, September 24, 2008.

Mathews, Donald and Jane Sharon DeHart. *Sex, Gender and the Politics of ERA*. New York: Oxford University Press, 1992.

Mayo, Edith P. "Motherhood, Social Service, and Political Reform: Political Culture and Imagery of American Woman Suffrage." *National Women's History Museum*. http://www.nwhm.org/online-exhibits/votesforwomen/tour_02-02j.html (accessed April 2, 2012).

McCain, John. "McCain Announces Sarah Palin as His VP." Speech given at a rally in Dayton, OH, August 29, 2008.

McDermott, Monika. "Voting Cues in Low Information Elections: Candidate Gender as a Social Information Variable in Contemporary United States Elections." *American Journal of Political Science* 41 (1997): 270–283.

McGinley, Ann C. "Hillary Clinton, Sarah Palin, and Michelle Obama: Performing Gender, Race and Class on the Campaign Trail." *Scholarly Works* (paper 171). http://scholars.law.unlv.edu/facpub/171 (accessed July 27, 2011).

McRobbie, Angela. *The Aftermath of Feminism: Gender, Culture and Social Change*. Thousand Oaks, CA: Sage, 2009.

Miller, Lisa. "Hear Them Growl: Sarah Palin Says a New Crop of Conservative Women Will 'Rise Up' to Protect Their Cubs. But Will They?" *Daily Beast*, September 27,

2010. http://www.thedailybeast.com/newsweek/2010/09/27/what-does-mama-grizzly-really-mean.print.html (accessed March 25, 2012).

Mohler, R. Albert, Jr. "Palin Can Serve Family and Country." *The Washington Post* blog. http://newsweek.washingtonpost.com/onfaith/panelists/r_albert_mohler_jr/2008/09/a_tale_of_two_offices.html (accessed March 24, 2012).

Morin, Rich and Paul Taylor. "Revisiting the Mommy Wars: Politics, Gender and Parenthood." *Pew Research Center*, September 15, 2008. http://pewresearch.org/pubs/950/mommy-wars (accessed March 25, 2012).

Morris, Celia. *Storming the Statehouse: Running for Governor with Ann Richards and Dianne Feinstein.* New York: Macmillan, 1992.

Mueller, Carol M. "Nurturance and Mastery: Competing Qualifications for Women's Access to High Public Office?" In *Women and Politics: Activism, Attitudes, and Office-Holding*, Gwen Moore and Glenna D. Spitze eds. Greenwich, CT: JAI Press, 1986.

Mundy, Liza. "Women, Money and Power." *Time*, March 26, 2012.

Murphy, Jen. "Gov. Sarah Palin: Midnight Runs and Caribou Dinners." *Wall Street Journal*, September 22, 2008. http://online.wsj.com/article/SB122002155637283431.html?KEYWORDS="midnight+runs+and+caribou+dinners" (accessed March 9, 2012).

Nelson, Michael. *PS. Political Science and Politics* 21, no. 4 (Autumn 1988): 858–868.

Nesmith, Bruce. *The New Republican Coalition: The Reagan Campaigns and White Evangelicals.* New York: Peter Lang, 1994.

Newport, Frank. "Americans Today Much More Accepting of a Woman, Black, Catholic, or Jew as President." *Gallup News Service*, March 29, 1999.

Noll, Mark. *American Evangelical Christianity: An Introduction.* Malden, MA: Blackwell Publishers, 2001.

Noonan, Peggy. "A Servant's Heart." *Wall Street Journal*, September 6, 2008. http://online.wsj.com/article/SB122059352189503479.html?KEYWORDS=Peggy+Noonan (accessed April 1, 2012).

Obama, Michelle. Speech given in Milwaukee, WI, February 18, 2008.

Omero, Margie. "The Marriage and Gender Gaps." *Huffington Post*, August 1, 2008. http://www.huffingtonpost.com/margie-omero/marriage_gender_gaps1_b_729194.html (accessed March 24, 2012).

Page, Susan. "Married? Single? Status Affects How Women Vote," *USA Today*, August 25, 2004. http://www.usatoday.com/news/politicselections/nation/polls/2004-08-25-female-vote_x.htm (accessed April 2, 2012).

"Palin as Proud Redneck." Time/CNN's *The Page*, October 23, 2008. http://thepage.time.com/2008/10/23/palin-as-proud-redneck/ (accessed April 5, 2012).

Palin, Sarah. Speech given at a rally in Dayton, OH, August 29, 2008.

Palin, Sarah. "Vice-Presidential Nomination Acceptance Speech." Speech given at the Republican National Convention, in Saint Paul, MN, September 3, 2008.

Palin, Sarah. Interview with Sarah Palin. By Katie Couric. *CBS News*, September 30, 2008.

Palin, Sarah. *Going Rogue: An American Life.* New York: Harper, 2009.

Palin, Sarah. "Resignation Speech." Speech given at Wasilla, AK, July 4, 2009. Full text of speech found at http://www.huffingtonpost.com/2009/07/03/sarah-palin-resignation-s_n_225557.html (accessed March 25, 2012).

Palin, Sarah. *America by Heart: Reflections on Family, Faith, and Flag.* New York: Harper Collins, 2010.

Palin, Sarah. "2010 Susan B. Anthony List Speech." Speech given at the Susan B. Anthony Celebration of Life Breakfast at Washington, DC, May 14, 2010. Full video of speech found at http://www.c-spanvideo.org/program/293509-1 (accessed March 24, 2012).

Palin, Sarah. Speech given at Annual National Rifle Association Meeting in Washington, DC, May 14, 2010.

Palmer, Lindsey. "The Debut of the Hockey Mom." *Redbook*, October, 2008.

Parker, Kathleen. "Palin Problem: She's Out of Her League." *National Review*, September 26, 2008. http://www.nationalreview.com/articles/225784/palin-problem/kathleen-parker (accessed September 29, 2008).

Parrish, Karen. "Letter to the Editor." *Charisma*, November, 2008.

Patterson, Troy. "The Sarah Palin Show." *Slate*, September 2, 2008.

Paul, David and Jessi L. Smith. "Subtle Sexism: Examining Vote Preferences When Women Run Against Men for the Presidency." *Journal of Women, Politics & Policy* 29, no. 4, (2008): 451–476.

Pelosi, Nancy. Interview by Jim Lehrer. *News Hour with Jim Lehrer*. March 30, 2006.

Perrotta, Tom. "The Sexy Puritan." September 26, 2008. http://www.slate.com/id/2200814/ (accessed March 24, 2012).

Pitney, Nico. "Palin Misquotes Albright: Place in Hell Reserved for Women Who Don't Support Other Women." *Huffington Post*, October 5, 2008. http://www.huffingtonpost.com/2008/10/05/palin-misquotes-albright_n_131967.html (accessed April 2, 2012).

Plotz, David. "I Dream About Sarah Palin. Do You?" *Slate*, September 9, 2008.

Pollitt, Katha. "Lipstick on a Wing Nut." *Nation*, September 29, 2008.

Posner, Sarah. "Where She Was Saved." *Slate*, September 11, 2008. http://www.salon.com/2008/09/11/assemblies_of_god/ (accessed March 24, 2012).

Prentice, Deborah and Erica Carranza. "What Women and Men Should Be, Shouldn't Be, Are Allowed to Be, and Don't Have to Be: The Contents of Prescriptive Gender Stereotypes." *Psychology of Women Quarterly* 26 (2002): 269–281.

Press, Andrea L. and Elizabeth R. Cole. *Speaking of Abortion: Television and Authority in the Lives of Women*. Chicago, IL: University of Chicago Press, 1999.

Price, Vincent and David Tewskbury. "News Values and Public Opinion: A Theoretical Account of Media Priming and Framing." In Vol. 13 of *Progress in Communication Sciences: Advances in Persuasion*, George A. Barnett and Franklin J. Boster eds., 173–212. Greenwich, CT: Ablex Publishing Corporation, 1997.

Przybyla, Heidi. "Giffords Shooting in Arizona May Cool U.S. Political Rhetoric, Hurt Palin." *Bloomberg*, January 10, 2011. http://www.bloomberg.com/news/2011-01-09/lawmakers-urge-end-to-political-rhetoric-after-tucson-shootings.html (accessed March 25, 2012).

Quayle, Marilyn. Speech given at the Republican National Convention, Houston, T, August 19, 1988.

Quindlen, Anna. "Can You Say Sexist?" *Newsweek*, September 15, 2008. http://www.newsweek.com/id/157543 (accessed March 20, 2012).

Reagan, Ronald. "Inaugural Address." Speech given at the West Front of the Capitol, Washington, DC, January 20, 1981.

Reitman, Ivan, dir. *Dave*. DVD. Burbank, CA: Warner Bros. Pictures, 1993.

Rohter, Larry. "Palin Criticizes Obama as Faux Feminist." *New York Times* political blog "The Caucus," October 21, 2008. http://thecaucus.blogs.nytimes.com/2008/10/21/palin-criticizes-obama-as-faux-feminist/ (accessed March 25, 2012).

Romano, Lois. "Gov. Mom: The Land of the Midnight Sun's Claim to Fame: Being Led by a 24-Hour Mother." *The Washington Post*, September 2, 2008.

Rose, Melody. "Pro-Life, Pro-Woman? Frame Extension in the American Abortion Movement." *Journal of Women, Politics & Policy* 32, no. 1 (2011): 1–27.

Rosen, Ruth. *The World Split Open.* New York: Penguin, 2006.

Rosin, Hanna. "What Scarlet Letter?" *Slate*, September 4, 2008. http://www.slate.com/articles/double_x/xxfactor_xxtra/2008/09/what_scarlet_letter.html (accessed April 2, 2012).

Rosenwasser, Shirley and Norma Dean. "Gender Role and Political Office." *Psychology of Women Quarterly* 13 (1989): 77–85.

Rosenwasser, Shirley M. and Jana Seale. "Attitudes toward a Hypothetical Male or Female Presidential Candidate: A Research Note." *Political Psychology* 9 (1988): 591–598.

Rucker, Philip and Eli Saslow. "Sarah Palin to Resign as Alaska Governor, Citing Probes and Family Needs." *The Washington Post*, July 4, 2009. http://www.washingtonpost.com/wp-dyn/content/article/2009/07/03/AR2009070301738.html (accessed March 25, 2012).

Russo, Nancy Felipe. "The Motherhood Mandate." *Journal of Social Issues* 32, no. 3 (1976): 143–153.

Sanbonmatsu, Kira and Kathleen Dolan. "Do Gender Stereotypes Transcend Party?" *Political Research Quarterly* 62 (2009): 485–494.

Sanchez, Leslie. "Palin is a VP for the rest of us." CNN, September 4, 2008. http://articles.cnn.com/2008-09-04/politics/sanchez.palin_1_sarah-palin-life-choices-life-support?_s=PM:POLITICS (accessed March 24, 2012).

Sapiro, Virginia. "If U.S. Senator Baker Were a Woman: An Experimental Study of Candidate Images." *Political Psychology* 2 (1982): 61–83.

"Sarah Palin: New Face of Feminism?" *All Things Considered*, National Public Radio, September 7, 2008. http://www.npr.org/templates/transcript/transcript.php?storyId=94369835 (accessed March 25, 2012).

SarahPAC.com. "Sarah Palin—'Mama Grizzlies.'" July 8, 2010. http://www.youtube.com/watch?v=oF-OsHTLfxM (accessed March 25, 2012).

Saturday Night Live: Primetime Election Special. NBC, October 4, 2008.

Saturday Night Live. NBC, November 1, 2008.

Schaffner, Brian F. and Mary Layton Atkinson. "Taxing Death or Estates? When Frames Influence Citizens' Issue Beliefs." In *Winning with Words: The Origins & Impact of Political Framing*, Brian F. Schaffner and Patrick J. Sellers eds, 121–135. New York: Routledge, 2010.

Schaffner, Brian F. and Patrick J. Sellers, eds. *Winning With Words: The Origins & Impact of Political Framing.* New York: Routledge, 2010.

Schofield, Mary Anne. "Miss America, Rosie the Riveter, and World War II." In *"There She Is, Miss America": The Politics of Sex, Beauty and Race*, Elwood Watson and Darcy Martin eds. New York: Palgrave MacMillan, 2004.

Schrobsdorff, Susanna. "Sister, Sister: What Some of America's Smartest, Most Successful Women Have to Say about Sarah Palin, Hillary Clinton and the Meaning of the Word 'Feminist' in 2008." *Newsweek* October 9, 2008. http://www.newsweek.com/id/163219 (accessed March 24, 2012).

Seib, Gerald. "Palin Pitches Sam's Club Tent." *Wall Street Journal*, September 3, 2008. http://www.online.wsj.com/article/SB122039959157792985.html?KEYWORDS=gerald+seib (accessed March 12, 2012).

Seem, Susan Rachael and M. Diane Clark. "Healthy Women, Healthy Men, and Healthy Adults: An Evaluation of Gender Role Stereotypes in the Twenty-first Century." *Sex Roles* 55 (2006): 247–258.

Seltzer, Sarah. "A Feminist Appalled by Palin." *Huffiington Post*, August 29, 2008. http://www.huffingtonpost.com/sarah-seltzer/a-feminist-appalled-by-pa_b_122489.html (accessed April 2, 2012).

Severson, Kim. "The Spotlight Arrives, to Some Unease, in a State that Savors its Isolation." *New York Times,* August 31, 2008.

Shriver, Maria and the Center for American Progress. *The Shriver Report: A Women's Nation Changes Everything.* Heather Boushey and Ann O'Leary eds. October 16, 2009.

Siegel, Deborah. *Sisterhood Interrupted.* New York: Palgrave MacMillan, 2007.

Silverman, Stephen M. "Republicans Spent $150,000 on Sarah Palin's Wardrobe." *People*, October 22, 2008. http://www.people.com/people/article/0,20234976,00.html (accessed April 2, 2012).

Slatta, Richard W. *The Cowboy Encyclopedia.* New York, NY: W. W. Norton, 1994.

Smidt, Corwin, Kevin R. den Dulk, Bryan T. Froehle, James M. Penning, Stephen V. Monsma, and Douglas L. Koopman. *The Disappearing God Gap: Religion in the 2008 Presidential Election.* New York: Oxford University Press, 2010.

Smith, Jessi L., David Paul, and Rachel Paul. "No Place for a Woman: Evidence for Gender Bias in Evaluations of Presidential Candidates." *Basic and Applied Social Psychology* 29 (2007): 225–233.

Snow, Kate and Imtiyaz Delawala. "Palin a Diva: Ruffled Feathers in McCain Camp." *ABC News* "Political Radar" blog, October 25, 2008.

Sofia, Anna and Elizabeth Botkin. "Q&A Regarding Our Position on Sarah Palin." *Visionary Daughters* website, October 19, 2008. http://visionarydaughters.com/category/female-magistrates (accessed March 24, 2012).

Stanley, Alessandra. "On 'SNL' It's the Real Sarah Palin, Looking Like a Real Entertainer." *New York Times*, October 20, 2008.

Stanley, Susie. *Holy Boldness: Women Preachers' Autobiographies.* Knoxville: University of Tennessee Press, 2004.

Steffensmeier, Janet Box and Steven E. Schier, eds. *The American Elections of 2008.* Lanham, MD: Rowman and Littlefield, 2009.

Steinem, Gloria. "Wrong Woman, Wrong Message." *New York Times*, September 4, 2008.

Stone, Gigi. "Palin's Spec-tacular Fashion Statement." *Good Morning America*, September 7, 2008.

Sullivan, Amy. "Does Sarah Palin Have a Pentecostal Problem?" *Time*, October 9, 2008. http://www.time.com/time/politics/article/0,8599,1848420,00.html (accessed March 25, 2012).

Sullivan, Maureen. "What, If Any of This, Is Justified?" The XX Factor, *Slate*, October 20, 2008. http://img.slate.com/blogs/blogs/xxfactor/archive/tags/Sarah+Palin+SNL/default.aspx (accessed April 2, 2012).

Swers, Michele. *The Difference Women Make: The Policy Impact of Women in Congress.* Chicago, IL: University of Chicago Press, 2002.

Swindoll, Charles. *Improving Your Serve.* Nashville, TN: Thomas Nelson, 1981.

Tagle, Ximena. "Mail Call and Corrections." *Newsweek*, September 22, 2008. http://www.thedailybeast.com/newsweek/2003/08/17/mail-call-and-corrections.html (accessed March 24, 2012).

Tancer, Bill. "Searching for Sarah Palin's 'Hot Photos.'" *Time*, September 2, 2008.

Tate, Ryan. "Sarah Palin's $150,000 Fashion Spree." *Gawker*, October 21, 2008. http://gawker.com/5066894/sarah-palins-150000-fashion-spree (accessed April 2, 2012).

The View. ABC, October 22, 2008.

Thomas, Evan. "Alienated in the U.S.A." *Daily Beast*, March 12, 2008. http://www.thedailybeast.com/newsweek/2008/03/12/alienated-in-the-u-s-a.html (accessed March 25, 2012).

Thomas, Evan and Karen Beslau. "McCain's Mrs. Right: Gov. Sarah Palin Came Out of Nowhere to Win the John McCain Veep Sweepstakes. Well, Not Quite Nowhere." *Newsweek*, September 8, 2008.

Thomas, Sue. *How Women Legislate*. New York: Oxford University Press, 1994.

Thornburgh, Nathan. "The Education of Sarah Palin." *Time*, September 15, 2008.

Traister, Rebecca. "Palin, Pregnancy and the Presidency." *Salon.com*, September 1, 2008. http://www.salon.com/2008/09/01/palin_baby/ (accessed March 25, 2012).

Traister, Rebecca. "Zombie Feminists of the RNC." *Salon.com*, September 11, 2008. http://www.salon.com/2008/09/11/zombie_feminism (accessed March 25, 2012).

Traister, Rebecca. "The Sarah Palin Pity Party." *Salon.com*, September 30, 2008. www.salon.com/mwt/feature/2008/09/30/palin_pity/print.html (accessed March 25, 2012).

Traister, Rebecca. *Big Girls Don't Cry*. New York: Free Press, 2010.

Tumulty, Karen. "Maxed-Out Moms." *Time*, September 29, 2008.

Turner, Frederick Jackson. "The Significance of the Frontier in American History." In *Frederick Jackson Turner: Wisconsin's Historian of the Frontier*, Martin Ridge ed. Madison: State Historical Society of Wisconsin, 1986.

Valenti, Jessica. "Opinion: The Fake Feminism of Sarah Palin." *The Washington Post*, May 30, 2010. http://www.washingtonpost.com/wp-dyn/content/article/2010/05/28/AR2010052802263.html?sid%3DST2010060501883&sub=AR (accessed March 24, 2012).

Waggenspack, Beth. "Deceptive Narratives in the 2008 Presidential Campaign." In *Studies of Identity in the 2008 Presidential Campaign*, Robert E. Denton, Jr. ed, 155–200. Lanham, MD: Lexington Books, 2010.

Walker, Rebecca. *To Be Real: Telling the Truth and Changing the Face of Feminism*. New York: Anchor Books, 1995.

Warner, Judith. "Emotion without Thought in New Hampshire." *New York Times* Opinionator blog, January 10, 2008. http://opinionator.blogs.nytimes.com/2008/01/10/emotion-without-thought-in-new-hampshire/ (accessed April 2, 2012).

Warner, Judith. "The Mirrored Ceiling." *New York Times*, September 4, 2008.

Warren, Rick. *The Purpose-Driven Life*. Grand Rapids, MI: Zondervan, 2002.

Watson, Elwood and Darcy Martin, eds. *"There She Is, Miss America:" The Politics of Sex, Beauty and Race*. Elwood Watson and Darcy Martin ed. New York: Palgrave MacMillan, 2004.

Wayne, Stephen J. *The Road to the White House 2004: The Politics of Presidential Elections*. Belmont, CA: Wadsworth/Thomson Learning, 2004.

Weiner, Jay. "She's Now a Household Phrase, but What is a Hockey Mom?" *MinnPost*, September 5, 2008. http://www.minnpost.com/stories/2008/09/05/3407/shes_now_household_phrase_but_whats_a_hockey_mom (accessed March 25, 2012).

Westen, Drew. *The Political Brain: The Role of Emotion in Deciding the Fate of the Nation*. New York: Public Affairs, 2007.

Westfall, Sandra Sobieraj. "John McCain and Sarah Palin on Shattering the Glass Ceiling." *People*, August 29, 2008.

Williams, Daniel K. *God's Own Party: The Making of the Christian Right*. New York: Oxford University Press, 2010.

Williams, Joan. "Is Sarah Palin Working Mother of the Year?" *Huffington Post*, September 5, 2008.

Wilson, Cintra. "Pissed About Palin." *Salon.com*, September 10, 2008.

Winter, Nicholas J. G. *Dangerous Frames: How Ideas About Race & Gender Shape Public Opinion*. Chicago, IL: University of Chicago Press, 2008.

Witt, Linda, Karen M. Paget, and Glenna Matthews. *Running as a Woman: Gender and Power in American Politics*. New York: Free Press, 1994.

Worthen, Molly. "Housewives of God." *New York Times Magazine*, November 12, 2010.

Yano, Christine R. *Crowning the Nice Girl: Gender, Ethnicity, and Culture in Hawaii's Cherry Blossom Festival*. Honolulu: University of Hawaii Press, 2006.

Yardley, William. "Sarah Heath Palin, an Outsider with Charms." *New York Times* (August 29, 2008).

Yerman, Marcia G. "Women Respond to Palin: Part One." *Huffington Post*, September 15, 2008.

Young, Cathy. "A Great Moment for Women." *Boston Globe*, September 12, 2008.

Ziganto, Lori. "Taking Feminism Back: Sarah Palin Endorses Nikki Haley for SC Governor." *News Real Blog*, May 14, 2010. http://www.newsrealblog.com/2010/05/14/taking-feminism-back-sarah-palin-endorses-nikki-haley-for-sc-governor/ (accessed March 24, 2012).

Zoonen, Liesbet van. *Entertaining the Citizen: When Politics and Popular Culture Converge*. Lanham, MD: Rowman & Littlefield, 2005.

INDEX

#0057 - 080817 - C0 - 229/152/12 [14] - CB - 9780415893336